PIPE FITTINGS

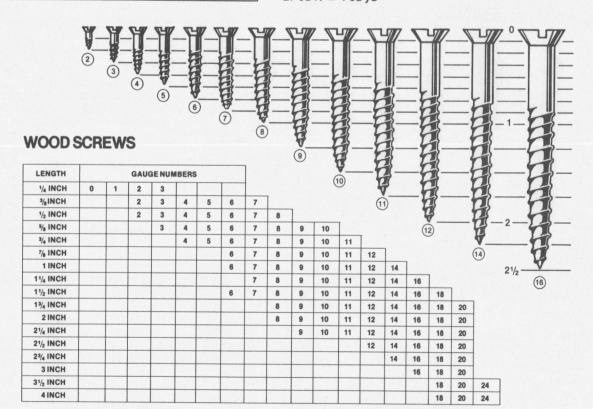

NIPPLES

PIPE LENGTHS UP TO 22 FT.

STRAIGHT COUPLING

REDUCING COUPLING

COUPLING

NUT

CAP

STRAIGHT TEE

REDUCING TEE

STREET TEE

STRAIGHT CROSS

REDUCING CROSS

90° ELBOW

90° ELBOW

90° ELBOW

45° ELBOW

REDUCING ELBOW

90° STREET ELBOW

45° STREET ELBOW

45° Y-BEND

REDUCING TEE

REDUCER

UNION (3 PARTS)

PLUG

BUSHING

CAP

RETURN BEND

90°

45°

UNION ELBOWS

STREET

UNION TEES

PLUG

45° ELBOW

TEE

Here are the common steel pipe fittings. Nipples are simply short lengths of pipe threaded on both ends. Reducing fittings join two different sizes of pipe.

Compression fittings of the flared-tube type are the easiest for the novice to handle when working with copper tubing.

STANDARD STEEL PIPE
(All Dimensions in Inches)

Nominal Size	Outside Diameter	Inside Diameter	Nominal Size	Outside Diameter	Inside Diameter
1/8	0.405	0.269	1	1.315	1.049
1/4	0.540	0.364	1 1/4	1.660	1.380
3/8	0.675	0.493	1 1/2	1.900	1.610
1/2	0.840	0.622	2	2.375	2.067
3/4	1.050	0.824	2 1/2	2.875	2.469

SQUARE MEASURE
144 sq in = 1 sq ft
9 sq ft = 1 sq yd
272.25 sq ft = 1 sq rod
160 sq rods = 1 acre

VOLUME MEASURE
1728 cu in = 1 cu ft
27 cu ft = 1 cu yd

MEASURES OF CAPACITY
1 cup = 8 fl oz
2 cups = 1 pint
2 pints = 1 quart
4 quarts = 1 gallon
2 gallons = 1 peck
4 pecks = 1 bushel

WOOD SCREWS

LENGTH	GAUGE NUMBERS													
1/4 INCH	0	1	2	3										
3/8 INCH			2	3	4	5	6	7						
1/2 INCH			2	3	4	5	6	7	8					
5/8 INCH				3	4	5	6	7	8	9	10			
3/4 INCH					4	5	6	7	8	9	10	11		
7/8 INCH							6	7	8	9	10	11	12	
1 INCH							6	7	8	9	10	11	12	14
1 1/4 INCH								7	8	9	10	11	12	14	16
1 1/2 INCH							6	7	8	9	10	11	12	14	16	18
1 3/4 INCH									8	9	10	11	12	14	16	18	20
2 INCH								8	9	10	11	12	14	16	18	20
2 1/4 INCH									9	10	11	12	14	16	18	20
2 1/2 INCH												12	14	16	18	20
2 3/4 INCH													14	16	18	20
3 INCH														16	18	20
3 1/2 INCH															18	20	24
4 INCH															18	20	24

WHEN YOU BUY SCREWS, SPECIFY (1) LENGTH, (2) GAUGE NUMBER, (3) TYPE OF HEAD—FLAT, ROUND, OR OVAL, (4) MATERIAL—STEEL, BRASS, BRONZE, ETC., (5) FINISH—BRIGHT, STEEL BLUED, CADMIUM, NICKEL, OR CHROMIUM PLATED.

POPULAR MECHANICS DO-IT-YOURSELF YEARBOOK
1985

HIGH TECH IN THE HOME

CRAFT PROJECTS

HOME IMPROVEMENTS

CAR CARE GUIDE

LAWN AND GARDEN PROJECTS

SHOP PROJECTS AND EXPERT KNOW-HOW

GUIDE TO NEW TOOLS AND EQUIPMENT

HOME ENERGY GUIDE

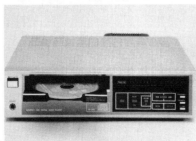

HEARST BOOKS New York, NY

CREDITS:

Computer Monitors, page 11, by Walter Salm
Compact Disc Players, page 20, by Christopher
  Greenleaf
Electronic Typewriters, page 22, by Louis Alexander
Stereo System Music Box, page 26, by David
  DeCristoforo
Expert Ways to Make Butcher Block, page 29, by
  Rosario Capotosto
Build an Old-time Icebox, page 34, by John Capotosto
Home Office Telephone Organizer, page 38, by Rosario
  Capotosto
Classic Lap Desk, page 39, by Ralph Wilkes
Secrets of a Master Woodcrafter, page 43, by C. E.
  "Doc" Banister
An Heirloom Wagon, page 50, by Mark C. DiBona
Joinery with Invisible Nails, page 51, by Jorma Hyypia
Wainscoting, page 53, by Steven Willson
Create Period Molding, page 57, by Rosario Capotosto
Pantry on Wheels, page 58, by Walter Alan Kerr
Home Wiring, page 60, by Richard Nunn
How to Frame and Finish a Basement Window, page 64,
  by Gene and Katie Hamilton
Reglazing Windows, page 65, by Rosario Capotosto
How to Beam a Ceiling, page 66, by Joseph Truini;
  Decorator's Guide to Beam Installation, by Gabe
  Herrick
Install Your Own Phone, page 70, by Marc Stern
Multipurpose Wall Cabinets, page 73, by Steven
  Willson and Steve Fay
Workbench from PM's Supershop, page 76, by Rosario
  Capotosto

Redwood Barbecue Cart, page 89, by Rosario
  Capotosto
Garden Benches, page 95; Patio Bench by Joseph
  Truini; Park Bench by Dave Smith
A Deck for Anywhere, page 97, by Joseph Truini
How to Season Firewood, page 104, by Jeffrey L.
  Wartluft
Picking Lumber, page 105, by John H. Ingersoll
What Is Wood, page 108, by R. Bruce Hoadley
Plywood and Other Building Panels, page 112, by
  Joseph Truini and John H. Ingersoll
Plywood Edge Treatments, page 116, by Rosario
  Capotosto
Draw Better Plans, page 119, by Ralph S. Wilkes
Measuring and Marking, page 120, by Rosario
  Capotosto
Adhesives, page 121, by John H. Ingersoll
Master Craftsman Tips, page 127, by Rosario
  Capotosto
Shop Ideas, page 133: Low-cost Shelves by Kenneth
  Wells; Resaw Jig by Ken Brooks; Miterbox Guides,
  Saw Platform and Miterbox Holder by Ken Patterson
Perfect Joints from your Router, page 135, by Steven J.
  Anderson
Using Handsaws, page 136, by Rosario Capotosto
Using a Combination Square, page 137, by Rosario
  Capotosto
Light Control for Close Jobs, page 142, by Walter E.
  Burton
Discover the Pin Router, page 147, by Rosario
  Capotosto
Tools That Will Surprise You, page 151, Tool
  Consultant John Gaynor
Key to Smart Tool Buying, page 157, by Joseph Truini
Solar System-Heat Pump Water Heater, page 163, by
  David A. Warren

Editor: C. Edward Cavert
Art Director: Eric Marshall
Production: Layla Productions, Inc.

POPULAR MECHANICS ADVISORY BOARD
John Linkletter, Editor-in-Chief
Joe Oldham, Executive Editor
Bill Hartford, Managing Editor
Harry Wicks, Home and Shop Editor
Bryan Canniff, Graphics Director

Published by Hearst Books,
A Division of the Hearst Corporation
1790 Broadway
New York, New York 10019

ISBN 0-87851-089-3
ISSN 0360-2273

CONTENTS

HIGH TECH IN THE HOME

COMPUTER WORKSTATION

This three-piece desk keeps everything neat and gives you plenty of room to work.

As important as your computer and its periph-erals is a desk to put it on that is functional, attractive, inexpensive and ergonomically correct—that is, designed to put the compo-nents in the proper positions for the most com-fortable use. This computer workstation can be custom-tailored to your own requirements. It's easy to build, extremely versatile and will fit comfortably in almost any home office. It can even be built in sections and added to as your needs grow.

The workstation deliberately does not look high-tech so it can blend in with your home decor. Yet this home computer center is more

advanced than most office workstations. It's filled with clever features, most of which are hidden from view.

The workstation shown here was built for an Apple IIe, with a single disk drive and optional joystick. In addition to Apple's black and white monitor, a color monitor was added for games and graphics. The printer is a Gemini 15. The dimensions of the workstation modules were determined by the size of these components plus basic ergonomic measurements.

BUILDING THE WORKSTATION
The workstation is easy to build. The sides of each unit are higher than the tops so you have only a simple butt joint to make. There are no curves to cut, and all of the major surfaces—the tops, sides and backs—are formed from a single piece. All hardware is available at any hardware store.

The workstation is built of oak cabinet–grade plywood with Formica brand plastic laminate

Surge-protected power strip is the power station on the main desk.

MATERIALS LIST
COMPUTER MODULE

Key	No.	Size and description (use)
A	2	¾ x 30 x 55½" oak veneer plywood (sides)
B	2	¾ x 25¼ x 30" oak veneer plywood (inside end panel)
C	1	¾ x 29⅝ x 39¼" particleboard (desk top)
D	2	¾ x 15 x 39¼" oak veneer plywood (top and bottom shelf)
E	1	¾ x 18⅞ x 39¼" oak veneer plywood (back)
F	1	¾ x 2 x 39¼" pine (top support)
G	1	¾ x 5 x 39¼" pine (stretcher)
H	1	¾ x 12¾ x 16¼" oak veneer plywood (divider)
I	2	¾ x 2 x 16" pine (cleats)
J	1	¾ x 3 x 10" oak veneer plywood (drawer front)
K	2	½ x 3 x 17¼" lauan mahogany plywood (drawer sides)
L	1	½ x 2¼ x 9½" lauan mahogany plywood (drawer back)
M	1	¼ x 8½ x 17" lauan mahogany plywood (drawer bottom)
N		¹⁄₁₆" oak veneer
O	1	¹⁄₁₆ x 29⅝ x 39¼" plastic laminate*
P	1 pr.	16" center drawer slide
Q	1	Brass drawer pull
R	4	Floor glide
S	1	¾ x 23 x 30 x 30" particleboard (removable shelf)
T	1	¹⁄₁₆ x 23 x 30 x 30" plastic laminate*
U	2	¾ x ¾ x 27" pine (cleats)
V	2	¼"-dia. x 1" hardwood dowel
W	6	1¼" No. 10 flathead screw
Misc.		Carpenter's glue, linseed oil, paste wax, contact cement
(*)		Formica brand plastic laminate, tidal sand No. 917

tops. You could use solid hardwood or solid pine throughout, but costs will mount. Painted plywood would make a functional substitute. Don't use an oil finish for surfaces that may come in contact with floppy disks. Laminate is best, though polyurethane varnish or paint are okay.

With the ergonomic guidelines, you'll end up with furniture that's as advanced as the computer it holds.

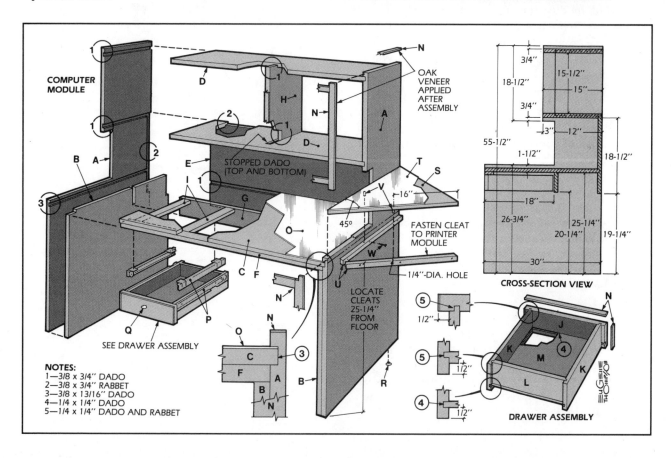

THE COMPUTER MODULE

The heart of the workstation is the terminal desk. If your space or funds are limited, you can build just this unit to support your keyboard, disk drives and monitor. If you have just one monitor, you can make your desk a bit narrower, although a desk for a single monitor still should be about 30 in. wide.

Otherwise, all the dimensions of the terminal desk are tailored to suit the computer. You'll need to measure your system components before modifying these plans. The most important dimensions are the height of the monitor and the distance between your eyes and the screen.

To support the weight of two monitors it was necessary to suspend the monitor shelf from a top shelf using a central divider. If your system includes two monitors, you *must* use both the top shelf and divider. All wiring is hidden behind the back, and brought into a filtered power strip and surge protector available at most electronic or computer stores. The pencil drawer is optional or can be switched to the other side of the desk.

THE PRINTER UNIT

The printer console is designed to hold a Gemini 15 or similar printer. Measure your printer and modify the dimensions accordingly. The console holds the printer on a fixed shelf, accessible from both front and top through the lift-up, counterbalanced lid. An optional window lets you check print quality without opening the soundproof lid.

Beneath the printer there's room for paper storage, accessible from the front of the console. A box of continuous-feed paper fits behind the paper storage.

Output paper falls onto a shelf behind the printer. This can be adjusted for the proper fall, has a lip to get the paper stack started and can be removed for access to the paper box. If you print single sheets rather than continuous-feed paper, the output paper shelf can be set in its highest position and used for storing input sheets.

The printer console can be positioned next to the terminal desk along the same wall, turned 90° to make an L, or as shown, on a 30° angle. The gap is filled with a removable triangular shelf matched to the terminal desk for height. If you select the L, a square filler piece adds extra space that is perfect for holding a telephone or disk-storage carousel.

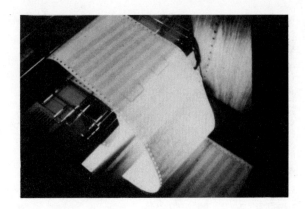

MATERIALS LIST
PRINTER MODULE

Key	No.	Size and description (use)
A	2	¾ x 29¾ x 30″ oak veneer plywood (sides)
B	1	¾ x 24 x 28⅛″ oak veneer plywood (back)
C	1	¾ x 23 x 29⅝″ oak veneer plywood (lid top)
D	1	¾ x 6⅝ x 23″ oak veneer plywood (lid front)
E	1	¾ x 24 x 29⅝″ oak veneer plywood (bottom)
F	1	¾ x 3⅜ x 24″ oak veneer plywood (kick)
G	1	¾ x 13⅜ x 24″ oak veneer plywood (shelf)
H	1	¾ x 6 x 24″ oak veneer plywood (shelf face)
I	1	¾ x 13 x 23″ oak veneer plywood (adjustable shelf)
J	2	¾ x 11⅜ x 18¼″ oak veneer plywood (doors)
K	2	¾ x ¾ x 5¾″ pine (lid stop)
L1	1	¼ x 1¼ x 23¼″ pine (shelf lip)
L2	1	¼ x 1¼ x 23″ pine (shelf lip)
M1	2	³⁄₁₆ x ⅝ x 11½″ pine (cleats)
M2	2	³⁄₁₆ x ⅝ x 3⅛″ pine (cleats)
N	1	⅛ x 3½ x 11½ glass
O	1	¹⁄₁₆ x 23⅛ x 30¹⁄₁₆″ plastic laminate*
P		¹⁄₁₆″ oak veneer
Q	1	1½ x 23″ brass continuous hinge
R	2 pr.	1¾ x 2″ brass butt hinge
S	3	Brass drawer pull
T	2	Magnetic catch
U	4	Shelf clip
V	4	Floor glide
W	1	13 x 23¼″ vibration pad
X	4	1¼″ No. 10 flathead brass screws
Y	1	Stanley 10″ lid support, No. SP 432
Misc.		Carpenter's glue, linseed oil, paste wax, contact cement
(*)		Formica brand plastic laminate, tidal sand No. 917.

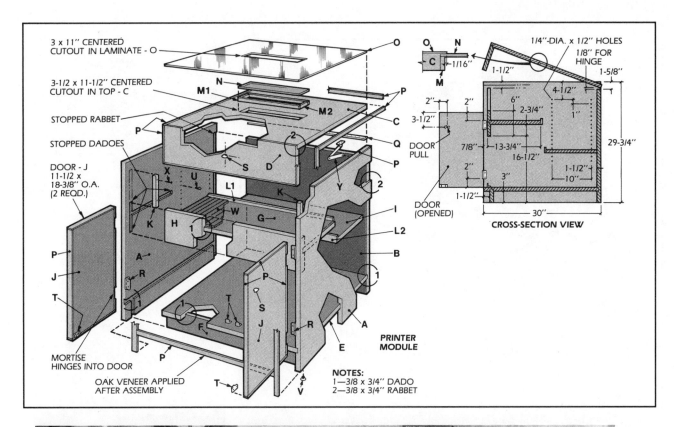

3 x 11" CENTERED
CUTOUT IN LAMINATE - O

3-1/2 x 11-1/2" CENTERED
CUTOUT IN TOP - C

STOPPED RABBET

STOPPED DADOES

DOOR - J
11-1/2 x
18-3/8" O.A.
(2 REQD.)

MORTISE
HINGES INTO DOOR

OAK VENEER APPLIED
AFTER ASSEMBLY

PRINTER
MODULE

NOTES:
1—3/8 x 3/4" DADO
2—3/8 x 3/4" RABBET

1/4"-DIA. x 1/2" HOLES
1/8" FOR
HINGE

1-5/8"

DOOR
PULL

1-1/2"
2"
6"
4-1/2"
2-3/4"
1"
13-3/4"
7/8"
16-1/2"
2"
1-1/2"
3"
10"
1-1/2"
30"
29-3/4"

DOOR
(OPENED)

CROSS-SECTION VIEW

The three modules can also be used in a straight-across configuration. You'll need more room with this arrangement.

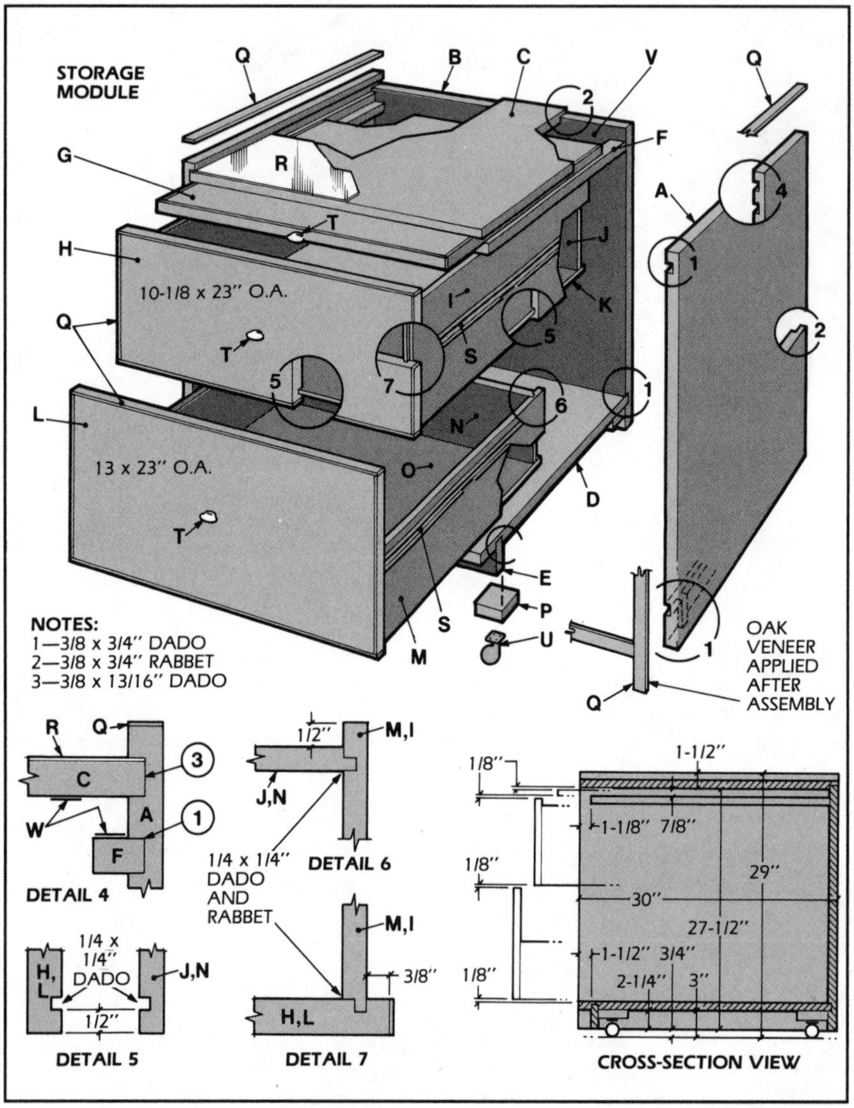
STORAGE MODULE
Q
B
C
V
Q
2
F
A
4
R
G
T
J
H
10-1/8 x 23" O.A.
1
K
Q
2
T
5
S
5
7
6
1
L
N
13 x 23" O.A.
O
D
T
E
P
NOTES:
1—3/8 x 3/4" DADO
2—3/8 x 3/4" RABBET
3—3/8 x 13/16" DADO
S
U
M
1
OAK VENEER APPLIED AFTER ASSEMBLY
Q
R
Q
3
C
A
1
W
F
DETAIL 4
1/2"
M,I
J,N
1/4 x 1/4" DADO AND RABBET
DETAIL 6
1/4 x 1/4" DADO
H, L
J,N
1/2"
DETAIL 5
M,I
3/8"
H,L
DETAIL 7
1/8"
1-1/2"
1-1/8"
7/8"
1/8"
29"
30"
27-1/2"
1/8"
1-1/2"
3/4"
2-1/4"
3"
CROSS-SECTION VIEW

MATERIALS LIST
STORAGE MODULE

Key	No.	Size and description (use)
A	2	¾ x 29 x 30" oak veneer plywood (sides)
B	1	¾ x 24 x 27⅞" particleboard (back)
C	1	¾ x 24 x 30" particleboard (top)
D	1	¾ x 24 x 29⅝" particleboard (bottom)
E	1	¾ x 2⅝ x 24" oak veneer plywood (kick)
F	2	¾ x 1⅛ x 28⅛" pine (shelf support)
G	1	¾ x 23 x 29" oak veneer plywood (pull-out shelf)
		UPPER DRAWER
H	1	¾ x 10 x 23" oak veneer plywood (front)
I	2	½ x 9¼ x 19" lauan mahogany plywood (sides)
J	1	½ x 8½ x 21¾" lauan mahogany plywood (back)
K	1	¼ x 18½ x 21¾" lauan mahogany plywood (bottom)
		LOWER DRAWER
L	1	¾ x 12⅞ x 23" lauan mahogany plywood (front)
M	2	½ x 6¾ x 19" lauan mahogany plywood (sides)
N	1	½ x 6 x 21¾" lauan mahogany plywood (back)
O	1	¼ x 18½ x 21¾" lauan mahogany plywood (bottom)
P	4	¾ x 3½ x 3½" plywood (mounting blocks)
Q		1/16" oak veneer
R		1/16 x 24 x 30" plastic laminate*
S	2 pr.	18" full extension drawer slide
T	3	Brass drawer pulls
U	4	Casters
V	2	¾" No. 8 roundhead screw (adjusting screw)
Misc.		Carpenter's glue, linseed oil, paste wax, contact cement
(*)		Formica brand plastic laminate, tidal sand No. 917

STORAGE CABINET

The rolling storage cabinet matches the printer console. It can be pushed back against the wall or rolled forward next to you. The bottom drawer is sized to hold two rows of standard ring binders, and the drawer sides are cut down so you can read the spines of the notebooks easily. The top drawer holds disk-storage boxes—three rows of 5¼-in. disks or two rows of 8-in. disks.

Tucked beneath the top is a pull-out writing surface. And behind the drawers is a hidden compartment accessible only by removing the drawers. It's perfect for a small safe or fireproof storage box for valuable papers. The casters are hidden behind the recessed kick panel.

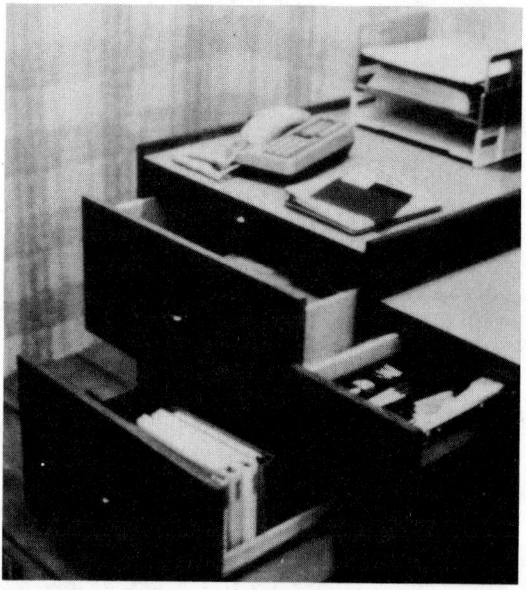

Storage module holds everything from manuals to disk cases.

This computer workstation, built by a PM reader, has the printer module on the left side and a storage module on the right. There is a fluorescent light under the lid using a tilt-sensitive mercury switch to turn it on and off. The light comes on automatically as you lift the lid.

HOW TO THINK ERGONOMICALLY

The whole point of a custom-designed workstation is to ensure maximum comfort. You may have to modify the dimensions to accommodate your equipment and yourself. These guidelines will help.

Start with your chair. It should have an adjustable seat, lumbar (lower back) support and backrest. Armrests should be removable, if you have them at all. Adjust the chair so that when you sit erect, with feet flat on the floor, your thighs are parallel to the floor.

The home row keys of the keyboard should be at or just above your elbow height when

you're seated properly. Usually, this means from 28 to 31 in. from the floor.

Remember to leave enough room for your thighs under the desk top. About 95 percent of American men require 25¼ in. from the floor to the bottom of the desk top for leg clearance, and 25 in. generally is considered the minimum. The angle between your upper and lower arms should be 90°, through a range of 80° to 120° up or down.

The position of the monitor is especially critical if you expect to avoid eyestrain. The top of the screen should be at or just below the horizontal plane of your eyes when you're sitting erect. The center of the screen should be 10° to 20° below the horizontal plane of your eye height, and the bottom of the screen within 40°.

Perhaps the most important of all, the distance between your eyes and the monitor should be 18 to 20 in. The screen should *never* be more than 27 in. from your eyes. Printed text should be the same distance from your eyes as the screen.

The biggest cause of eyestrain is glare from the monitor screen. You can minimize this by keeping your work area at a low ambient light level—between 500 and 700 lux—using indirect lighting. For printed material, use adjustable spot lighting.

Ideally, your work area should be 68° to 72° F and 30 to 40 percent humidity. Bright colors are distracting. Neutral colors should be used, especially for the desk top. Even under the best conditions, working at a computer for six hours without a break is about the limit. Otherwise, you risk eyestrain.

NEW HIGH-TECH PRODUCTS

New products add comfort and convenience to high-tech equipment in the home.

COMPUTER CHAIR

New ergonomic design of a computer chair gives natural support to your spine and muscles. You automatically sit more comfortably, breathe more easily, finish your work without strain and discomfort. Because all parts of your body are in perfect balance, no back rest is required. Unlike conventional seating, which cramps body organs into an unnatural 90° angle, this chair uses the body's own structure to give maximum comfort and support.

Ergonomic design positions muscles and skeletal structure in natural, relaxed position, very similar to the way children sit instinctively.

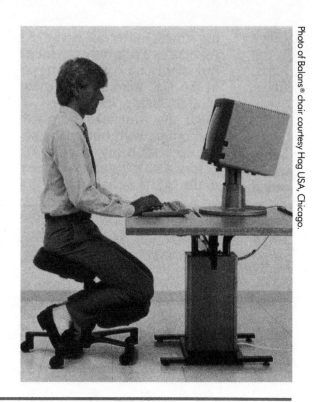

Photo of Balans® chair courtesy Hag USA, Chicago.

EASY TO MAKE PRINTED CIRCUITS

Dry transfers are a popular way to fabricate your own printed-circuit boards. The transfers are rubbed onto a blank copper board. Like press-on lettering, the circuit traces, pads and dots are easily positioned.

After the transfers are on the board it is dipped in ferrochloride for about 20 minutes. The solution eats away the copper that's not under the transfers. Clean off the board and you have a finished PC board.

NEW KEYBOARD CUTS TYPING PAIN

Every full-time typist knows that after a couple of hours, an ache climbs from the small of your back to your shoulders, then travels down your elbows toward your wrists.

Based on studies of typists' muscle actions, a research team has proposed a solution: Split the keyboard.

The standard typewriter, say scientists at the Technical School in Darmstadt, West Germany, turns the typist into a contortionist: To support the fingers, the shoulders must be lifted, the elbows splayed outward and the wrists twisted sideways almost to their limit.

Instead, the researchers, writing in *Applied Ergonomics*, propose dividing the keyboard up the middle and pivoting the bottom of each half outward by 10°. They say that the keyboard should also be tilted toward the typist by 60°. This, however, would make it difficult for the novice, who must look at the keys to find the right one. Even a 10° or 20° tilt would help, according to the designers. And the outermost keys (like the carriage return and shift keys) could be placed between the two keyboard halves to be hit with the thumb rather than the little finger.

Have any manufacturers looked into this idea? "I don't know of any in the United States who have tested it," says Richard Hirsch of IBM. "We've experimented with a number of keyboards, but none seems significantly better than the standard design."

Typing strains arm and wrist muscles, forcing them to bend unnaturally (top). But a keyboard that has been split and angled appears to relieve the discomfort (bottom).

FIRST AID FOR COMPUTER DISKS

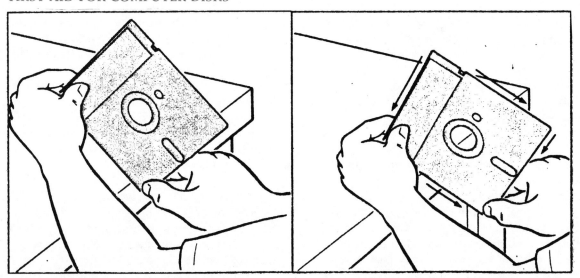

If a floppy disk won't boot (start up), it may not be moving within its jacket. Carefully grasp the disk by two corners and hold it upright on the edge of a desk (above, left). Press lightly and draw the edges of disk along the desktop (right). This will flatten edges back into shape long enough for you to recopy data to another disk.

COMPUTER MONITORS

If your computer has been sharing the family's TV set, it's time to get it a monitor of its own. Computer and video game images will be sharper and easier on your eyes.

If you're using your computer hooked up to the family TV set, you've already discovered this arrangement is far from ideal. Not only does it upset family TV viewing habits but it gives you less-than-ideal screen display of text, graphics and games from your computer. A TV set is designed to pull in programs off the airwaves, not for high-precision computer display.

TYPES OF DISPLAY DEVICES

There are three basic types of display devices for computers in use today, with promise of technology breakthroughs for other types of displays in the near future. The output from your computer can be displayed on a standard television receiver, a composite video monitor, or an RGB display screen. The type of display device you can use with your computer depends on the internal circuits of the computer itself. So before you run out to buy the very best, be sure your computer has the circuitry to drive it.

FACTORS AFFECTING SCREEN DISPLAY

A gun in a cathode ray tube fires a beam of electrons at a phosphor on the face of the tube as the beam moves left to right, top to bottom forming ideal-size fields of 262½ lines interlaced in pairs for 525-line frames—each frame repeated 30 times a second.

In a color tube, there are clusters of red, green and blue dots, bars or strips etched on the face. The size of these triads obviously limits the number of lines the electron can scan to form each image. The result is a sacrifice in picture sharpness or resolution. Monochrome screens, with a continuous phosphor coating, do not share this problem.

The intensity of the picture at any one point depends on how strong the electron beam is at that given point. Color depends also on where the beam is aimed. This is analog control, varying the intensity and aim of the electron beam to form the picture.

Most computers, on the other hand, generate on/off digital information. Instead of varying

Photo Courtesy of Data General Corporation. DATA GENERAL/One™ is a trademark of Data General Corporation.

The DATA GENERAL/One™ (above) features a full-size liquid-crystal display monitor in a 10-pound portable package.

the intensity of a continuous sweep of the electron beam, the computer looks at the scanning of the tube as a series of dots or pixels to turn on or off depending on the display desired. Each row of dots is "written" by the electron beam as it scans across the tube.

Computers form letters or numbers on the screen in a matrix of dots or pixels, most in a 63-dot matrix that is 7 dots wide by 9 dots high. This can range from as coarse as a 35-dot matrix (5 by 7) to a high resolution matrix of more than 300 dots. When you allow for blank rows of dots between lines of characters, it can take 10 to 12 scanning lines to draw a row of characters. Patterns of these dots or pixels are turned on for graphic displays.

Clarity or sharpness of the picture on the screen can be thought of in terms of how many vertical lines of these dots can be seen across the tube and how many horizontal lines of dots can be seen down the face of the screen.

Horizontal resolution, determined by the bandwidth of a display device, tells how many vertical lines across the screen can be displayed. Bandwidth is a measure of how fast information can be written to the screen. The faster a complete screen of information can be written, the more vertical lines will be seen. Bandwidth is expressed in how many millions of times the screen is written each second (MHz). To display a screen with 25 rows of 80 characters (each character in a 7 by 9 matrix), a video display device must have a 9 MHz bandwidth. A 40-column display would require only half the speed—4.5 MHz.

Vertical resolution tells how many horizontal lines down the face of the tube the device will display. In practice, the standard 525-line screen will have a vertical resolution of only 343 lines. You probably are seeing only about 260 lines of resolution on your TV set when you watch the nightly evening news. This is okay for family TV entertainment viewing but not so good for the display of text from a computer's word processing program.

Dot size is another factor affecting sharpness. When the electron beam hits the phosphor on the face of the tube, other electrons are forced off the layer of phosphor, hit the face of the tube and bounce back. This creates a "halo" around the dot. When these halos get too big, or halos on adjacent lines overlap, the picture loses sharpness. The smaller the spot turned on by the electron beam, the sharper the picture. The dot size of a TV set can be as much as 0.10mm. On a high resolution color monitor it can be half that—0.05mm—which is one reason why monitors generally give sharper, clearer pictures.

TV RECEIVERS
When television pictures are broadcast, the signal controlling the electron beam is wrapped in an envelope called a radio frequency carrier

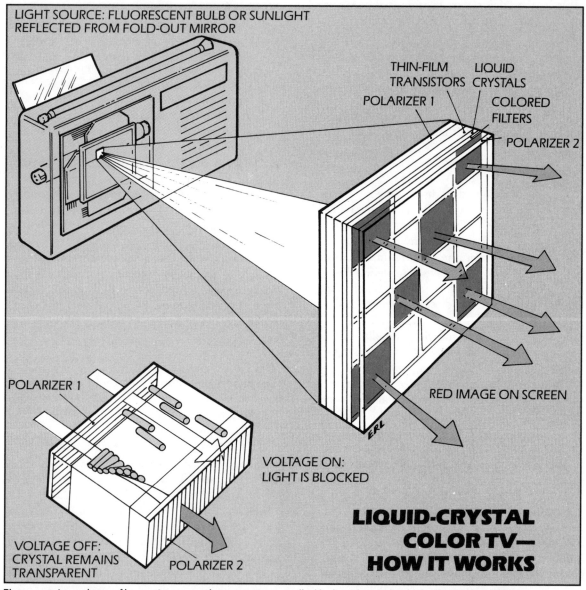

LIGHT SOURCE: FLUORESCENT BULB OR SUNLIGHT REFLECTED FROM FOLD-OUT MIRROR

THIN-FILM TRANSISTORS
LIQUID CRYSTALS
POLARIZER 1
COLORED FILTERS
POLARIZER 2
RED IMAGE ON SCREEN

POLARIZER 1
VOLTAGE ON: LIGHT IS BLOCKED
VOLTAGE OFF: CRYSTAL REMAINS TRANSPARENT
POLARIZER 2

LIQUID-CRYSTAL COLOR TV— HOW IT WORKS

Flat screen is made up of layers. Image on the screen is controlled by liquid crystals which allow polarized light to illuminate desired portions of screen through appropriate color filters, or they can be "untwisted" to block light.

wave (RF signal). There's a different envelope frequency for each TV channel. The tuner in your receiver strips away the carrier wave envelope for the channel you select leaving only the composite of the video signal for each color to be sent to the picture tube.

The amount of information for both the video signals and the carrier waves must be contained within a limited band of frequencies for broadcast. The broadcast of these signals requires receivers to have greater tolerances, and a lot of unwanted signals and noise is picked up along the way. Generally, the greater the bandwidth of your TV set, the greater will be the sharpness or resolution of the picture. But, you can't expect to see more than what's left after the tuner strips away the RF signals.

Computers that allow you to use a television receiver as the video display terminal have a built-in modulator that combines the 3 color signals and other information then wraps the composite signal in an envelope for either Channel 3 or Channel 4 (usually switchable) where it is sent by wire to the antenna terminals on your TV set to be unwrapped by the tuner, decoded and displayed.

With a color TV set, resolution of a computer image is seldom more than 16 rows of 40 characters each.

COMPOSITE VIDEO MONITORS

A monitor is designed to display the video signals from a computer, VCR or camera with a higher resolution and without the complicating and limiting circuits used to unwrap the RF carrier frequency from the picture information. Because monitors don't have to leave tolerances for the tuner to translate broadcast signals, they can be made to much closer specifications resulting in higher resolution. Connections to a monitor go directly to the video amplifiers, bypassing the antenna terminals and tuner circuits.

They are called *composite* video monitors because the red, green and blue signals are combined with other information the tube needs to be sent over a single wire bypassing any tuner circuits in the device then split apart to be sent to the appropriate place on the screen for a color display.

Almost always substituting a monitor for a TV set (if your computer has a composite video output) will mean a noticeable increase in picture sharpness and often an increase in the number of lines that can be displayed. Monochrome monitors can give you a readable screen

of at least 25 rows of 80 characters each, while some color displays of text may still be limited to 40 characters in less expensive color monitors because of the limited bandwidth or resolution. Graphic displays on monochrome monitors can display 320 rows of 640 dots each—or more in some specialized graphic terminals.

RGB DISPLAYS

With an RGB display screen, each of the three primary signals—red, green and blue—and the luminance signal controlling brightness—are sent out of the computer from different circuits over separate wires. These connections are made with a multiple-pin connector from your computer. The signals are never combined into a composite signal in the computer so they never have to be separated in the monitor. Each enters its own circuit to fire an electron gun when it scans the tube in the exact location of that color dot. The result is greatly increased sharpness of the picture. Because of the preciseness of these circuits, manufacturers of RGB displays such as Taxan can give you a color picture that is 400 lines of pixels, 720 across—but at a premium cost.

The RGB circuits in the computer can deliver a digital signal for each of the colors. These displays are restricted to the 8 colors that can be made from the red, blue and green phosphor dots lit in combination at the same intensity. Some RGB display circuits deliver analog information to the tube. The result is almost unlimited variations in the colors and brightness levels. Most offer "pallets" of 512 colors, but the potential is much greater. Your computer must be able to send each of the 3 color signals separately or you cannot use an RGB monitor. The type of connections available between the computer and the monitor can usually tell you if it can.

WHAT TO LOOK FOR

The factors you should look for in a display unit for your computer are computer capacity, bandwidth, dot pitch, screen size, color, accessories and cost.

Computer capacity will determine the kind of display device you should invest in. Adding a high resolution Taxan Model 440 monitor will do little good with an Atari computer that only sends out 191 lines of information. A high-res color RGB is a waste of money with the Sanyo MBC-1250 computer which has the high-res graphics, but no circuits to drive a color signal. In a similar manner, your picture sharpness is not going to be great by adding the 80-column board to a Commodore 64 if the color monitor you're using has a bandwidth limiting the display to 40 characters.

Bandwidth determines the sharpness or resolution of the picture displayed. It is usually measured in millions of cycles per second (MHz). As a rule of thumb, you can expect about 80 lines of horizontal resolution from each MHz of bandwidth. TV sets typically have a bandwidth of 3.8 to 4.5 MHz; a good monitor can have a bandwidth of 50 MHz. Most manufacturers of computer monitors and RGB displays specify bandwidth as lines of resolution while TV sets are more likely to express this in MHz, if at all.

Dot pitch is the size of each red, green and blue dot and the space between them. A color display is limited to the number of triads of red, green and blue dots, bars or stripes etched on the face of the tube. Monochrome screens, with a single continuous phosphor, can have a much smaller dot pitch and higher resolution. High resolution color monitors can have a dot pitch of 0.05mm but a color TV set can be twice that. Manufacturers of computer monitors often express dot pitch in terms of the matrix of dots or pixels on the entire screen. Typical specs range from the 320 by 200 pixels of the Commodore C-1702 monitor to the 720 by 420 pixels of Amdek's Color IV RGB display.

Screen size does not follow the rule that more is better. The best screen size for a monitor for close-in work is 12 inches diagonal measure whether it's monochrome or color. This is because most computing is done with your eyes approximately 18 to 20 inches from the screen. If you plan to use the monitor for a lot of game play, then 13 inches is an ideal size. The extra inch *does* make a difference. As screen size gets too small, however, the "halos" of the dots overlap producing a fuzzy picture.

Color depends what you use your computer for. If you do a lot of business-type work, you're much better off getting a monochrome display which typically has much higher resolution. If you also plan to do color bar charts or play some computer games you need a color monitor. You might want to get both kinds of monitors and connect them to the computer using a selector switch, an inexpensive item available in most computer stores.

Monochrome displays are not called black & white screen any more. A screen with a green phosphor (green letters on a black background) is now almost the monochrome standard in the

U.S. Amber screens are gaining in popularity because they're very legible and cause less eyestrain. They are about the only kind you can buy in Europe.

Accessories. Some monitors are really bare bones when it comes to controls. Some have two knobs on the front labels PULL-On and BRIGHT. Others have enough control knobs to operate a Space Shuttle. The brightness and contrast of the image on the screen can affect the sharpness of the picture. The brighter you turn up these controls, the harder the electron beam hits the phosphor. This creates dots with bigger halos and less sharpness.

Some monitors have a window-screen-like mesh attached to the front. This is an anti-glare shield and its very effective in eliminating annoying reflection. It's available built-in to both monochrome and color monitors or can be added as an accessory later. Some of these anti-glare screens can create an optical resolution loss because the brightness control is turned up to compensate for the light filtered out.

Cost is a factor we all consider. Monochrome models range from $99 to about $250, and color models retail from $300 to $700. If you prefer, you can spend thousands of dollars on a color RGB display device designed for special scientific uses, but it's not likely that you'll find such units in your department or computer store.

NEW TECHNOLOGY BREAKTHROUGHS
The fall of 1984 saw several lap-sized computers introduced with full 80 column, 25 line

Flat screen is sandwich of microcomponents.

monochrome display screens less than an inch thick. These larger flat screens are a second generation of the 40 by 8 displays vying for acceptance in the computer marketplace for the past year or so. These screens use a technology called liquid-crystal-display (LCD)—something you've seen on pocket calculators and digital watches for a long time but just recently perfected to the point where they can be used as television screens or computer displays.

Two factors have affected their limited acceptance in the computer community: First, they had (until now) limited screen capacity. They were also limited to a monochrome display, and that often a very coarse matrix of dots or pixels.

Getting a workable liquid-crystal display (LCD) image on a monochrome screen was child's play compared to getting it in color. Unlike regular TV tubes, an LCD display doesn't generate its own light, so an external light source is needed. LCD watches and clocks have a tiny light bulb that reflects its light from the front of the crystal display. The technology for the LCD color TV was developed by Seiko and the company holds all patents for the sandwich-type television screen.

In the Epson Elf and the Seiko TFT (Thin Film Technology), transmitted light is used instead of reflected light. Light coming from a built-in fluorescent bulb, or reflected from a fold-down mirror, passes through the LCD elements. The screen uses polarized light to operate. Light coming through the rear glass of the screen's sandwich is filtered into parallel light waves by passing through the glass' polarizing structure. The light can be stopped by another screen or screen element that is polarized at a 90° angle.

The tiny TV's 2-inch (diagonal measure) screen is made up of 52,800 pixels or picture elements, and each of these is a fast-acting liquid-crystal element. The manufacturer has gone to great lengths to develop a special invisible transistor that's mounted on each picture element. This transistor provides the voltage to change the crystal's alignment to polarize the light in about 300 milliseconds (thousandths of a second). The transistors are indeed invisible, or at least transparent, and are deposited as thin films on the LCD elements. According to the manufacturer, each transistor is only 0.3 microns thick.

Each of the screen elements has a color filter in front—one for the three primary TV colors of red, blue and green. These in turn are grouped in threes, and each group is a triad.

Light shining through the screen from behind passes through one of these positions, and the filter gives that element its particular color. Where color is not called for (image is supposed to be dark), the LCD element electronically rotates its axis 90° and the light is blocked by the second polarizer.

The light source can be ordinary daylight, reflected from a fold-down mirror, or it can come from an internal fluorescent source, which you can switch on as needed. The battery drain is considerably lower when the set is sun-powered (1.1 watts vs. 1.9 watts in the Epson Elf).

The system runs on five AA-size penlight batteries or from an a.c. adapter that comes with the set. Optional power sources include a rechargeable battery pack and a cigarette lighter plug-in for the car.

The pocket-size TV is only slightly larger than a standard microcassette stape recorder. The Elf is 3 inches high by 6¼ inches wide by 1⅛ inches thick, and weighs 1.1 pounds with batteries in place. The Seiko TFT is 3.15 by 6.3 by 1.22 inches and is less than a pound. The Epson uses a single fluorescent bulb mounted at the top of the screen. The Seiko model has a pair of fluorescent bulbs mounted at the screen's two sides.

Conventional battery life is rated at about five hours for a set of alkalines. A collapsible monopole antenna is attached to the top of the set. Controls include on-off/volume, brightness, continuous-dial tuning and a light on-off switch.

Color and tint controls on the side of the set are difficult to adjust—made that way on purpose to prevent accidental changes in settings.

An easel snaps out of the back to support the set on a tabletop, and there are four jacks on the side: 7.5 volts d.c. (input from the a.c. or cigarette-lighter adapter), earphone jack, and inputs for video and audio signals from such external sources as a video cassette or your computer.

See color illustrations of computer monitors on pages 18-19.

In actual use, flat screens of Seiko TFT and Epson Elf color television sets are illuminated from behind, but simulated images were used for this photograph

18

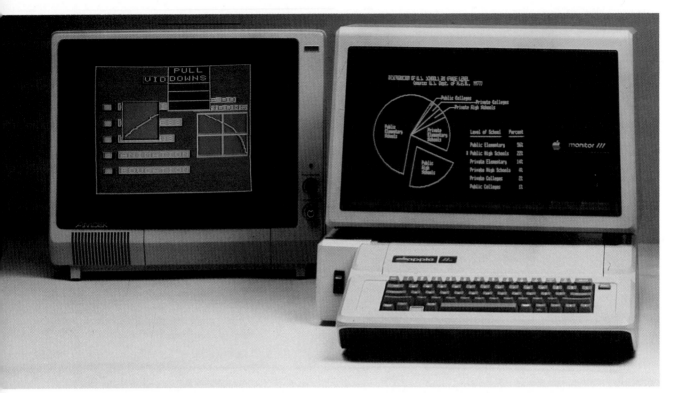

Amdek Color-1 Plus (left) is currently the top-selling computer monitor for full-color display. The Apple III monitor (with the Apple IIe computer, right) is a 12-inch green phosphor monochrome unit that is particularly suited for text and word processing work.

COMPUTER WORKSTATION

This three-piece computer desk keeps everything neat and gives you plenty of room to work. Storage module, left of the main desk, holds everything from manuals to disk cases. Desk module holds color and black and white monitors, as well as computer and disk drive. Printer module to the right of the main desk has shelves for printer and paper. See page 4.

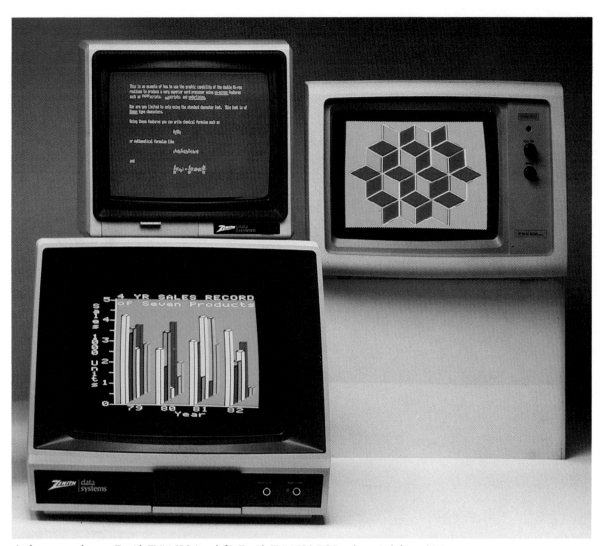

Amber monochrome Zenith ZVM-122 (top left), Zenith ZVM-133 RGB color unit (left) and Princeton Graphic HX-12 (right) are popular monitors. Driving all the monitors is the Apple IIe computer shown with the Kensington SystemSaver. Inside the IIe is the new Video 7 RGB hi-res graphics color board, providing color graphics quality previously thought to be impossible with the Apple. Screen photo on the HX-12 was created with Koala touch pad and Coloring Series I software. Other screens were taken from a demonstration disc supplied by Video 7. Multiple screen shots were possible with an Amdek-supplied hand-wired demonstration monitor box.

Amdek Color-1 Plus is a low-res color set good for games and some graphics, poor with text.

The green monochrome hi-res Apple III monitor works well with text and mono graphics.

Zenith ZVM-133 is a hi-res R-G-B color monitor with many controls to zero in on good picture.

Zenith ZVM-122 is a top-selling hi-res monochrome monitor, especially good for business use.

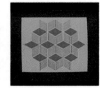

PGS HX-12 is a hi-res R-G-B color monitor which is especially popular with IBM computer owners.

COMPACT DISC PLAYERS

New laser turntables with controls that let you
cue your music with the skill of a disc jockey
and the purest sound you've ever heard from
your stereo system.

*When a Compact Disc lands in the front-loading drawer of any one of these second-generation players,
it'll deliver the purest sound you've heard from your stereo system.*

The drawer glides open without a sound, inviting you to drop in your latest laser disc. It slides closed just as quietly, and the disc spins up to speed. You can then listen to the music without lifting a finger, or you can take over, playing the panel controls to pick off the disc just what you want to hear. Select any track with the touch of a button, skim through all the selections, hearing a snippet of each; or punch in a program to hear the tracks in the order you want.

Easy operation and versatile manipulation of the laser disc are common to all the second-generation $500 to $700 Compact Disc players, sometimes called laser turntables. The newest players are technically better and lower priced than their $1,000 ancestors, which were introduced in 1983. Here's where you'll find some of the improvements.

STRONG NERVES AND MUSCLES
Optical guidance systems and electronics are more sophisticated. The lasers that read digital information off the disc and keep the beam on track, and the microprocessors that change light to sound, are cheaper to produce, lighter in weight and more reliable. Large-scale integrated circuits have replaced entire boards of electronic components. Tiny servos now guide the arm that carries the laser and do it more accurately than the massive linkages that were used originally.

AMAZING MEMORIES
The latest digital logic circuitry can track the tiny micro-pits engraved on the spinning CD with exceptional single-mindedness. When dirt or scratches cause brief information dropouts, the decoding circuitry pulls replacement information from computer memories to patch these chuckholes before the audio circuits of the player get the shock or dead spots of silence. There is so much compensating circuitry that audible glitches are rare, except when playing damaged or unusually faulty discs.

SPEED READERS
Readout panels show you how much time has elapsed or remains on a whole disc or just one track. All the information is on the discs, just waiting to be read. There are even four ways of repeating music: You can replay a whole disc, just one song, selections in the programmable memory or all music between two programmed points (A-B repeat). One final control feature is for the do-it-yourselfer who wants to locate music manually, as opposed to programming it in. This is music search, which samples brief bits of music as the laser skims over the disc.

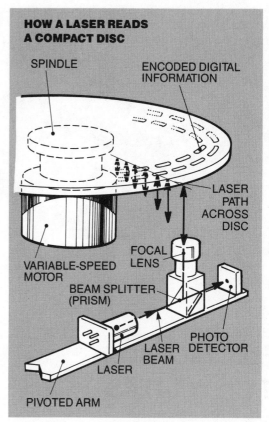

HOW A LASER READS A COMPACT DISC

SPINDLE

ENCODED DIGITAL INFORMATION

LASER PATH ACROSS DISC

VARIABLE-SPEED MOTOR

FOCAL LENS

BEAM SPLITTER (PRISM)

PHOTO DETECTOR

LASER BEAM

LASER

PIVOTED ARM

Digitally recorded music is stored on the underside of a Compact Disc as microscopic pits etched into a perfectly reflective foil, laminated into the disc's transparent protective coating. The pits are arranged along a spiral, like a phonograph-record groove, but they start at the inside of the disc. The disc rotates slower when the laser moves toward the edge because the pits must pass the finely focused laser beam at a constant linear velocity. The laser beam is reflected up through a prism and focused onto the whirling disc's reflective layer. The beam, interrupted by the speeding pits, is reflected back down through the lens and prism, and is perceived by the photo detector as incredibly rapid on/off pulses—pure digital information that provides flawless audio signals to your amplifier.

COMPONENT SYSTEMS
Some manufacturers design entire interrelated component systems, including CDs. Record synchronization lets you start a CD player and a cassette deck (set to record) with the touch of one button. Both stop at the same time. What about the possibility of future audio *and* video information packed onto CDs? Small as they are, Compact Discs have room enough for more than just the 70 minutes of stereo sound they currently can hold, and manufacturers have been searching for a technical standard for video images on CDs.

Some electronic typewriters are computerlike. The IBM Model 95 accommodates a floppy-disk drive for added word-storage, and a communications module (far right) to send documents to another unit over the phone.

ELECTRONIC TYPEWRITERS

The latest electronic typewriters put speed and precision at your fingertips.

Most of us probably look upon typing as a chore—hardly a source of enjoyment or entertainment! But it's true—technology has made the latest generation of electronic typewriters absolutely fascinating to use. The combination of programmable memory and high-speed printing takes the most tedious burdens off the typist's hands, and the computerlike features of today's electronic typewriters enable the user to correct, revise and even rearrange a document with a minimum of retyping.

Electronic typewriters—ETs for short—aren't limited to busy corporate offices. They're widely available now in a broad range of models that offers varying degrees of sophistication. The simplest portable can help a student correct mistakes or perform minor revisions while typing a term paper. A more advanced, stationary model would have enough internal memory to store the entire assignment, allowing the student to restructure the piece, add footnotes or even new blocks of text to the paper. The most sophisticated ETs can be hooked up to an external memory-storage device as a computer floppy-disk drive. This means a student could record the entire content of a doctoral thesis (or even a novel) and make revisions electronically on a video monitor instead of on paper. When deadline approaches, pressing a button would send the final draft onto the paper at high speed.

Compared to conventional electric typewriters, the appearance of an ET is at once familiar and strange. Most ETs are wider than the electric and the manual typewriters from which they evolved—usually wide enough to accommodate computer paper 17 in. wide. The keyboard looks similar too, but you'll find banks of additional program keys on either side of the ET's alphanumeric keyboard. Lift the ET's lid, though, and you're in for a surprise.

In place of the familiar rods and levers, the ET substitutes a mass of circuit boards and a single, mobile printing unit. The latter is the only part you'll see: Most manufacturers conceal the circuit boards beneath the keyboard or behind the platen. One company boasts its machines have 30 moving parts, down from 300.

HOW IT WORKS

When you depress a character key, you activate a switch on a layer just below the keyboard. This sends an electrical signal to the circuit board, which relays the signal to a microprocessor.

Up to this point, everything is quiet, invisible and instantaneous as the signal moves along wires or flat, ribbonlike cables to the printing unit. At the printing unit, the ET begins to sound off and show its mechanical dexterity.

PRINT WHEELS

On most ETs, the business end of the printing unit is a "daisy wheel" about 3 in. in diameter. The daisy is composed of typebars or "petals" with a letter, number or symbol at the tip of each. (Some machines use a golf-ball-like element for printing; the simpler portables use a dot-matrix mechanism.

In response to keyboarded instructions, the daisy wheel spins at high speed to position the selected petal before the ink ribbon. The daisy takes its directions from a stepper motor (see technical illustration). Once the petal is in position, it's struck by a plunger and hammer assembly. The petal, in turn, strikes the ink ribbon to make an impression of its character on the paper.

CHARACTER PREVIEW DISPLAY

Most models will let you preview what you're composing through a visual display window similar to electronic calculators. You can then backspace, on the visual display, to correct your spelling or revise your text *before* you command the ET to print on paper.

The character capacity of the display window varies with the particular ET model. Portables show you a few words at a time, intermediate models an entire line, and the most sophisticated ETs display half a page or more at a glance.

COPY STORAGE

Compared to the amount of copy you can see, the amount you can revise before printing depends on how much internal memory the machine offers.

With many inexpensive portables, you're usually limited to the character capacity of the display window. Most manufacturers' intermediate, stationary models can store between 10 and 20 pages in their internal memory. If you write lengthy documents, or if your work involves producing many versions of a similar document (a standard legal contract or form letter, for example), you might consider a more sophisticated ET—one that allows you to add external storage devices (floppy-disk drive or cassette recorder) with virtually unlimited memory. In this case, you'll probably want a video display monitor, too.

Typical ET printing unit: Encoder changes keyboard signal to light, tells motor to find the desired petal and to print.

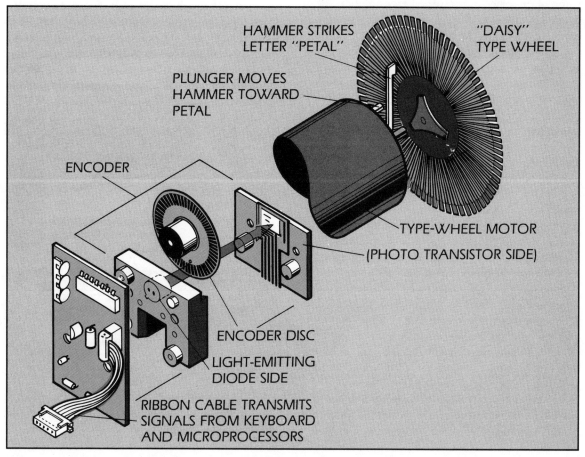

HAMMER STRIKES LETTER "PETAL"

"DAISY" TYPE WHEEL

PLUNGER MOVES HAMMER TOWARD PETAL

ENCODER

TYPE-WHEEL MOTOR

(PHOTO TRANSISTOR SIDE)

ENCODER DISC

LIGHT-EMITTING DIODE SIDE

RIBBON CABLE TRANSMITS SIGNALS FROM KEYBOARD AND MICROPROCESSORS

Royal-Adler's Model 1035 electronic typewriter has a separate keyboard with video display window for flexible placement.

SPECIAL FUNCTIONS

One feature made possible by the ET's internal memory is the ability to store frequently used phrases. You can type a phrase (such as "payment due upon receipt") once and assign it to a particular program key in memory. When you come to the place in a letter where the phrase is needed, you simply press the key and the ET types your phrase for you.

Those program keys are capable of numerous automatic functions, depending again on the ET model. Besides the usual margin, tab, indent and backspace functions, the program keys can perform time-consuming tasks such as underlining each word as you type it and erasing one character at a time or an entire line at once. ETs can center titles in your document, or even justify right-hand margins to give the appearance of a printed page. With some ETs you don't even have to strike the carriage return at the end of the line, but your copy will automatically "wrap around" to the next line when your right margin is reached. This feature alone can speed up your typing time dramatically.

Some worthwhile functions involve pressing several program keys in sequence. For example, you might press the search and replace keys to make your ET find a word or phrase you wish to change. It will print out your text up to that point, then stop and wait for your orders. You simply add the new or revised text and press the insert key. What if you discover you've misspelled a word throughout your document? Simply program your ET to perform global search and replace, and it will locate and correct the mistake everywhere the word appears. Some ETs are so sophisticated they can transmit your finished copy to another ET. This is done over phone lines through the addition of an accessory telephone modem.

COMPUTER FEATURES WITH TYPEWRITER EASE

With disk drives, video display monitors and telephone modems, the somewhat understated ET begins to take on the appearance of a computer. It isn't. An ET won't perform accounting programs for you, nor will it let you play computer games. It doesn't tie into as many telephone-line data networks as computers do. A computer, though, will perform the word-processing chores an ET will.

So why not buy a computer? One reason is convenience. If all you're going to do is type, there's no point in mastering the complexities of a computer's word-processing program. Another reason is cost: With a computer, you'll be paying for functions you don't intend to use.

For those who already own computers for word-processing chores, the ET can be an inexpensive alternative to a letter-quality printer to supplement the higher-speed dot matrix printer you use for rough drafts. Most ETs can be modified to accept the output of your computer through the familiar printer ribbon cable connections without losing the advantages of having a sophisticated typewriter for tasks where the computer's storage or word-processing capabilities are not needed.

The Penman De Luxe ET from Silver-Reed is a light-duty, stationary machine. Built-in handle makes the machine easily portable.

SUPERDENSITY DISKS AND DRIVES

A new way of packing information onto the familiar 5¼-inch floppy disk will turn it into a megabyte storage system.

A new superdensity floppy disk drive developed by Eastman Kodak makes it possible to store four to eight times as much computer data on a conventional-size floppy disk.

The superdensity disk drive can pack up to 3.3 megabytes (million characters) on a 5¼-in. floppy disk—a disk that until now has been able to hold a maximum of about 800 kilobytes (thousand characters).

The technology involves using an extra-fine, ultra-pure thin magnetic coating to create a superdensity floppy disk. It also involves a new servo-driven disk drive with newly developed read/write heads that can write and read tracks of data packed so closely together that 1 inch of disk surface contains 192 parallel tracks (192 tracks per inch, or tpi).

Not long ago 91 kilobytes of disk storage on a 5¼-in. disk was a lot. This was what you got on the old Osborne I, and even today on the typical single-density Atari. Track spacing for this kind of storage is 20 TPI, and only one side of the disk is used.

Other computer manufacturers have opted for double-density storage, which puts about 180K on a single side of a disk. Double-density systems use track spacing of 40 to 48 TPI.

Double-sided disk drives have two sets of read/write heads and work on both sides of a disk at the same time. They double the disk's storage space—usually to 320K instead of 160K while keeping the same track spacing of 40 to 48 TPI.

There's also *quad* density, which can pack up to 390K on one side of a disk and 780K on double-sided versions. These units use track spacing of 90 to 96 TPI and use either heads with more finely spaced gaps or two sets of read/write heads on the same side of the disk.

The very fine coatings used on the 780K disks are nothing compared to the precision of the new superdensity floppies. The superdensity disks have to be preformatted at the factory—with special magnetic "sector" dividing lines and magnetic signals that tell the disk drive where its heads are at any time.

At the moment, at least three companies are

The Kodak superdensity disk looks like any other floppy disk, but when used on the new disk drive it will pack in four to eight times the storage of conventional disks.

involved in producing these systems. The first to actually put an add-on product on the market, Rana Systems, has introduced a floppy disk drive that stores 2.5 megabytes on each disk. The first unit in the line is a $1,550 add-on for IBM-PC computers, but an Apple version is also coming, and compatibility with others may follow.

You get a 10-pack starter set of superdensity disks when you buy the Rana drive. Extra disks now cost $16 each, which works out to $160 a box—compared to $30 to $60 a box for conventional disks.

If you pay $30 for a box of disks for the IBM-PC at 360K per disk, that comes to about 83 cents per 100K. Using the same formula, the new Rana disks cost about 64 cents per 100K. They're 23 percent less in cost, and they're probably a lot easier to use, since you have fewer disks to contend with. One 10-pack will hold as much as 50 conventional floppies.

Kodak has been quietly making disk drives, now being marketed by Data Technology Corporation. DTC, which specializes in making disk controller plug-in cards, is offering the new superdensity drives (called the "3.3") in versions for other manufacturers to use and is also marketing them separately through computer dealers. The detail version, called "TeamMate," is available without a case for building into an IBM-PC or Apple. You can also get it in a box for add-on installations.

According to Data Technology, the new drives will also "read down"—working with more conventional disks that use quad format (780K per disk) and double density (360K per disk).

To make the whole scene even more interesting, Kaypro is now selling its first desktop computer, called "Robie," with *two* of these superdensity drives at 2.6 megabytes each.

STEREO SYSTEM MUSIC BOX

Quality stereo equipment deserves to be shown off in style. This rack-type cabinet does just that.

Owning a multicomponent home stereo system creates one immediate problem—where do you store all the components? The current solution to this problem is the stereo rack—a cabinet sold to stack stereo components on shelves vertically. But here's an alternative: Use these plans to build your own solid oak rack-style stereo cabinet.

MEASURE EQUIPMENT

Before starting construction, measure your stereo equipment to ensure that the cabinet will accommodate it all. The cabinet is designed to accept many standard-size components, but you may have to alter sizes for your equipment.

CABINET SIDES

Begin by building the cabinet sides. Each side consists of a frame with a solid panel insert. Cut the frame pieces. Notice the top and bottom pieces are 2 in. wider than the sides. This is to allow for the inside radius cutouts. To make the

The contemporary oak cabinet provides storage space that's custom fitted to your audio equipment plus a tape drawer and shelves for components and records.

radius cutouts, first pencil the cutout profile on the frame top and bottom pieces. Then rough-cut the waste using a band saw or sabre saw. Next, make a ¼-in. plywood template ½ in. wider and ½ in. longer than the desired cutout. Clamp the template in place as shown. Now use a router fitted with a ½-in. guide bushing and a ¼-in. straight bit to smooth the cutout's rough inside edge. Steer the bushing against the template's edge to control the bit.

Next, dry-assemble the two frames with bar or pipe clamps. Using a router fitted with a ¼ x ⁹⁄₁₆-in. slotting cutter, groove the inside edge of both frames for installing the side panels. Then, round the inside frame edges with a ½-in. rounding-over bit. Also, mark the dowel locations at both of the frames' four joints. Disassemble the frames and use a drill press or a doweling jig to bore ⅜-in.-dia. x 1⅛-in.-deep holes at these locations. Before reassembling the frames, you must make and install the side panel inserts.

To form each side panel insert, edge-glue and clamp together two ½ x 6 (or wider) x 36-in. oak boards. After the glue has dried, cut the panels ¾ in. wider and ¾ in. longer than the inside frame openings. Then, cut off the four corners of both panels to match the frame inside curves. Next, rout a ¼-in.-deep x ¾-in. rabbet around the perimeter of both panels using a ¾-in. straight bit. Clamp a wood block to the router base to serve as a fence and prevent the bit from cutting beyond ¾ in. Round the panels' raised edge using a block plane. Use a belt sander to smooth all surfaces of both panels.

Reassemble the frames with the side panels in place. Join the frame pieces using ⅜-in.-dia. x 2-in. hardwood dowels. Apply glue to the dowels and joints. Clamp the frames square.

BUILDING THE SHELVES

Form the top and bottom shelves by edge-gluing oak boards to the desired width. Then, assemble the three middle shelves and the cabinet back as frames with doweled joints. The framed design allows air to circulate around the stereo components. It also makes it easier to wire connections between components. Be sure to make the middle shelf members at least 3 in. wide to provide a solid support for the components' feet.

ASSEMBLE THE CABINET

After the glue has dried on the cabinet sides, cut the outside corners round as shown. Sand all surfaces of both sides smooth using a belt sander and 120-grit paper. Next, use a ¾-in. straight bit to rout a mating pair of stopped dadoes into the cabinet sides for each shelf. Be sure to clamp a straightedge in place to guide the router. Notice the dadoes are cut to within 1 in. of the cabinet front edge. Make certain the dadoes are cut into the side frame members *only* and not into the panel inserts.

Using the same router setup, groove the sides for receiving the cabinet back. Also dado the cabinet back for accepting all shelves. Shape both edges of each side with a ½-in. rounding-over bit.

Before assembling the cabinet, notch the front-corner details on all shelves—except the bottom shelf—as shown. To cut the notches,

first bore a ½-in.-dia. hole located ¾ in. in from the shelf front and side edges. Then, use either a band saw or sabre saw to remove the waste. Shape the front edges of all shelves (except the bottom shelf) with a ½-in. rounding-over bit.

Dry-assemble the cabinet to make certain all joints fit properly. Start final assembly by gluing the cabinet shelves and back into the side dadoes. Then, clamp the cabinet square. Counterbore ⅜-in.-dia. holes at all screw-hole locations on both sides. Bore ⅛-in.-dia. pilot holes and screw the cabinet together with 1¼-in. No. 8 flathead screws.

COVE DETAILS

Make the rounded cove details used at the cab-

Trim the side radii cutouts using a router fitted with a ½-in. guide bushing. Guide the bushing against a plywood template to control the cutter.

With the side frames dry-assembled, rout the panel grooves with a ¼ x ⁹/₁₆-in. slotting cutter. Then, shape the frame opening's edge using a ½-in. rounding-over bit. Also mark the dowel locations at each joint before disassembling.

Rout the stopped dadoes for the shelves and the cabinet back with a ¾-in. straight bit. You must clamp a straightedge in place to guide the router. Be certain the bit cuts into the frame members only and not into the side panels.

Assemble the cabinet with glue and then clamp it square. Use glue sparingly to avoid excess squeeze-out. Secure the shelves with screws turned into the cabinet's sides. Conceal the screwheads with ⅜-in.-dia. walnut plugs.

Glue and clamp the three cove pieces in a plywood jig. Cut joining edges at 22½° angles. The top board serves as a clamping block to ensure even pressure.

The cabinet back is designed to allow easy wiring among components. Notice the back is recessed for additional space to store excess wire.

First use a bench plane to round the cove's outside surface. Then, finish-sand to remove all of the planing marks.

Notch drawer front to match the shelf edge detail and to serve as drawer pulls. Join sides to front with dovetail joints.

inet's top rear and bottom front. Form each cove by edge-gluing together three 2½ x 21-in. oak boards. Cut the joining edges with the saw blade set at a 22½° angle. Then, glue and clamp the cove pieces into the plywood jig as shown. Use a clamping block to provide even clamping pressure.

After the glue has dried, round the outside cove surface, using first a bench plane and then sandpaper. Cut the cove length to equal the cabinet interior dimension. Secure each cove with four 1¼-in. No. 8 flathead screws. Conceal the screwheads by plugging all counterbores with ⅜-in.-dia. walnut plugs.

ASSEMBLING THE STORAGE DRAWER

The front of the tape cassette storage drawer is notched at each end to match the shelf detail. To make the drawer, first lay out the dovetail joints used to join the drawer sides with the drawer front. Mark the 5° sloped dovetails onto the side pieces. Then, cut along the sloped lines using a dovetail saw or a fine-tooth backsaw. Next, use a coping saw to rough-cut out the waste in the joint sockets. Trim the sockets clean with a sharp ¼-in. chisel. Use the finished drawer side to mark the dovetail pins onto the mating front drawer end. Be sure to keep all edges aligned. Round out the waste area from the drawer front joint using a ¼-in. straight bit. Finish trimming the sockets clean with a sharp ¼-in. chisel.

Cut the rabbets into the drawer sides for accepting the drawer back. Groove all drawer pieces for installing the ¼-in. oak veneer plywood drawer bottom. Assemble the drawer with glue and clamp it square. Once the glue has dried, belt sand all surfaces and shape the drawer front's edges with a ½-in. rounding-over bit. The finished drawer fits snugly between the second and third shelves and operates without using slide hardware. Apply paste wax to the drawer bottom edges occasionally to ensure smooth operation.

BUILDING THE CABINET BASE

Cut the cabinet base members as shown and assemble them with glue. To install the base, first counterbore ⅜-in.-dia. x 1-in.-deep holes into the base stretchers. Then, use four 1½-in. No. 8 roundhead screws to secure the base to the underside of the cabinet bottom shelf.

After finish-sanding the cabinet, apply several hand-rubbed coats of Watco Danish oil finish. Allow the oil to dry, then apply a protective paste wax coat. Install and wire up your stereo equipment, then sit back and enjoy.

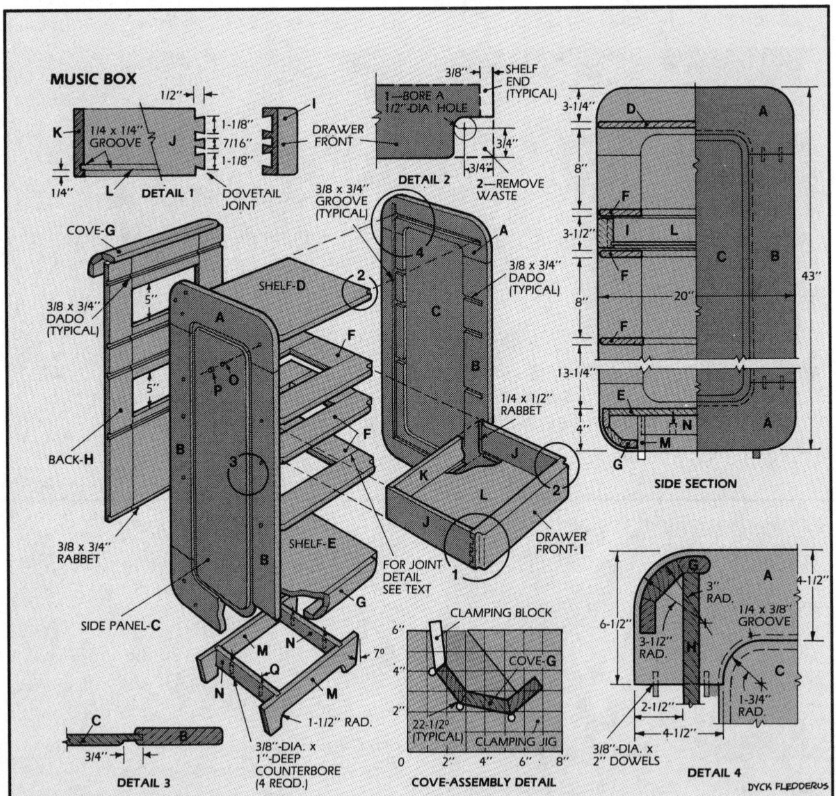

MATERIALS LIST
STEREO SYSTEM BOX

Key	No.	Size and description (use)
A	4	⅞ x 6½ x 20" oak (frame top and bottom)
B	4	⅞ x 4½ x 43" oak (frame sides)
C	2	½ x 11¾ x 34¾" oak (side panels)
D	1	¾ x 17⅛ x 20" oak (top shelf)
E	1	¾ x 16⅛ x 20" oak (bottom shelf)
F	3	¾ x 17⅛ x 20" oak (framed shelves)
G	2	¾ x 2½ x 21"* oak, six pieces required (cove)
H	1	¾ x 20 x 38¾" oak (back)
I	1	1¾ x 3⅜ x 19⅞" oak (drawer front)
J	2	½ x 3⅜ x 15" oak (drawer sides)
K	1	½ x 3⅜ x 19⅜" oak (drawer back)
L	1	¼ x 15 x 19⅜ oak veneer plywood (drawer bottom)
M	2	¾ x 4 x 16" oak (base front and back)
N	2	¾ x 2 x 11¾" oak (base stretcher)
O	28	1¼" No. 8 flathead screws
P	28	⅜"-dia. x ⅜" walnut plugs
Q	4	1½" No. 8 roundhead screws

Misc.: Carpenter's glue, Watco Danish oil finish, 600-grit wet/dry abrasive paper, paste wax.
(*) Trim to fit.

CRAFT PROJECTS

EXPERT WAYS TO MAKE BUTCHER BLOCK

Wood-joining techniques for building butcher block tops.

Butcher blocks are now enjoying a renaissance. These attractive hardwood surfaces are durable, versatile and easy to make.

Butcher blocks are most commonly used for active work surfaces such as kitchen counter-tops, chopping blocks and workbenches. The warm, hand-crafted look of butcher blocks also makes them a popular choice for furniture. Vir-

Dowel pins. Fluted dowel pins are used to join lengths of ¾ × 2-in. cherry. Note that they're joined in pairs first. Cross section (top) reveals dowel locations.

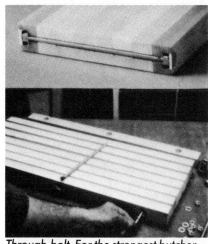

Through-bolt. For the strongest butcher block joint, bolt each part together with a threaded rod. Counterbore end pieces (top) to accept a nut, washer and plug.

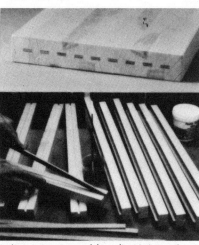

Spline joint. Assemble spline joints using mahogany plywood splines. Groove each member on both sides, except the end pieces (top), to accept the splines.

Nail pins. Cut pins from finishing nails using a pair of end-cut nippers. The pins strengthen the glued joint and prevent the wood from slipping when clamped.

Glue joint. Use a glue-joint bit to cut mating edges on all parts. Then glue the parts ot a plywood base. Cross section (top) shows the tight-fitting joints.

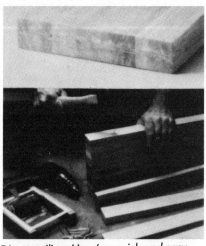

Direct nailing. Here's a quick and easy way to make a strong joint. Simply glue and nail one board to the next until the desired width butcher block top is formed.

Parquet flooring. Glue hardwood floor-ing to a plywood base. After assembly, add trim around the butcher block to conceal the plywood edge (top).

tually any hardwood can be used to make butcher blocks, either alone or in combination with other species for a contrasting appearance.

These butcher block techniques are described: dowel pins, through-bolt, spline-joint, nail pins, glue-joint, direct-nailing and a top made using teak parquet flooring. Each technique provides an easy way to assemble strong, durable butcher block tops. The particular technique you choose depends on the size and function of the butcher block, the tools you have available and the desired finished appearance. For example, the through-bolt technique provides the strongest top and is recommended for large surfaces subjected to heavy poundings. If thin boards are used to make a smaller butcher block top, try the easy, direct-nailing method. In most situations, many of the techniques shown would be suitable.

ASSEMBLY

After milling the butcher block pieces to the same width and thickness, cut them ½ in. longer than needed to allow for final trimming with a portable circular saw or radial-arm saw. Next, arrange the pieces with the best side up. Then orient the pieces so that the wood grain of each piece is pointing in the same direction. Mark an arrow on each piece to indicate the grain direction. By pointing the grain in the same direction, the plane won't gouge the wood.

Now mark each board with a number or letter to help you arrange them for final assembly and to assure that you machine each piece from the same face or edge. This is especially important for techniques that require boring holes or cutting grooves.

Since most butcher block surfaces are exposed to water, use a water-resistant glue during assembly, such as plastic resin. Simply mix the powdered resin with water as per label instructions. Use a miniature paint roller to apply the glue evenly and quickly.

After planing and sanding the assembled top smooth, apply several coats of mineral oil or Wood Bowl Seal, a non-toxic sealer.

If you don't own a drill press, use a portable drill with a doweling jig to bore dowel pin holes. Note depth-stop collar on the drill bit.

Apply glue to the walls of the holes and then tap in the pins using a wooden or plastic mallet so you don't damage the ends.

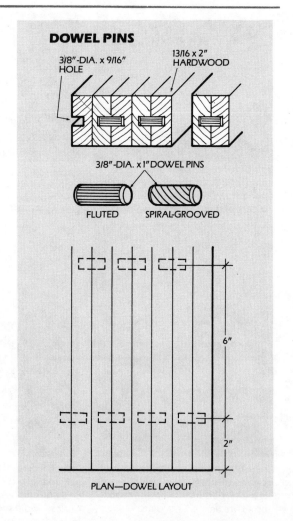

DOWEL PINS

3/8"-DIA. x 9/16" HOLE

13/16 x 2" HARDWOOD

3/8"-DIA. x 1" DOWEL PINS

FLUTED   SPIRAL-GROOVED

6"

2"

PLAN—DOWEL LAYOUT

DOWEL PINS

This technique uses hardwood dowel pins to join the butcher block members. The wood members are first joined in pairs, and then into blocks of four using a staggered dowel pattern. Continue joining the pieces this way until the desired width butcher block is obtained. It's important to use only fluted or spiral-grooved dowel pins, not sections or ordinary hardwood dowels. The flutes and spirals cut into the pins allow excess glue to escape the dowel hole during clamping. Otherwise, clamping pressure may cause the trapped glue to split the wood.

First, lay the butcher block members edge-to-edge on a flat surface. Then, using a framing square or T-square, draw centerlines for the first set of dowel holes every 6 in. Be sure to code each board with a number or letter to aid the final assembly.

Next, bore the dowel holes using a drill press or a portable drill with a doweling jig. Note that for a 1-in.-long dowel pin you must bore a 9/16-in.-deep hole in each board. The extra 1/16 in. retains a small amount of glue, just enough to make a strong joint. During assembly, be certain to apply glue to the walls of the dowel holes and along the faces of the mating boards. Clamp the pieces with bar or pipe clamps placed under and over the butcher block to prevent bowing. Be certain to scrape off hardening glue squeezed out before planing and sanding.

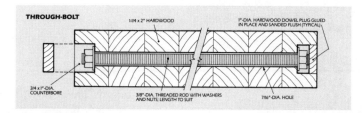

Use a small paint roller to spread the glue quickly and evenly. Glue and stack all pieces and then insert threaded rods.

Use two socket wrenches to draw the joints closed. Mark the threads on one end to prevent the nut from running off.

THROUGH-BOLT

When you're building a butcher block surface that's going to get a lot of abuse, such as a workbench, the through-bolt technique shown here is the one to use. The wood members are held together solidly by threaded steel rods that pass through holes bored in each board. Space the rods between 12 and 16 in. apart, depending on the size of the butcher block. For very wide butcher blocks, you can save money by using plain steel rod and threading the ends yourself.

Start by carefully center-boring holes in each piece using a drill press and fence. If the holes don't align the error will produce an uneven butcher block top. Next, counterbore the two boards to receive the washer, nut and wood plug. Then continue boring through the end pieces for the rod.

Glue and stack all the pieces and insert the rods through the holes with a nut and washer on one end. Position the last end piece and add the washer and nut. Tighten each rod little by little until the wood joints are closed tight. Finally, glue the wood plugs in place and sand them flush.

SPLINE JOINT

The spline-reinforced joint is one of the easiest to cut and assemble, yet it produces one of the strongest butcher blocks. Note that ¼-in. mahogany plywood is used for the splines because the inner plies run crosswise and resist splitting.

Start by cutting ⅜-in.-deep grooves in both sides of each board using a ¼-in.-wide dado blade on a table saw. Don't be concerned with cutting grooves in the *exact* center of the piece.

It's more important to keep the same face of the piece against the saw fence when cutting both grooves. Simply flip the piece end for end so the grooves will match, centered or not.

There are two ways to assemble spline-joint butcher blocks. Glue the splines into one side of all the pieces and then assemble the top, or build up the butcher block progressively by adding one board and spline at a time.

Cut the spline grooves on a table saw. Feather-board applies side pressure.

Splines are visible on end grain.

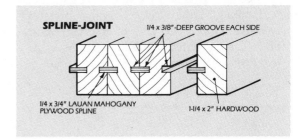

SPLINE-JOINT
1/4 x 3/8"-DEEP GROOVE EACH SIDE
1/4 x 3/4" LAUAN MAHOGANY PLYWOOD SPLINE
1-1/4 x 2" HARDWOOD

NAIL PINS

Short sections of finishing nails are used to align the boards of the butcher block and prevent slippage during gluing and clamping.

Bore a hole near each end on one side of

every board. Then insert a nail pin, blunt end first, into each hole. Clamp the pieces together so the pin points make indentation marks. Unclamp the assembly, apply glue and reclamp, driving the pins in fully.

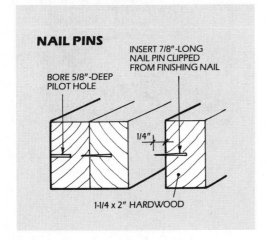

NAIL PINS
INSERT 7/8"-LONG NAIL PIN CLIPPED FROM FINISHING NAIL
BORE 5/8"-DEEP PILOT HOLE
1/4"
1-1/4 x 2" HARDWOOD

Use bar clamps to drive nail pins into adjacent pieces. Note board clamped across the top to keep the butcher block flat and even.

GLUE JOINT

This tight-fitting joint is made with a glue-joint cutter on a shaper or on a table saw with a glue-joint molding cutter head. Note that a ¾-in. plywood base supports the butcher block.

Carefully adjust the cutter so that it's cen-

tered on the work piece edge. Next, shape the edges of each board. Assemble the butcher block onto the base with glue, then nail through the plywood and into the wood members. Add 1½-in.-wide trim around the butcher block to conceal the plywood edge.

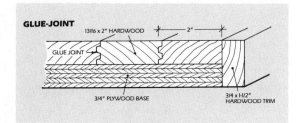

Cut the tight-fitting glue joint on a shaper. Glue-joint molding cutter heads are also available for a table saw.

DIRECT NAILING

The direct-nailing technique is used when making butcher blocks from boards less than 1 in. thick. Bore pilot holes in each board about 6 in. apart. Then glue and nail one board to the next using 1¼-in. finishing nails. Be sure to stagger the nails so you don't strike a nail in the preceding board. Finally, clamp the assembled butcher block until the glue dries.

Direct-nailing technique is a quick and easy way to make a butcher block. Be certain to bore nail pilot holes first.

PARQUET FLOORING

Hardwood parquet flooring is available in a wide variety of patterns and wood species and makes attractive butcher blocks. Since most parquet flooring is only ¼ or ⅜ in. thick, a base is needed to support the butcher block. Make the base from two pieces of ¾-in. plywood.

Glue the parquet to the plywood base with flooring adhesive. If teak parquet is used, as shown here, be sure to use an adhesive formulated specifically for teak, which is very oily. Complete the top by nailing on ½ x 1¾-in.-wide hardwood trim to conceal the plywood edge.

Glue parquet flooring to a plywood base using the appropriate adhesive. Add a second plywood base for additional support.

BUILD AN OLD-TIME ICEBOX

This handsome oak icebox stores glasses and beverages in style with room to spare.

Old-time iceboxes, once a necessity, are now expensive collector's items. These plans incorporate many of the details used in turn-of-the-century ice chests in a handsome bar and storage cabinet. Like all 11 models shown in Sears' 1902 catalog, this icebox features frame-and-panel construction, brass hardware and casters. This slightly scaled-down version has a hinged lid that opens to reveal a mixing compartment lined with plastic laminate.

MATERIALS NOTES

The solid oak used in the icebox shown came dressed to 13/16 in. If you choose stock of different thickness or assemble it with different joints, alter the dimensions to compensate for the changes.

Lid of icebox opens to reveal plastic-lined mixing compartment. Adjustable, recessed shelf (lower left) allows flexible storage.

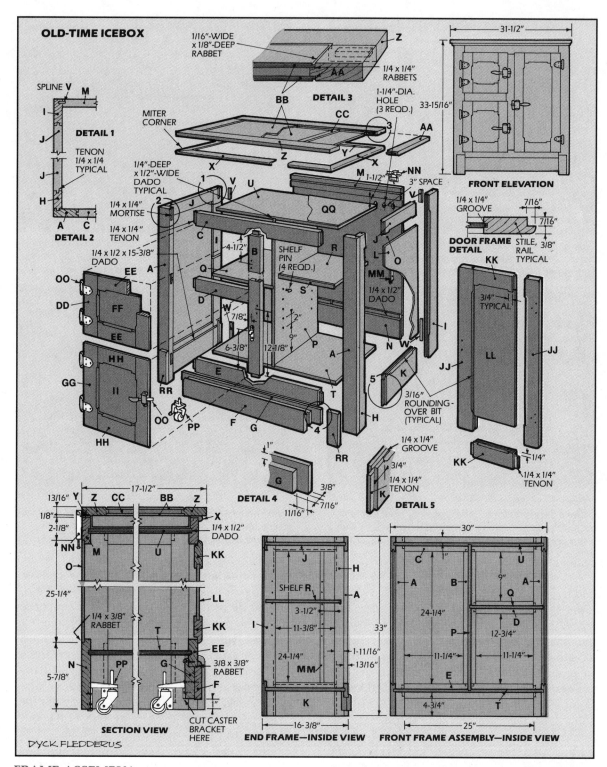

OLD-TIME ICEBOX

1/16"-WIDE x 1/8"-DEEP RABBET

DETAIL 3

1/4 x 1/4" RABBETS

31-1/2"

33-15/16"

FRONT ELEVATION

SPLINE V M

DETAIL 1

TENON 1/4 x 1/4 TYPICAL

DETAIL 2

MITER CORNER

1/4"-DEEP x 1/2"-WIDE DADO TYPICAL

1/4 x 1/4" MORTISE

1/4 x 1/4" TENON

1/4 x 1/2 x 15-3/8" DADO

1-1/4"-DIA. HOLE (3 REQD.)

3" SPACE

1/4 x 1/4" GROOVE

7/16"

7/16"

DOOR FRAME DETAIL   STILE, RAIL TYPICAL   3/8"

3/4" TYPICAL

SHELF PIN (4 REQD.)

1/4 x 1/2" DADO

4-1/2"

7/8"

6-3/8"

12-1/8"

9"

2"

3/16" ROUNDING-OVER BIT (TYPICAL)

1/4 x 1/4" GROOVE

3/4"

1/4 x 1/4" TENON

1/4 x 1/4" TENON

1/4"

DETAIL 5

DETAIL 4

1"

3/8"

7/16"

11/16"

17-1/2"

13/16"

1/8"

2-1/8"

25-1/4"

1/4 x 3/8" RABBET

5-7/8"

1/4 x 1/2" DADO

3/8 x 3/8" RABBET

1"

SECTION VIEW

CUT CASTER BRACKET HERE

DYCK FLEDDERUS

SHELF

3-1/2"

11-3/8"

24-1/4"

1-11/16"

13/16"

16-3/8"

END FRAME—INSIDE VIEW

30"

9"

24-1/4"

12-3/4"

11-1/4"

11-1/4"

4-3/4"

25"

33"

FRONT FRAME ASSEMBLY—INSIDE VIEW

FRAME ASSEMBLY

Rip front frame rails and stiles (A,B,C,D and E) to the specified width. Then cut each part to length. Cut the mortises and tenons with a table saw, shaper, router or by hand. To ensure the frame fits together with tight glue lines, cut or sand 1/32 in. off the end of each tenon. Seal the end grain on the three rails (C,D and E) and the center stile (B) with a 1:1 mixture of water and

white glue. Apply the runny mixture to the tenon ends and shoulders. Let it dry about 15 minutes. Then apply full-strength glue to the tenon at one end of the center rail (D) and join it with the mortise of the center stile (B). Fit a scrap block with a mortise cut into it over the unjoined end of D to protect it, then clamp the parts. Check for squareness and let the glue set. Join the upper and lower rails (C and E) to the

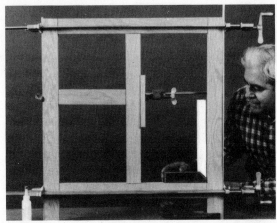

Gluing the outer stiles completes assembly of the front frame. Use protective glue blocks to cushion stile edges from clamp jaws. Check the frame for squareness.

Panels for cabinet ends fit into grooves cut into inner edges of rails and stiles. Check to make sure the panels slide in easily before joining the end frames with glue.

Groove the inside faces of the cabinet's front frame to accept the inner compartment parts. Use a router with a straight cutter. Guide it on edge of straight board.

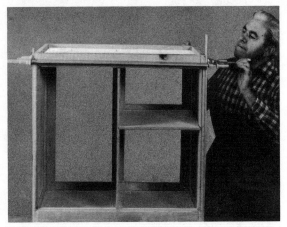

After the inner parts are assembled and glued into front frame and ends, add the back rails. Clamp them as shown above. Splines will be driven into the mortises.

center stile. Then add the outer stiles (A).

Cut stiles (H and I) and rails (J and K) for the end frames. The front stiles (H) must have a ¼ x ¼-in. tongue milled into the front edge. Cut tenons in the end of the rails and cut grooves ¼ in. wide and ¼ in. deep into the inner edges of all end frame parts. The rear stiles are rabbeted to receive the back. Also cut mortises for the splines in these pieces. Cut end panels (L) from ¼-in. plywood with veneer that matches the solid stock. Dry-assemble the end frames without the panels and round over the inside edges with a ³⁄₁₆-in.-rad. rounding-over bit. Stop the cuts at a uniform distance (¾ in.) from each corner. Finish-sand all end parts before gluing assembly.

Follow the same gluing procedures as described for the front frame.

MAKING THE COMPARTMENTS

Parts for the inner compartments of the icebox (P,Q,R,T and U) are cut from ½-in. fir plywood. Face the front of the adjustable shelf (R) with

solid edging (S). Bore ¼-in.-dia. holes ⁵⁄₁₆ in. deep for adjustable shelf pins in the divider. Prepare a solid oak strip (MM) and fasten it to the inside of the large compartment end since the ¼-in. panel is too thin for the shelf pin.

The divider (H), bottom (T) and top (U) must all have dadoes ½ in. wide by ¼ in. deep. Cut a panel for the back (O) from ½-in. plywood and the upper and lower back rails (M and N) from solid stock. Rabbet the back rails to accept the back panel. Cut grooves in the ends of the rails so they can be joined to the end frames with spline (V and W). Also cut the dummy drip pan door (F and G) and leg blocks (RR). Groove the inner faces of all frame parts and cut dadoes.

ASSEMBLY

Join the assembled cabinet ends to the front frame, clamp and let the glue set. Slide the bottom, top, divider and fixed shelf into what, at this point, is a three-sided box. Then, join the upper and lower back rails to the cabinet. Attach the back panel with ½-in. No. 4 flathead

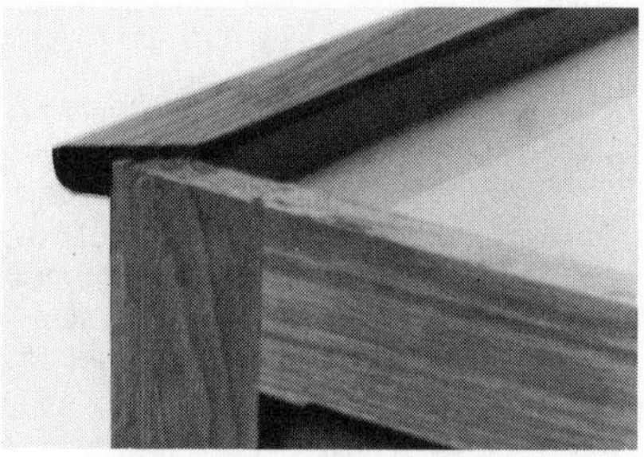

J-molding, made up from solid stock that's rabbetted and rounded over, is applied to the mixing compartment's edges after lamination. Miter front corners, butt rear joints.

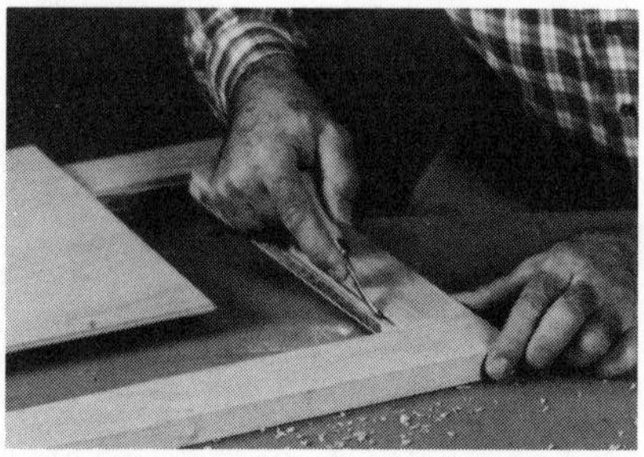

Since the top frame is rabbetted with a router after being glued, round corners must be squared with a chisel before the plywood insert can be installed.

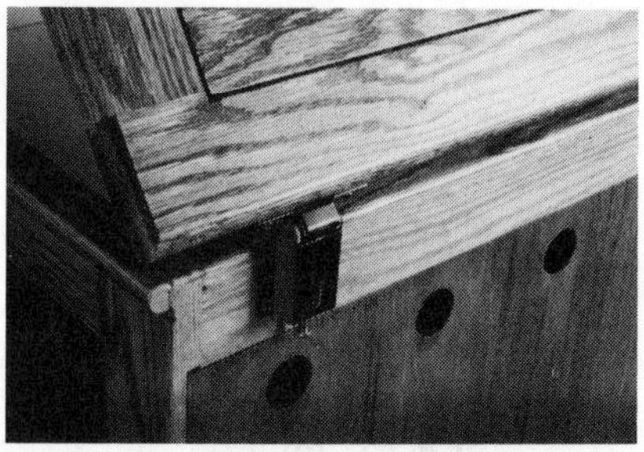

The lid is attached with spring-loaded hinges that can be adjusted to compensate for its weight. Turning the screw clockwise increases tension that holds the lid open.

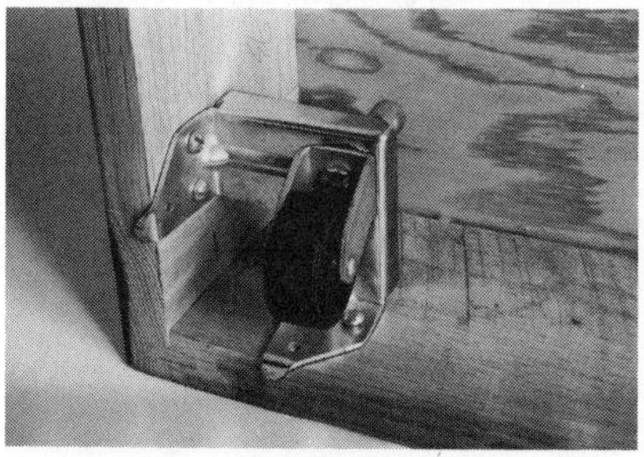

Concealed swivel casters have mounting brackets that attach to corners of the base. See the order box for the supplier of this and other special hardware.

MATERIALS LIST

OLD-TIME ICEBOX

Key	No.	Size and description (use)
A	2	13/16 x 2½ x 33″ oak (front stile)
B	1	13/16 x 2½ x 24¾″ oak (center stile)
C	1	13/16 x 2½ x 25½″ oak (front top rail)
D	1	13/16 x 2½ x 11¾″ oak (center rail)
E	1	13/16 x 2½ x 25½″ oak (drip pan door)
F	1	13/16 x 3½ x 25″ oak (drip pan door)
G	1	¾ x 3½ x 28⅜″ scrap (drip pan door backer)
H	2	13/16 x 1 15/16 x 33″ oak (front end stile)
I	2	13/16 x 2½ x 33″ oak (rear end stile)
J	2	13/16 x 2½ x 11⅞″ oak (end top rail)
K	2	13/16 x 6¼ 11⅞″ oak (end bottom rail)
L	2	¼ x 11 13/16 x 24 1/16″ oak veneer plywood (end panel)
M	1	13/16 x 2½ x 28⅜″ oak (rear top rail)
N	1	13/16 x 6¼ x 28⅜″ oak (rear bottom rail)
O	1	¼ x 25 x 29⅛″ fir plywood (back)
P	1	½ x 15⅜ x 27⅜″ fir plywood (divider)
Q	1	½ x 14 7/16 x 15⅜″ fir plywood (fixed shelf)
R	1	½ x 12½ x 13 ⅞″ fir plywood (adjustable shelf)
S	1	¼ x ¾ x 12½″ oak (shelf edging)
T	1	½ x 15⅜ x 28⅞″ fir plywood (bottom)
U	1	½ x 15⅜ x 28⅞″ fir plywood (top)
V	2	¼ x ½ x 2½ plywood scrap (spline)
W	2	¼ x ½ x 6¼″ plywood scrap (spline)
X	1	⅜ x 1 5/16 x 72″ oak (J-molding, rabbetted and shaped)
Y	1	⅛ x ⅞ x 29″ oak (trim)
Z	2	13/16 x 2½ x 31½″ oak (lid frame front and rear)
AA	2	13/16 x 2½ x 13″ oak (lid frame end)
BB	2	¼ x 13 x 27″ oak veneer plywood (lid insert)
CC	2	5/16 x ½ x 12½″ oak (lid stiffener)
DD	2	13/16 x 2½ x 9¾″ oak (top door stile)
EE	2	13/16 x 2½ x 7½″ oak (top door rail)
FF	1	¼ x 7 11/16 x 5 3/16″ oak veneer plywood (top door panel)
GG	2	13/16 x 2½ x 13½″ oak (bottom door stile)
HH	2	13/16 x 2½ x 7½″ oak (bottom door rail)
II	1	¼ x 7 11/16 x 8 15/16″ oak veneer plywood (bottom door panel)
JJ	2	13/16 x 2½ x 25″ oak (large door stile)
KK	2	13/16 x 2½ x 7½″ oak (large door rail)
LL	1	¼ x 7 11/16 x 20 7/16″ oak veneer plywood (large door panel)
MM	1	5/16 x ¾ x 24¼″ oak (adjustable shelf strip)
NN	2	Brass adjustable tension hinge*
OO	set	Brass hardware including door hinges and latches*
PP	4	Concealed swivel casters*
QQ	6 sq. ft.	Plastic laminate
RR	2	13/16 x 2¼ x 5″ oak (foot)

Misc.: ⅝-in. No. 4 flathead screws, ¾-in. No. 8 roundhead screws, white carpenter's glue; contact cement; pigmented paste filler; sanding sealer or thinned shellac, semigloss lacquer; furniture rubbing compound.

(*) See order box for source.

screws driven into the rabbets and divider. Attach the drip door assembly by screwing the ends of the backer to the back of the face frame stiles. Install the casters (PP). Caster brackets on the front pair must be cut.

To line the mixing compartment, first cut large bottom piece of laminate (QQ) to size and attach it with contact cement. Then cut narrow strips for the sides and attach them. The J-molding (X) is attached around the top edges of the mixing compartment. Join the front corners of the J-molding with 45° miters; butt the rear joints.

TOP LID AND DOORS

The top lid is of frame construction with a hollow center section. Cut solid stock for the rails and stiles (Z and AA) and prepare the mortises and tenons. Rabbet the inner edges of the frame after the pieces are joined. Use a chisel to square round corners left by the router bit. Glue the ends of the two stiffeners (CC) and fit them into the frame. Rabbet edges of the lid panels with kerfs 1/32 in. deep and 1/16 in. wide.

Construct the doors by using the same procedure used for the cabinet ends. After assembly, door front edges are shaped with a ⅜-in. rounding-over bit, and rabbets are cut in the back. Fasten the lid with tension hinges (NN) and attach doors with brass hardware (OO).

Once assembly is complete, remove the hardware. Fill the pores with paste filler and follow with two coats of sanding sealer and two coats of semigloss lacquer.

HOW TO ORDER HARDWARE

Order hardware for old-time icebox from Armor Products, Box 260, Deer Park, N.Y. 11729. Check with supplier first for latest prices and availability of material.

HOME OFFICE TELEPHONE ORGANIZER

Here is a way to turn your telephone into a family communications center.

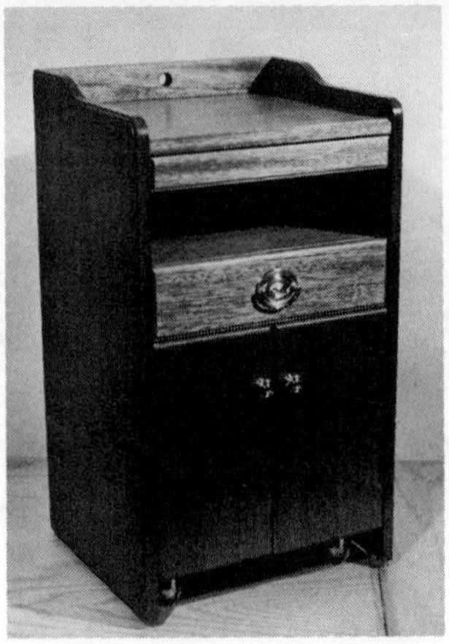

This mahogany home office organizer holds an office-model phone and answering machine; has storage drawer, cabinet, and pullout writing surface. It provides a lot of storage—all in only 1½ sq. ft. of floor space.

This handsome mahogany cabinet is a smart way to store phone equipment in a home office, library or den while providing valuable storage space. The dimensions can be altered easily to conform to your specific equipment.

MAKING THE CABINET

Make the cabinet from mahogany hardwood; use ¼-in. lauan mahogany plywood for the cabinet back and drawer bottom. Start by cutting the cabinet sides to the dimensions given. Mahogany is commonly available in 16-in.-wide boards, but you can edge-glue two boards together to form each side.

Rout stopped dadoes into the sides using a router and a straight bit to accept the horizontal cross members. Then chisel the rounded ends of the dadoes square. Cut the top shelf and cabinet bottom to size and rabbet the back edges of both to accept the cabinet back. Note that the front corners of the shelf are notched to extend past dadoes. Rout decorative profile in the front edge of the top shelf using a ¼-in.-rad. cove bit.

Make the frame to support the pullout tray. Assemble frame with half-lap joints and then slot the four inside corners as shown for the tray-stop screws. Dry-assemble the cabinet with clamps so you can fit the doors properly.

The doors operate on invisible barrel or cylinder hinges inserted into 14-mm-dia. holes bored into the door edge and cabinet side. The 14-mm-dia. drill bit is available from the hinge supplier. First, bore hinge holes into the doors, then insert ½-in.-dia. dowel centers (wrap the dowel centers with masking tape so they fit snugly into the holes). Next, press each door against the cabinet side so the dowel center points transfer the hinge hole centers to the cabinet sides. Disassemble the cabinet and bore the hinge holes. Then use the ¼-in.-rad. cove bit to rout the edges of the sides and doors as shown. Reassemble and clamp the cabinet using glue only.

Assemble and install the drawer. Before nailing the cabinet back, mark rear slot locations against the underside of the pullout tray. Bore pilot holes at these two marks for the tray-stop screws. Apply three coats of polyurethane varnish to all parts. Then nail on the back and install the pullout tray. Use an offset screwdriver to turn in the tray-stop screws.

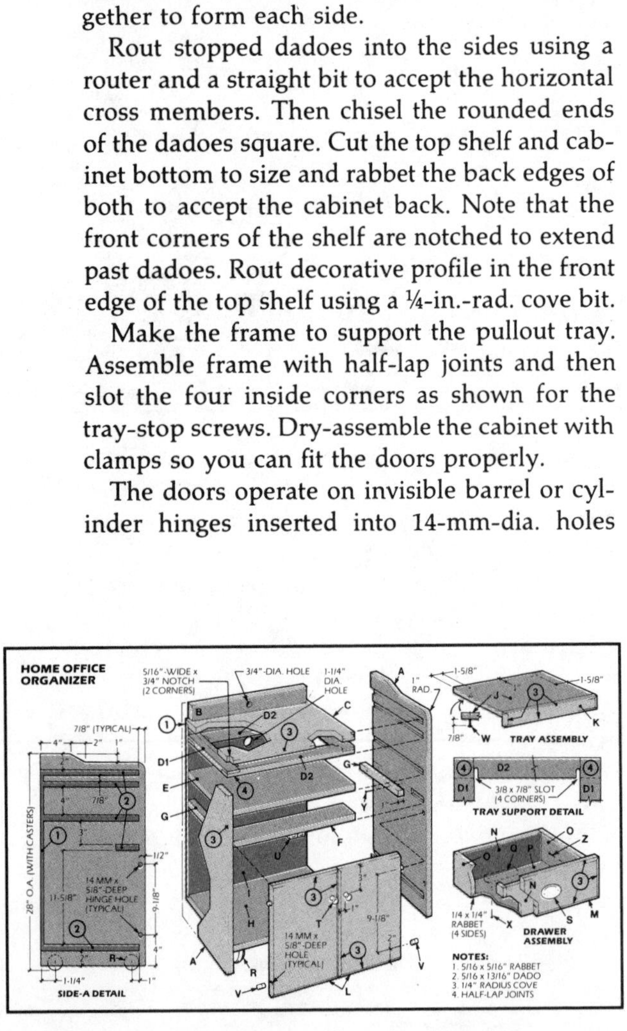

MATERIALS LIST
HOME OFFICE TELEPHONE ORGANIZER

Key	No.	Size and description (use)
A	2	13/16 x 14 x 27½" mahogany (side)
B	1	13/16 x 2 x 14½" mahogany (upper back)
C	1	13/16 x 13⅞ x 15" mahogany (top)
D1	2	13/16 x 1¾ x 12¾" mahogany (side rail)
D2	2	13/16 x 1¾ x 15" mahogany (front and rear rail)
E	1	13/16 x 12¾ x 15" mahogany (shelf)
F	1	13/16 x 3 x 15" mahogany (cabinet rail)
G	2	¾ x 1 x 9¾" mahogany (drawer guide)
H	2	13/16 x 13⅞ x 15" mahogany (bottom)
I	1	¼ x 15 x 22¾" lauan plywood (back)
J	1	13/16 x 12 11/16 x 14 5/16" mahogany (pullout tray)
K	1	13/16 x 1¾ x 14⅜" mahogany (tray front)
L	2	13/16 x 7⅛ x 13¼" mahogany (door)
M	1	13/16 x 3 13/16 x 14 5/16" mahogany (drawer face)
N	2	½ x 2⅞ x 13 5/16" mahogany (drawer front and back)
O	2	½ x 2⅞ x 12⅝" mahogany (drawer side)
P	1	¼ x 12⅛ x 13 13/16" lauan plywood (drawer bottom)
Q	1	¾ x ¾ x 5" mahogany (drawer stop)
R	4	2" plate-type casters
S	1	2" brass pull
T	2	1"-dia. brass knob
U	2	Magnetic catch
V	4	Invisible barrel hinge
W	2	1½" No. 14 roundhead screw (tray stop)
X	2	1½" No. 6 flathead screw (drawer stop)
Y		1½" finishing nails
Z		1" brads

CLASSIC LAP DESK

This is a reproduction of the desk that Mark Twain used. You can build one in two weekend sessions.

This mahogany lap desk is a close reproduction of Mark Twain's desk, now in his collection at Elmira College in New York. This little piece of furniture must have played a significant role in Twain's daily life. Perhaps on the velvet panel he wrote *The Adventures of Tom Sawyer.* The compartments may have held the notes for *Life on the Mississippi.*

Today, a lap desk is still a convenient box to store the essentials for writing. When opened, the slanted, velvet-covered panels provide a handy writing surface.

BUILDING THE BASIC CABINET
The corners of the lap desk are mitered so they show no end grain. Glue and nail the front, back and ends; then add the top and bottom. Be careful to locate corner nails where they won't interfere with sawing the box into two parts. On the hinged side keep nails far enough from the

With few variations, this lap desk is reproduced from the one Mark Twain used. The original desk is among the best in quality of workmanship seen in antique shops and museums today. Changes from the original piece incorporated into the copy include the brass corners of the lid (ones similar to the original weren't available), the size of the box and the material in the top. The copy is ¾ in. deeper from front to back to store 8½ in.-wide paper. Mahogany plywood is used in the top. If 10-in.-wide solid mahogany, as in the original, is readily available, you can plane it to ¼-in. thickness. Compartments provide storage for supplies.

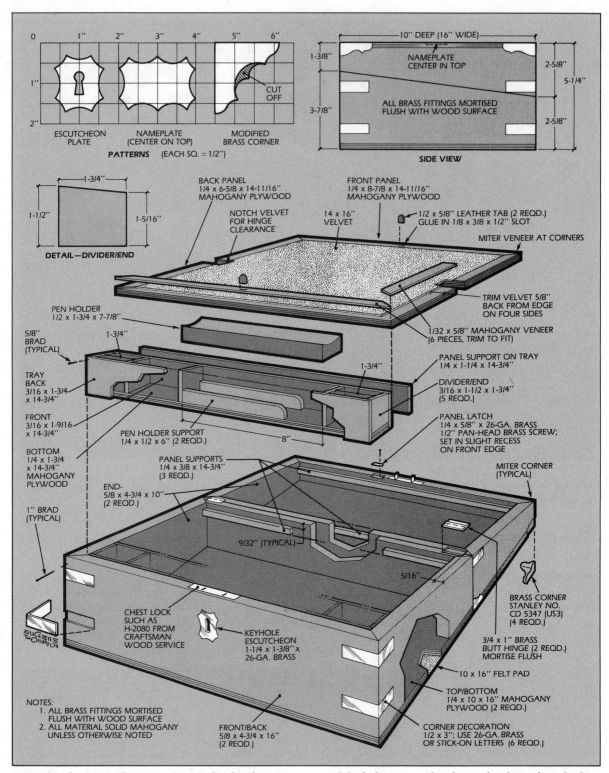

PATTERNS (EACH SQ. = 1/2")

ESCUTCHEON PLATE

NAMEPLATE (CENTER ON TOP)

MODIFIED BRASS CORNER

CUT OFF

SIDE VIEW

10" DEEP (16" WIDE)

NAMEPLATE CENTER IN TOP

ALL BRASS FITTINGS MORTISED FLUSH WITH WOOD SURFACE

1-3/8"
3-7/8"
2-5/8"
5-1/4"
2-5/8"

DETAIL—DIVIDER/END

1-3/4"
1-1/2"
1-5/16"

BACK PANEL
1/4 x 6-5/8 x 14-11/16"
MAHOGANY PLYWOOD

NOTCH VELVET FOR HINGE CLEARANCE

FRONT PANEL
1/4 x 8-7/8 x 14-11/16"
MAHOGANY PLYWOOD

14 x 16" VELVET

1/2 x 5/8" LEATHER TAB (2 REQD.)
GLUE IN 1/8 x 3/8 x 1/2" SLOT

MITER VENEER AT CORNERS

TRIM VELVET 5/8" BACK FROM EDGE ON FOUR SIDES

1/32 x 5/8" MAHOGANY VENEER
(6 PIECES, TRIM TO FIT)

PEN HOLDER
1/2 x 1-3/4 x 7-7/8"

5/8" BRAD (TYPICAL)

1-3/4"

1-3/4"

PANEL SUPPORT ON TRAY
1/4 x 1-1/4 x 14-3/4"

TRAY BACK
3/16 x 1-3/4 x 14-3/4"

FRONT
3/16 x 1-9/16 x 14-3/4"

PEN HOLDER SUPPORT
1/4 x 1/2 x 6" (2 REQD.)

8"

DIVIDER/END
3/16 x 1-1/2 x 1-3/4"
(5 REQD.)

PANEL LATCH
1/4 x 5/8" x 26-GA. BRASS
1/2" PAN-HEAD BRASS SCREW;
SET IN SLIGHT RECESS
ON FRONT EDGE

BOTTOM
1/4 x 1-3/4 x 14-3/4"
MAHOGANY PLYWOOD

1" BRAD (TYPICAL)

PANEL SUPPORTS
1/4 x 3/8 x 14-3/4"
(3 REQD.)

END-
5/8 x 4-3/4 x 10"
(2 REQD.)

9/32" (TYPICAL)

5/16"

MITER CORNER (TYPICAL)

BRASS CORNER
STANLEY NO.
CD 5347 (US3)
(4 REQD.)

CHEST LOCK
SUCH AS
H-2080 FROM
CRAFTSMAN
WOOD SERVICE

KEYHOLE ESCUTCHEON
1-1/4 x 1-3/8" x
26-GA. BRASS

3/4 x 1" BRASS
BUTT HINGE (2 REQD.)
MORTISE FLUSH

10 x 16" FELT PAD

TOP/BOTTOM
1/4 x 10 x 16" MAHOGANY
PLYWOOD (2 REQD.)

NOTES:
1. ALL BRASS FITTINGS MORTISED FLUSH WITH WOOD SURFACE
2. ALL MATERIAL SOLID MAHOGANY UNLESS OTHERWISE NOTED

FRONT/BACK
5/8 x 4-3/4 x 16"
(2 REQD.)

CORNER DECORATION
1/2 x 3"; USE 26-GA. BRASS
OR STICK-ON LETTERS (6 REQD.)

sawed edges so they won't touch the hinge screws.

After the glue dries, sand with 150- and 220-grit abrasive in a portable or stationary belt sander, or with an orbital sander. Using fine 220-grit sandpaper on a block, ease all corners. Then sand the top edges a little more. It's important to shape the wood to the slightly rounded brass corners.

Mark lines on the front, back and ends for separating the box into two parts (see drawings). You'll need to remove the guard from the table saw for this job. Tilt the blade about 7° from vertical, lower the blade so only ¾ in. extends above the table, and make the front and back cuts, using the rip fence. Make a simple jig to hold the box at the proper angle to the rip fence while making the diagonal end cuts.

Move the blade back to the vertical position and use the jig against the rip fence to make these cuts. A fine-tooth plywood blade works well for this job.

Install the lock before gluing and nailing the tray in place. Lock No. H-2080 from Craftsman Wood Service Co. can be used. Chisel away the wood and shape the keyhole, following instructions supplied by the maker. A high-speed hand grinder with a flat end burr is helpful in doing the final smoothing.

BUILDING THE ACCESSORY TRAY

Rip 3/16-in.-thick strips of mahogany on the table or radial-arm saw for the accessory tray. Sand both sides. Cut pieces to the dimensions shown and assemble, checking the fit inside the box. Make a concave insert to hold pens and pencils. Apply glue to the ends and to the side that's adjacent to the box and nail in place with a wire brad at each end.

Attach the other three panel support strips 9/32 in. from the edge. Cut two 1/4-in. mahogany panels to fit. Stain and apply satin finish polyurethane to the backs of both panels and to the entire assembly.

You can duplicate the original's slightly brownish mahogany stain by mixing 2/3 Minwax red mahogany to 1/3 special walnut. After the stain dries, fill nail holes with matching color. Weldwood blend stick works well for this.

Since mahogany is open-grained wood, you'll get a smoother surface if you next apply paste wood filler that has been tinted with the same stain used for the first coat. Follow instructions on the can, rubbing across the grain.

Follow up by using two or three coats of satin finish polyurethane. Do not apply stain or finish to the hinged edges because velvet will be glued to them later.

JIG CONSTRUCTION

1—DRAW GUIDE LINE ON FOUR SIDES OF BOX

2—MATCH ENDS, TRACE OUTLINE ON JIG

10"

5-1/4"

1"

3"

3—DRAW LINE 1" FROM OUTLINE; CUT OUT ON THIS LINE

CUTTING PROCEDURE

SAW TABLE

RIP FENCE

BLADE

1—TILT BLADE 7° TO ALIGN WITH LINES ON BOX

2—SAW FRONT AND BACK OF BOX

7°

RIP FENCE

SAW BLADE

JIG

BOX

3—ADJUST BLADE TO VERTICAL POSITION AND CUT FIRST END

4—FLOP JIG AND TURN END-FOR-END

5—CUT SECOND END WITH BLADE IN VERTICAL POSITION

To prevent glued surfaces from sliding out of position, you should prebore holes before nailing. Take care not to use any nails near the diagonal cutline which divides the box into top and bottom.

Make the lengthwise cuts at a 7° angle (see drawings). Then return the blade to the vertical position and use a jig to make the two end cuts.

INSTALLING THE HINGES

Using a sharp wood chisel to mark the locations and to pare away the wood, set the ¾ x 1-in. brass hinges in ⁵⁄₁₆ in. from the ends and flush with the surface. This allows for two thicknesses of velvet when the lap desk is closed. Bore the holes and then screw the hinges in place.

INSTALLING THE VELVET

On the upper or unfinished side of the two panels, draw lines ⅝ in. from the edge, parallel to the ends and outsides of the opened box. With the panels in place, apply to the larger one a thin, smooth coating of glue, extending it just to the outside of the line you have drawn.

Lay the velvet in place, brushing out wrinkles. Coat the smaller panel with glue in the same way, draw the velvet fairly tight across the center, lay it on the glued surface of the smaller panel and brush out any wrinkles.

After the glue has dried, remove the panels from the box and use a steel straightedge and razor blade or sharp utility knife to remove excess cloth.

Cut mahogany veneer to shape with sharp household shears and glue it to the ⅝-in. margin around three sides of each panel. If you use carpenter's glue you'll have to clamp wood over each strip until it dries. Follow the maker's directions for contact cement. Stain and varnish the veneer trim and edges. Cut the slot and install leather tabs.

Trim the velvet to fit between the two hinges, apply glue to the box edges between the hinges and set the two panels in place. Press the velvet down on the glued edges and leave the box open until the glue is dry. Install the catch to hold the large panel when the box is opened. Glue a piece of felt or corduroy to the bottom of the lap desk so it won't scratch the surface you set it on.

INSTALLING THE BRASS TRIM

If you attach an escutcheon around the keyhole

and stop right there, you will have a nice-looking lap desk. If you want an even more beautiful one, however—a reasonably true reproduction of the Mark Twain lap desk—you'll need to add some brass trimming: a name or initial plate, decorative escutcheon, brass corners and brass corner straps.

The corners and corner straps cannot be surface-mounted, as this would interfere with opening the lap desk to its fullest extent. A raised nameplate could scratch a tabletop. All brass should be flush-mounted.

Before you begin chiseling for the brass mountings, it's a good idea to practice on scrap wood. Use sharp ⅛-in. and ¼-in. wood chisels. Keep a cloth under the box to protect the finish and anchor the box with some blocking. As you work, keep both hands behind the sharp chisel edge.

Lay the brass corner (or other brass trim) in the proper location and outline it with an awl. Using the ⅛-in. wood chisel, bevel toward the part to be removed; cut straight down around the outline to establish the edge. Then remove enough wood within the boundary to permit the brass to fit evenly, flush with the wood surface.

On the corners, you'll find it necessary to make a new perimeter line just outside the original as you remove a layer of wood. After you fit each piece, remove it and apply a thin line of stain around the edge of the cut.

Secure all brass parts with contact cement. Apply it to the wood and to the back of the brass, wait for the period of time recommended by the maker and press the brass in place.

To make the ½ x 3-in. straps around each corner, you can use the same 26-ga. brass or you can purchase 3-in.-high brass stick-on sign letters. The letters save time and are difficult to differentiate from thicker brass. Cut portions of the letters to give you the dimensions you need and stick them in place. With the last piece of brass trim in place, you are ready to use the handsome lap desk.

Fit the lock into the front of the box. Remove most of the wood with a chisel then use a high-speed hand grinder in the finishing stages. You may prefer to do this job before you start assembling the desk.

Using a mallet, ⅛- and ¼-in. wood chisels, remove the wood to a ⅟₃₂-in. depth. Fit the brass frequently to check depth.

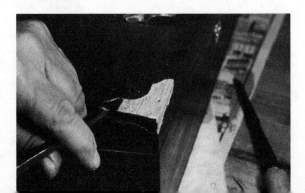

SECRETS FROM A MASTER WOODCRAFTER

Share the secrets of a master woodcrafter who has devoted many hours toward perfecting his craft.

Strike the screw shaft to peen the end over.

CLAMP REPAIR

If the swivel pads on your C-clamps become loose and fall off, try this method for replacing them.

First, open the clamp wide and place it in a vise, as shown. Now, strike the end of the screw shaft with a ball-peen hammer to peen the shaft over. Be sure to strike the shaft accurately, for an errant blow could fracture the casting of the clamp.

Once the screw shaft is sufficiently peened, remove the clamp from the vise and position it on a hard surface. Hold the swivel pad in place and tighten the clamp, driving the peened shaft into the swivel pad collar.

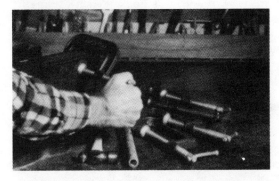

Hold the swivel pad in place and tighten the clamp to drive the peened shaft into the collar of the pad.

EXTENDED PIPE CLAMPS

When your pipe clamps are too short to use on a particular project, don't invest in an additional set of longer clamps. Simply extend your existing clamps with lengths of black pipe.

Keep your workshop well supplied with various pipe lengths—threaded on both ends—plus several standard pipe couplings, and you'll be able to clamp almost any project. You're limited only by the length of pipe you have on hand; this procedure works with either ½- or ¾-in.-dia. pipe clamps. You'll obtain more professional results by creating the correct clamp for each job.

To lengthen a clamp, disengage the clamp's tail-stop assembly and slide it off the pipe. Choose the desired length of extension pipe and join it to the "short" clamp with a coupling. Do not use a wrench when adding an extension to a clamp. Hand-tightening is sufficient. Replace the tail-stop assembly and you've got a "new" clamp.

Lengthen your pipe clamps to suit any job. Add the desired length extension to the clamp with a standard pipe coupling.

SCREW-EYE DRIVER

These homemade tools are great for driving screw eyes and hooks of all sizes. Each driver is a 4¼-in.-long hardwood birch dowel. Make four different-size drivers: ⅜-, ½-, ⅝- and ¾-in.-dia.

Start by cutting a ½-in.-deep saw kerf centered in one end of each driver. Cut the kerf narrow enough to provide a snug fit around the screw eye. Measure 1½ in. down from the other end of each driver and center-bore a ¼-in.-dia. hole to accept a ¼-in.-dia. x 2½-in.-long dowel handle. The handle adds leverage when you turn in a screw eye or hook. When driving a screw eye into very hard material, you may need to establish a starting point with an awl, or by first boring a pilot hole with a drill.

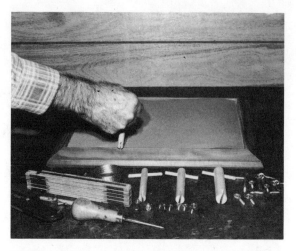

To drive screw eyes, cup hooks and screw hooks of all sizes, use these hardwood birch dowel drivers.

Make glue spreaders from nylon brushes.

Cut bristles down to 1 in. long.

GLUE SPREADER

Here's an easy and effective way to apply glue to wordworking projects. Take several inexpensive nylon paint brushes—from ½ to 2½ in. wide—and cut the bristles down to 1 in. long. The shorter, more rigid bristles spread glue evenly and quickly. The different-width brushes let you pick the best brush for each job. When you use water-soluble glues, store brushes in a jar of water to keep them pliable. But first apply a coat of rust-resistant paint to the metal ferrules to prevent rust from contaminating the glue.

MASKING-TAPE STOP

This simple idea provides a temporary stop for a radial-arm or table saw.

Use a razor knife to make a ¼-in.-deep cut into a roll of masking tape (½ or ¾ in. wide). Position a piece of the ¼-in.-thick tape on the fence or table at the desired distance from the blade. Abut the wood to the stop on each cut to produce identical-length pieces without measuring each one. You'll find many shop uses for this stop, such as cutting sandpaper with a paper trimmer. To reuse the stop, peel off the bottom layer of tape to reveal a clean adhesive surface.

Try this masking-tape stop on a paper trimmer when you cut sheets of sandpaper.

IDENTIFYING DOWEL JOINTS

Correctly identifying and aligning dowel joints can be tricky. Try this method to avoid misaligned joints when you build a frame.

After you cut the frame's stiles and rails, lay them out on a workbench and clamp the frame square. Draw a pencil line across each joint using a try square to indicate the dowel locations. These marks will be used to align the doweling jig when boring the dowel holes. Identify each mating piece with a letter to help you match the joints correctly during final assembly.

Mark for dowels with a try square. Identify each mating piece with a letter.

DRAW KNOB AND PULL JIG

This homemade jig provides a quick, accurate way to mark knob or pull locations on cabinet drawers and doors.

To install drawer hardware, first mark a centerline lengthwise on the drawer face. Hold the jig with the stop bar against the edge of the drawer face, and align the centerline through the template holes. The ³⁄₁₆-in.-dia. hole is for laying out knobs. The two ¹⁄₈-in.-dia. holes are for laying out pulls. Note that the two pull template holes are 3 in. on center to accommodate standard hardware. You can easily alter the template to lay out hardware of all sizes.

To install hardware on cabinet doors, hold the stop bar on the top of the door, and keep the template edge flush with the door edge. Mark and bore the mounting holes.

To assemble the jig, pass the template through the stop bar's saw kerf and tighten the wingnut. The distance from the template holes to the stop bar should equal the distance from the desired mounting hole to the top of the door, or to the edge of the drawer face.

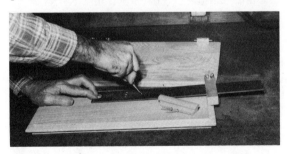

This jig is used to install knobs or pulls on doors and drawers.

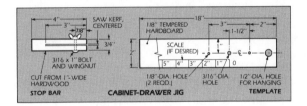

SANDBAGGED

Sandbags are a great help when you glue large or uneven projects. They're flexible enough to weigh down irregular shapes that are otherwise impossible to clamp. When gluing large areas of plywood or veneers, pile sandbags in the center to ensure total contact between surfaces until the glue dries.

Fold a 10 x 24-in. piece of lightweight canvas in half to form a 10 x 12-in. bag. Sew sides closed and turn the bag inside out. Add sand until it's three-quarters full, fold the top edges in ½ in. and sew the bag closed.

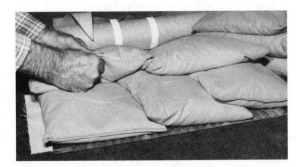

Gluing uneven projects, such as this tambour door, is easy with several sandbags.

Attractive, three-drawer pine mirror, left, is a simplified version of popular Early American piece. Old-time flavor of Chippendale Looking Glass, currently a favorite at antique shops, is captured in the reproduction shown above. Mirror shown on right frequently is listed in antique furniture guides under "dressing mirror" or "dressing glass."

ANTIQUE MIRRORS YOU CAN COPY

Using our plans, you can reproduce these three classic mirrors.

The mirrors shown here were popular in the late 18th century and throughout the 19th. All three are in great demand at antique shops these days. However, they are becoming more difficult to get. These mirrors duplicate the original antiques.

PINE DRESSING MIRROR

Designed for use on a table or chest of drawers, this attractive dressing mirror is mounted atop a three-drawer cabinet. It's made entirely of pine to look authentic.

Start by cutting the base cabinet pieces as shown. Notice the cabinet's sides receive rabbets along the back and bottom edges. The cabinet's top and bottom pieces are rabbeted along the back edge. Take the time to sand all pieces thoroughly before assembly. This way, the cabinet will require only light sanding after assembly.

The cabinet's designed so you don't nail through the top or sides. All visible nailing is done through the cabinet's bottom and back surfaces. First, glue and screw the cleats to the cabinet's sides and partitions. Be sure to keep the cleats ½ in. back from the front edge to allow the drawers to close. Next, attach the partitions and the sides to the cabinet top's underside by screwing through the cleats. Finally, glue and nail the cabinet's bottom in place.

Cut lengths of ¾ x ¾-in. vinyl corner molding for drawer slides. If you can find rounded corner molding, plane the two outside surfaces flat before using it. Secure the slides in the cabinet with one ⅝-in. brad at each end. Next, cut all the drawer pieces according to the materials list. To avoid the cleats, the two smaller drawers' sides are narrower than the center drawer's.

Dry-assemble the drawers to be sure they fit smoothly into the cabinet. Make any adjustments before gluing and final assembly. With the cabinet assembled and the drawers fitting properly, glue and nail the cabinet's back in place using ⅝-in. brads.

Cut the pieces needed for the mirror frame, supports and braces. Before assembling the frame, cut rabbets into the frame's pieces to hold the mirror and hardboard back. Shape the

MATERIALS LIST

PINE DRESSING MIRROR

Key	No.	Size and description (use)
A	1	¾ x 8 x 28" pine (cabinet top)
B	1	¾ x 8 x 27¼" pine (cabinet bottom)
C	2	¾ x 8 x 4¼" pine (cabinet sides)
D	2	¾ x 3½ x 7⅞" pine (partitions)
E	4	½ x ¾ x 7⅜ pine (cleats)
E1	11	1¼" No. 8 flathead screws
E2	8	1" No. 8 flathead screws
F	4	⅜ x 2⅞ x 7½" pine (drawer sides)
G	2	⅜ x 2½ x 5" pine (drawer back)
H	2	¾ x 4 x 6½" pine (drawer front)
I	2	⅛ x 5¼ x 7⅜" hardboard (drawer bottom)
J	2	⅜ x 3¼ x 7½" pine (drawer side)
K	1	⅜ x 2⅞ x 11¾" pine (drawer back)
L	1	¾ x 4 x 13½" pine (drawer front)
M	1	⅛ x 7⅜ x 12" hardboard (drawer bottom)
N	6	¾ x ¾ x 7½" vinyl corner molding (draw slide)
O	4	1¾"-dia. x 2⅛" pine (feet)
P	3	1"-dia. x 1" pine (drawer pull)
Q	2	1 x 1³⁄₁₆ x 20½" pine (support)
Q1	2	1" No. 8 roundhead screws
Q2	2	1½" No. 8 roundhead screws
R	2	¾ x 2½ x 5½" pine (braces)
R1	4	⅜"-dia. x 1½" pine dowels
S	2	1⅜ x 1½"-dia. pine (mirror adjusting knobs)
T	2	¼"-dia. x 2½" flathead stovebolts with nuts
U	4	¼"-dia. flat washers
V	2	¼"-dia. Teenuts
W	2	1 x 1³⁄₁₆ x 17¾" pine (frame sides)
X	2	1 x 1³⁄₁₆ x 21⅞" pine (frame top and bottom)
Y	1	⅛ x 16 x 20" mirror
Z	1	⅛ x 16 x 20" hardboard (mirror back)
Z1	1	⅛ x 4⅜ x 27⅜" hardboard (cabinet back)

Misc.: Carpenter's glue, 8d finishing nails, 1¾" 17-ga. wire brads, 220-grit sandpaper, ⅝" 16-ga. wire nails, polyurethane varnish, Minwax Early American stain (No. 230).

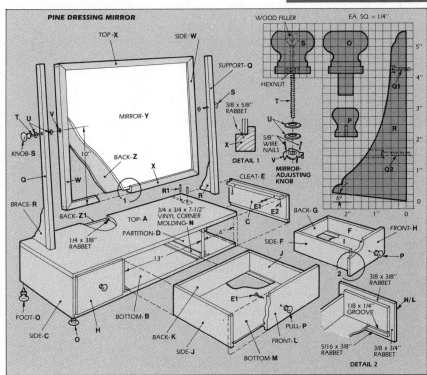

front edges of the frame and all four corners of the two support pieces with a ¼-in. rounding-over bit.

Next, cut the bottom edges of the supports and braces at a 6° angle. Attach the braces to the supports using No. 8 roundhead screws as shown. Use a doweling jig to bore each brace's bottom for accepting two ⅜-in.-dia. dowels. Also, bore a ¼-in.-dia. hole through each support for installing the mirror adjusting knobs.

Before assembling the mirror's frame, bore a 5/16-in.-dia. hole in each side piece for installing Teenuts. Since the Teenuts are installed backward from their designed use, bore two 1/16-in.-dia. holes in each Teenut as shown. Tap the Teenuts into the frame's sides, and then drive in two ⅝-in. wire nails to secure each one. Glue and nail the frame together with 1¾-in., 17-ga. wire nails at the corners. Clamp the frame square until the glue dries.

Before proceeding any further, use your lathe to turn the mirror adjusting knobs, drawer pulls and the cabinet feet. After turning the adjusting knobs, counterbore both ends of each knob as shown. Then, bore a ¼-in.-dia. through hole in each knob for installing a ¼-in.-dia. x 2½-in. stovebolt. Place a hexnut inside each knob and tighten the bolt to draw the nut flush with the knob. Fill the outside counterbores with wood filler to conceal the bolt heads.

Assemble the support members and the frame by screwing the mirror adjusting knobs through the supports and into the Teenuts in the frame's sides.

Now you're ready to join the mirror frame and supports with the base cabinet. Stand the frame and support members centered on the base cabinet's top. Position the braces ¼ in. from the cabinet's back edge. Outline the two brace locations lightly with a pencil on the cabinet top.

Remove the frame and insert dowel centers into the holes previously bored in the braces' bottoms. Then, reposition the frame according to the pencil lines on the cabinet. Push down on the braces so the dowel centers transfer the dowel locations onto the cabinet's top. Bore ⅜-in.-dia. x ½-in.-deep holes into the top at these locations. Glue and insert the dowels into the braces, and then glue the frame and support assembly to the cabinet's top. Clamp and let dry. Attach the feet and drawer knobs to complete the assembly.

Finish the project with a coat of Minwax Early American stain (No. 230). After the stain has dried for 24 hours, apply three coats of satin polyurethane varnish. Sand lightly between varnish coats with 220-grit abrasive paper.

After the surface has dried thoroughly, install the mirror. Then, carefully nail the hardboard back in place with ⅝-in. brads.

CHIPPENDALE LOOKING GLASS

This wall-mounted mirror is made entirely of rich, ribbon-stripe mahogany; ¾-in. stock is used for the frame, ¼-in. mahogany-veneer plywood for the decorative scrolls.

Begin by cutting the mitered frame pieces to size. The frame's corners are joined using spline-reinforced miter joints. Splines produce tight, strong joints and ensure flush surface alignment. Use a table saw tenoning jig to cut ⅛-in.-wide spline grooves in the frame's miters.

Next, cut ⅛-in.-thick solid mahogany splines to fit the spline grooves. Be sure the grain runs across the spline's width to prevent splitting. Each spline has an inside corner cutout. Install the splines so this cutout will fit flush with the frame's inside corners.

Assemble the frame by first gluing the splines into the grooves and then clamping the frame square. Let the frame dry, then sand it.

Turn the frame face down on the workbench and rout a ¼-in.-deep x ⅜-in. rabbet into the back inside edge. This recess holds the mirror and the hardboard back.

Next, using a ½-in.-dia. straight bit, rout the eight circular notches into the frame's back for holding the hardboard back's tabs.

Set up the table saw with a ¼-in.-wide dado head to groove the frame's edges to hold the decorative scrolls. Cut the grooves ¼ in. deep along the length of the frame's top and bottom and partially up the frame's sides, as shown. Next, cut the ¼-in. mahogany-veneer plywood scrolls using a band saw, jigsaw or sabre saw. Use a smooth-cutting 24-tpi saw blade for a cut that requires little or no sanding. Notice the scroll's corners are mitered to allow the scrolls to abut tightly. Dry fit all scrolls before final positioning and gluing.

Since mahogany is an open-grain wood, you must fill the grain before applying the finish. To save a finishing step, mix the red mahogany stain with a natural wood filler. You can stain and fill the wood's grain in one step.

Brush the stain/filler mix liberally into the wood's grain. Let the filler dull over (about 20 minutes), then wipe off the excess with a coarse rag, such as burlap or terry cloth. Wipe against the grain, rubbing the filler into the wood's pores. Be sure to remove all excess filler from the wood's surface before it dries or you'll have a lot of sanding to do. Allow the filler to dry overnight, then sand lightly with 220-grit abrasive paper. Brush off the sanding dust, wipe with a tack cloth and follow with two coats of clear finish.

Complete the project by installing the mirror after the finish has dried. Attach the hardboard back to the frame with one ½-in. No. 6 flathead screw in each of the back's eight circular tabs. Then, insert two No. 16 screw eyes in the frame's top as shown to anchor the picture-hanging wire.

CHERRY DRESSING MIRROR

The cherry dressing mirror is similar in design and construction to the three-drawer pine mirror. Often listed in antique books as a drawing glass, this late 19th-century piece is designed for use on a table or chest of drawers.

Start by cutting all the pieces to the sizes shown. Solid cherry hardwood is used through-

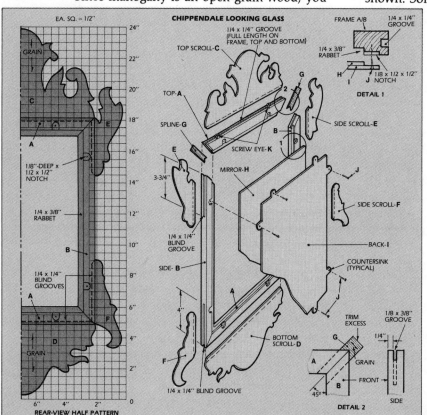

CHIPPENDALE LOOKING GLASS

MATERIALS LIST
CHIPPENDALE LOOKING GLASS

Key	No.	Size and description (use)
A	2	¾ x 1⅛ x 9¾" mahogany (frame top and bottom)
B	2	¾ x 1⅛ x 13⅛" mahogany (frame sides)
C	1	¼ x 6⅛ x 9⅞" mahogany plywood (top scroll)
D	1	¼ x 4⅞ x 9⅞" mahogany plywood (bottom scroll)
E	2	¼ x 2 x 5¾" mahogany plywood (side scroll)
F	2	¼ x 2 x 5¾" mahogany plywood (side scroll)
G	4	⅛ x ¾ x 2¼" hardwood mahogany (splines)
H	1	⅛ x 8⅛ x 11½" mirror
I	1	⅛ x 9¼ x 12⅝" hardboard (back panel)
J	4	½" No. 6 flathead screws
K	2	No. 16 screw eyes

Misc.: Carpenter's glue, picture-hanging wire, wood filler, 220-grit sandpaper, red mahogany stain, clear finish.
Note: Lumber and Wood-Glo clear finish from Constantine's, 2050 Eastchester Rd., Bronx, N.Y. 10461.

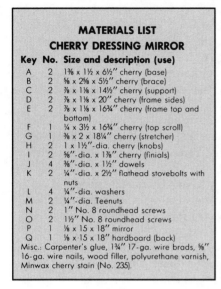

MATERIALS LIST
CHERRY DRESSING MIRROR

Key	No.	Size and description (use)
A	2	1⅜ x 1½ x 6½" cherry (base)
B	2	⅝ x 2⅝ x 5½" cherry (brace)
C	2	⅞ x 1⅛ x 14½" cherry (support)
D	2	⅞ x 1⅛ x 20" cherry (frame sides)
E	2	⅞ x 1⅛ x 16¾" cherry (frame top and bottom)
F	1	¼ x 3½ x 16¾" cherry (top scroll)
G	1	⅜ x 2 x 18¼" cherry (stretcher)
H	2	1 x 1½"-dia. cherry (knobs)
I	2	⅝"-dia. x 1⅞" cherry (finials)
J	4	⅜"-dia. x 1½" dowels
K	2	¼"-dia. x 2½" flathead stovebolts with nuts
L	4	¼"-dia. washers
M	2	¼"-dia. Teenuts
N	2	1" No. 8 roundhead screws
O	2	1½" No. 8 roundhead screws
P	1	⅛ x 15 x 18" mirror
Q	1	⅛ x 15 x 18" hardboard (back)

Misc.: Carpenter's glue, 1¾" 17-ga. wire brads, ⅝" 16-ga. wire nails, wood filler, polyurethane varnish, Minwax cherry stain (No. 235).

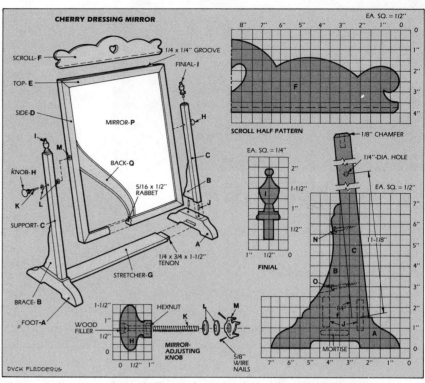

out. Before assembling the mirror's frame, rabbet the frame's pieces to hold the mirror and hardboard back. Also, shape the frame's two front edges and all four sides of both vertical supports with a ¼-in. rounding-over bit. The decorative scroll, feet and brace pieces are all shaped on a band saw, jigsaw or sabre saw. Use a lathe to turn the finials and the mirror adjusting knobs.

Next, cut the mortises in the feet using a router or shaper fitted with a ¼-in.-dia. straight bit. Make several passes, increasing the cutter's depth on each pass, until you reach a ¾-in.-deep mortise. You could also form the mortises by boring a series of ¼-in.-dia. holes and then chiseling out the waste.

Form the ⅛-in. chamfer on each support's top edge with a disc sander or block plane. Then, bore a ¼-in.-dia. hole in each support's top for installing the finials. Also, bore a ¼-in.-dia. hole through each support's side for installing the mirror adjusting knobs as shown.

Cut the bottoms of the supports and braces at a 6° angle (84° angle along the vertical plane). Then, attach the braces to the supports as shown. Use a doweling jig to bore each brace's bottom edge for two ⅜-in.-dia. wood dowels. The rear dowels are bored slightly deeper than the front dowels.

Transfer the braces' dowel hole locations to the two foot pieces using dowel centers. Bore ⅜-in.-dia. holes into the feet on these points. In this case, the rear dowels are bored into each foot *shallower* than the front dowels. This is to avoid boring into the foot pieces' mortises.

Glue and insert the dowels into the braces and then glue the braces onto the feet. The vertical support members are now completed, but they're not joined by the stretcher until after the mirror's frame is assembled and installed.

Before assembling the mirror's frame, bore a 5/16-in.-dia. hole in each frame's side for installing Teenuts. See the instructions for the pine dressing mirror for installing the Teenuts and the mirror adjusting knobs.

Glue and nail the frame together with 1¾-in., 17-ga. wire nails at the corners. Clamp the frame square until the glue dries. Then, glue the decorative scroll into the frame's top groove. Assemble the support members to the frame by screwing the mirror adjusting knobs through the supports and into the frame's Teenuts. Tighten the mirror adjusting knobs to hold the supports parallel to the frame's sides. Cut the stretcher to equal the exact distance between the two feet. Dry-fit the stretcher to be sure its length and tenons fit properly. Make any necessary adjustments before gluing and assembly.

Finish the project with a coat of Minwax cherry stain (No. 235). After the stain has dried 24 hours, apply three coats of satin polyurethane varnish. Sand lightly between varnish coats with 220-grit abrasive paper. After the surface has dried thoroughly, install the mirror. Carefully nail the hardboard back in place with ⅝-in. brads.

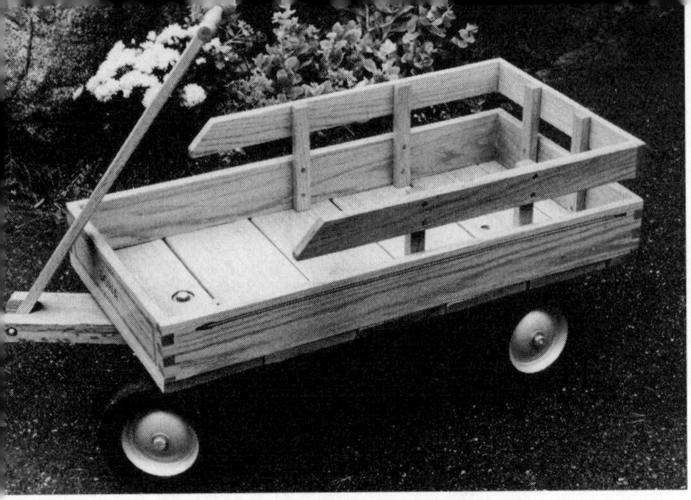

AN HEIRLOOM WAGON

An easy-to-build project that copies a familiar heirloom.

This sturdy child's wagon is built of solid oak to last for generations. It features a smooth-operating steering mechanism of a Lazy Susan.

Start by cutting all parts as shown. Make all 1½-in.-thick parts by gluing up two pieces of ¾-in. stock. Next, cut box joints into the wagon sides and ends using a box-joint jig on a table saw or router table. Glue and clamp together the wagon frame. Attach the six floorboards with 1½-in., No. 8 roundhead brass screws. Leave a ¼-in. space between the boards.

Next, glue and shape the front and rear suspensions. Then clamp the end caps to each suspension and bore a ½-in.-dia. hole for the axle. Remove the end caps and bore out all parts to hold a hexnut.

Reassemble the parts with the nuts embedded. Assemble the steering mechanism with the Lazy Susan in position. Then bore through the floorboard, steering tongue and front suspension to install the pivot bolt. Bore and chisel out the mortise in the handle block. Secure the handle by driving in two wedges. Attach the remaining parts and connect the wheels by screwing the axles into embedded nuts. Apply a waterproof finish.

MATERIALS LIST
HEIRLOOM WAGON

Key	No.	Size and description (use)
A	2	¾ x 4½ x 36″ oak (sides)
B	2	¾ x 4½ x 18″ oak (ends)
C	5	¾ x 6½ x 18″ oak (floor)
C1	1	¾ x 2¼ x 18″ oak (floor)
D	2	¾ x 2½ x 26″ oak (side rails)
E	1	¾ x 2½ x 18″ oak (back rail)
F	6	¾ x 1¼ x 8½″ oak (supports)
G	1	1½ x 6 x 14″ (rear suspension)
G1	1	1½ x 5¹¹⁄₁₆ x 14″ oak (front suspension)
H	4	¾ x 1½ x 3″ oak (end caps)
I	1	1½ x 4 x 18″ oak (steering tongue)
J	1	¾ x 1½ x 32″ oak (steering post)
J1	2	¼ x ½ x 1⅝″ maple (wedge)
K	1	1½ x 1⅝ x 3″ oak (handle block)
L	2	¾″-dia. x 5″ oak (handles)
L1	2	½ x 1¼″-dia. oak (handle caps)
M	1	5⁄16 x 6″ Lazy Susan
N	6	½″ No. 6 flathead screws with washers
O	1	½″-dia. x 6″ carriage bolt, 3 washers and locknut (handle pivot)
P	6	¼″-dia. x 3″ lagscrew and washer
Q		1½″ No. 8 oval or roundhead brass screws
R	4	8″-dia. wheel with ball bearing
S	4	½″-dia. x 6″ carriage bolts, two washers and locknuts (axle)
T	1	¼″-dia. x 4″ carriage bolts, washers, locknuts

Misc.: Carpenter's glue, pinstripe tape, sandpaper, waterproof finish or marine varnish.

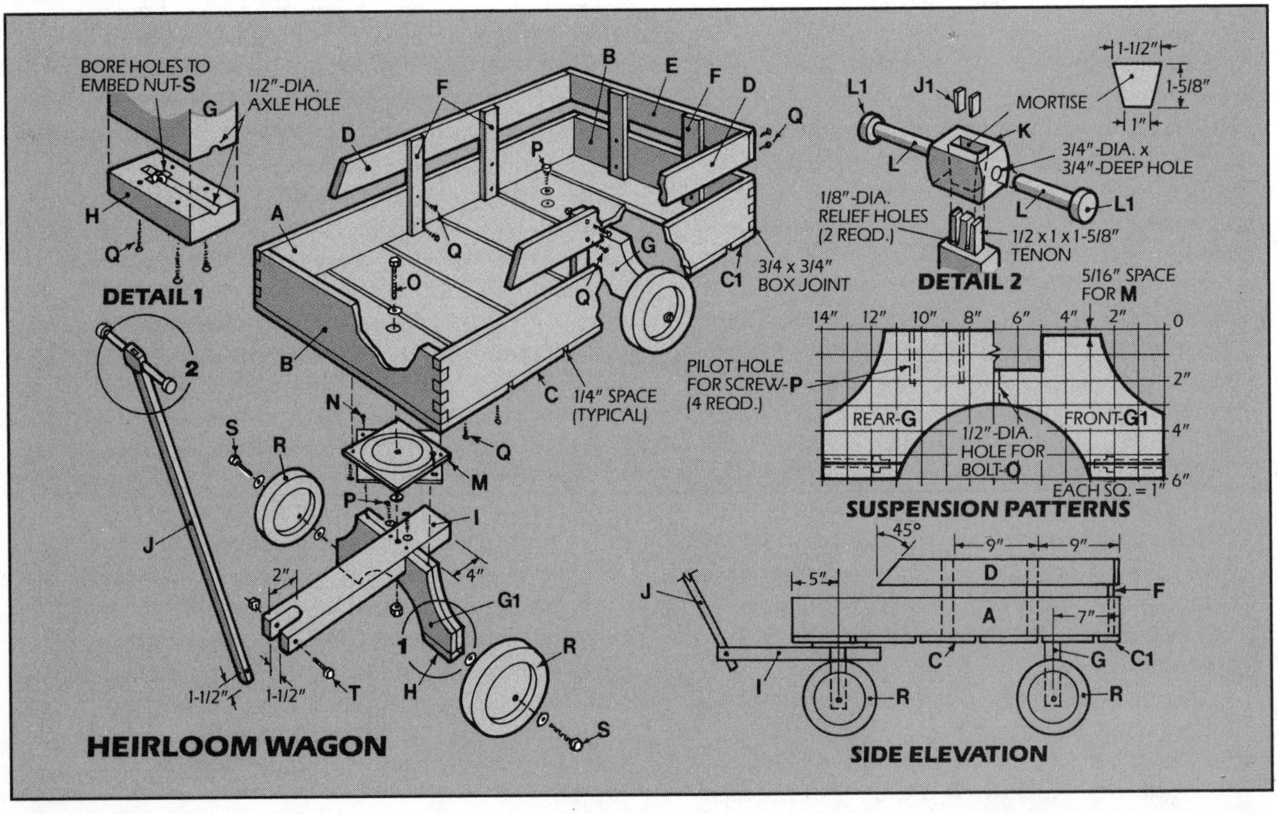

TIPS AND TOOLS FOR CRAFT PROJECTS

These handy tips will help you with an added touch of quality to your craft projects.

The next time you need to join two lengths of wood, but don't want the nailheads to show, try a technique called blind nailing. When combined with glue, blind nailing is a fast, easy means of making remarkably strong wood joints.

If you are unfamiliar with cabinet scrapers, you've been missing out on a good thing. These tools excel at smoothing wood and, when properly sharpened, can yield a ready-to-finish surface without the need for tedious sanding.

JOINERY WITH "INVISIBLE" NAILS
Blind nailing is most often used to produce a finished, L-shaped trim around countertops and table edges, and to conceal a plywood edge. You can also produce a wide variety of moldings—including baseboard, crown, chair rail and corner guard—by blind-nailing two, three or four routed pieces. Blind nailing is also used to edge-join boards to form wider panels.

First, be certain the two pieces to be joined form a tight-fitting joint. Sand or plane the wood where necessary. Next, mark the nail positions onto the larger, flatter piece. For most jobs, 1½- or 2-in. finishing nails spaced 6 in. apart work fine. In the photos, 4d (1½-in.) finishing nails are used to blind-nail ¾-in.-thick pine.

Blind nailing was used to make this remarkably strong, tight wood joint. Completed piece can be routed or sanded without hitting nailheads.

Cut off the nailheads with end-cut nippers or cutting pliers. Then hammer the nails partially into the edge of the first piece. You should make certain the nails don't protrude too far, or they'll pass through the second piece.

Next, grind sharp points onto the protruding nails using a stone grinding wheel in a drill press or portable electric drill. The sharpened tip offers less resistance to wood penetration than the blunt-end nail.

Apply carpenter's glue to the first piece and clamp it to the edge of a workbench. Place newspaper under the work to absorb any glue squeeze-out. The protruding nails with the sharpened ends should be facing the rear of the bench. Position the second piece against the nails and apply pressure gradually by squeezing the two parts together with C-clamps. Tighten the clamps little by little, starting at each end and working toward the center. After the glue has dried, the assembly is ready to be sanded, routed or planed without hitting the nailheads.

Snip off the nailheads before you hammer the nails into the edge of the workpiece.

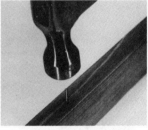
Space the nails as needed and drive them partially into the edge of the workpiece.

Use the mating workpiece as a guide to check the height of the protruding nails.

Grind the nails to a sharp point. A file can be used to sharpen the nails as well.

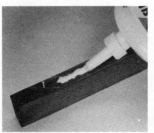
Apply carpenter's glue to the nailed edge. Be sure the surface is clean and dry.

Tighten C-clamps gradually to draw the two pieces together.

USING CABINET SCRAPERS

Cabinet scrapers can remove saw marks, tool burns and milling defects such as planer ripples in any kind of wood stock. They can eliminate ridge marks left by a smoothing plane and can also flatten wavy-grained stock that doesn't respond well to planing.

The scraper is nothing more than a flat piece of tough but malleable steel, about ¹⁄₃₂ in. thick. The steel lends itself to burnishing, or "turning over," the edge to form a slightly hooked flare of steel. When the blade is held at an angle of about 70° to the workpiece and pushed or pulled over the surface, this hook cuts the stock, producing very fine shavings. Despite its name, the only time the tool actually *scrapes* is when the edge is dull and produces dusty particles, not shavings.

Although using the scraper is easy, sharpening it is a bit tricky. When an edge just begins to dull, it can be revived with a few burnishing strokes. This will work several times before filing and honing must be repeated. To burnish

Cabinet scraper blades come in three basic shapes: rectangular, straight with concave and convex ends, and gooseneck. Your choice depends on the shape of the workpiece. For heavy-duty jobs, there's also a tool holder that accommodates a rectangular blade. Sharpening burnishers (left) come with either round or triangular blades.

properly, just make four or five progresive passes over each edge until you get a flare of about 10° relative to the blade edge.

To sharpen the gooseneck scraper and the blades with concave and convex ends, use the same method, but different tools: a round file, slip stone and round blade burnisher.

For normal use, the handled blades will work well. But for heavy-duty work, the frame-mounted type that looks much like a spokeshave is a better idea.

To sharpen scraper, first clamp blade in a vise, then file edges flat using a single-cut fine mill file. Be sure to use full, firm strokes.

Remove file marks on edge by honing blade on oilstone. Keep blade perpendicular to stone at all times. Avoid rocking motion.

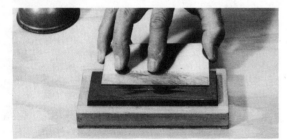

Once edge is honed, lay scraper flat on the stone and hone both blade faces. This will remove the fine wire edge left from filing.

Final step in sharpening is to clamp blade in vise, apply oil to edge and draw burnisher across each side of edge several times.

To use cabinet scraper, hold it firmly in both hands, bow blade slightly with thumbs. Tilt blade in cut direction and push.

Use straight blade with concave and convex ends, or gooseneck scraper, to smooth curved surfaces.

WAINSCOTING

Here is a step-by-step guide to redecorating with wainscoting.

Wainscoting is a general term applied to many different wall treatments. Some traditional examples are: flat-panel wainscoting, which consists of a series of flat panels surrounded with rails and stiles, much like cabinet doors; raised-panel wainscoting, fabricated in a similar manner, but which is usually considered more elegant because of the time and effort required; and the double V-joint and bead wainscoting (shown here), which is probably the most prevalent. It's still available in open stock at many lumberyards and is usually made of pine or fir, sometimes in different grades. If you plan to paint it, as done here, you can save money by using the less expensive grade. In fact, your choice of wainscoting materials is by no means limited to these traditional examples.

3 BASIC WAYS TO ATTACH WAINSCOTING

You need horizontal nailing for the boards at least every 24 in. This is required because the boards are narrow and applied vertically. The studs within the wall are aligned the same way, typically on 16-in. centers. Therefore, the voids between the wall studs have to be spanned to provide nailing surfaces for the wainscoting boards.

SURFACE-MOUNT FURRING

Probably the easiest way is to nail furring strips across the surface of the wall, hitting each wall stud with a nail. This method has one minor drawback. Because both the furring and the wainscoting are applied over the drywall or plaster, the finished surface extends at least 1 in. into the room, depending on the material you use—$^{11}/_{16}$ in. or ¾ in. for the furring and $^{9}/_{16}$ in. or ⅜ in. for the wainscoting.

RECESSED FURRING

A second method gains some space because the furring is recessed into the drywall or plaster. To do this, just position the furring strips in their proper place on the wall, trace their outlines, then cut out the wall covering material behind. Nail the furring directly onto the studs. Of course, you can remove all the drywall or plaster, but this is time-consuming and messy.

NAILING BLOCKS

If you do remove all the drywall or plaster, you have a third option that reduces the projection of the wainscoting to a minimum. This is to nail solid blocking between the studs, flush with the outside edge of the studs. Then nail the wainscoting directly across these framing members.

A variation of this method was used in our installation. The room had been gutted, solid blocking added between the studs, and new drywall installed on the walls and ceiling. We wanted the finished surface of the wainscoting boards to project the extra ½ in. into the room, so we installed the drywall over the lower part of the wall.

Solid wood wainscoting can change the appearance of any room. It's easy to work with and takes a natural finish, stain or paint well.

Begin by establishing height of boards. Mark wall at this point, then draw a level line through mark and continue it around room, maintaining precise level as you go.

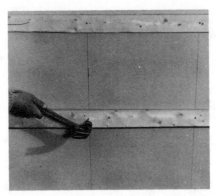

If you don't have horizontal blocking between studs, nail furring strips directly onto surface to receive the wainscoting. Nail into every wall stud.

If you'd rather recess the furring, draw an outline around each strip and cut out the drywall behind with a utility knife. Then nail furring directly onto the studs.

Start installing boards at room corner or door casing as shown here. For pro results, use level to plumb first board in place. Mark plumb position for reference.

If first board doesn't fit tightly to casing or room corner when held in plumb position, scribe back edge to conform to irregularities. Then plane edge to meet line.

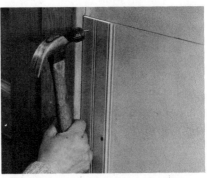

Once board is planed to fit, nail in place with finishing nails near back edge. The end boards are the only ones nailed through the surface. Set heads and fill nail holes.

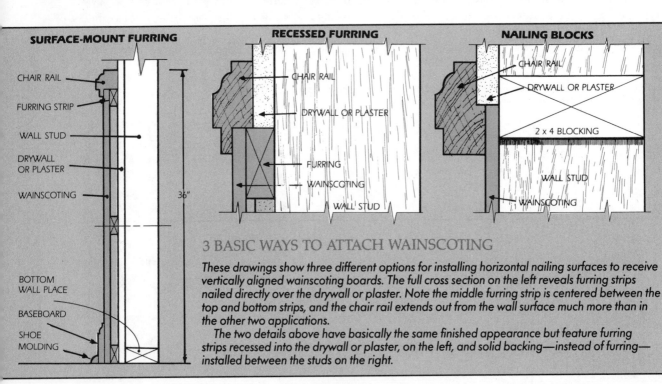

3 BASIC WAYS TO ATTACH WAINSCOTING

These drawings show three different options for installing horizontal nailing surfaces to receive vertically aligned wainscoting boards. The full cross section on the left reveals furring strips nailed directly over the drywall or plaster. Note the middle furring strip is centered between the top and bottom strips, and the chair rail extends out from the wall surface much more than in the other two applications.

The two details above have basically the same finished appearance but feature furring strips recessed into the drywall or plaster, on the left, and solid backing—instead of furring—installed between the studs on the right.

INSTALLING THE WAINSCOTING BOARDS

First, decide on what height you want your chair rail. We chose 36 in., which is fairly standard but by no means a rule.

Next, cut all the wainscoting boards to length using a radial-arm saw or a circular saw with a cutting jig. Start installation at a room corner or alongside a door casing. Plumb the first wainscoting board in place, scribe and plane it to fit flush, then nail it in place.

Keep in mind these boards have a tongue on one edge and a groove on the other. Because of this built-in joinery method, once the first board is nailed soundly in place, all following boards are nailed only through the tongue. These nails will be hidden by the groove of the next board. You must work carefully when nailing so you don't split the tongue. Angle the nails at approximately 45°.

For right-handed people, working left to right on the wall is generally more convenient. For

Attach tongue edge of board by driving nail through corner where tongue and bead meet. Angle nail at approximately 45° and set head.

Drive next board into place so groove fits over first board's tongue. Use scrap block of wainscoting to prevent damaging edge. Nail second board through tongue only.

If board is slightly warped, you can often pry it tight by driving a chisel into the wall or furring strip and pulling back on chisel. Hold in place while driving nail.

If you want to fabricate your own chair rail, use a router table to make the cuts. To duplicate our pattern, begin cutting the back rabbet with a straight cutter.

Next, cut bottom rabbet on board face, then turn board over and cut roman ogee shape near top. Don't cut full depth in one pass. Use two or three passes for a clean cut.

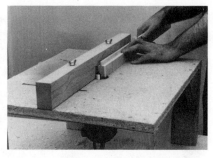

When ogee has been cut to depth shown in the drawing, install straight cutter in router and trim off waste below ogee to complete the finished shape.

Lightly sand rail to remove any sharp edges and you're done. Completed shape required only two cutters: roman ogee shown and straight cutter still in router.

left-handed people, the opposite direction is better.

When you come to an electrical outlet, turn off the power to that circuit at your fuse box or breaker box. Then remove the covering plate and the screws holding the receptacle in the wall box. Pull the receptacle away from the box, being careful not to damage any of the insulation on the wires. It is not necessary to remove the wires—you just need enough room to work around the receptacle.

Cut the board or boards so the perimeter of the box is just visible. Then nail the boards on the wall. Screw the receptacle back in place so its positioning ears, on the top and bottom, bear directly on the surface of the boards. Then attach the covering plate and turn on the power.

INSTALLING THE CHAIR RAIL

Once all the boards are nailed on the wall, cut and install a chair rail of your choice. You can either buy a stock rail at a lumberyard or cut one of your own design on a shaper or a router table.

Finish up by installing a baseboard at the floor and a shoe molding over it if you choose. Now you should sand the whole wall with 220-grit sandpaper, remove the dust and apply a finish of your choice. You could also sand each board after it is cut and before you nail it to the wall, saving you the discomfort of trying to sand a low, vertical surface.

CUTTING JIG FOR CIRCULAR SAW

If you're installing a lot of wainscoting, you've got a lot of straight cuts to make, all the same length. A radial-arm saw is the ideal tool, but if you don't have one, this simple-to-build jig for a circular saw will save a lot of time. Assemble the parts as shown in the drawing above, making sure the fence is installed square to the sides. Then just slide the boards into the jig and make the cuts. Clamp a stop block at the far end of the jig so you won't have to measure each board.

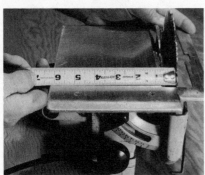

Measure distance from side of shoe to saw blade, then install fence on jig so blade just clears end of saw platform.

When parts are assembled, set blade to cut ⅛ in. into top of 2 x 4. Then make kerf cut, keeping shoe tight to fence.

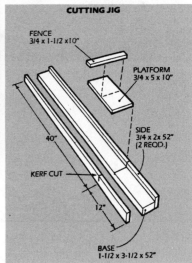

CUTTING JIG

FENCE
3/4 x 1-1/2 x 10"

PLATFORM
3/4 x 5 x 10"

SIDE
3/4 x 2 x 52"
(2 REQD.)

40"

KERF CUT

12"

BASE
1-1/2 x 3-1/2 x 52"

CREATE PERIOD MOLDING

Reproduce period baseboard, chair rail, door surround and cornice from stock items.

Re-creating authentic period moldings *exactly* would be frustrating. But, by using stock lumber, you can closely duplicate the moldings of yesteryear.

BASEBOARD

Shape the baseboard from 1 x 6 using a ¼-in. and ½-in. quarter-round molding head in a table saw. Make the first pass with the cutter tilted at 28°. Adjust the depth-of-cut so only the corner of the cutter projects above the table. Then readjust the cutter to the perpendicular position and make the second pass with the rounded portion of the molding head.

CHAIR RAIL

Shape the backboard from 1 x 3 using the same method as described above for the baseboard. Next, nail a 1 x 2 to the top surface of the backboard. Add ½-in. half-round and ½-in. cove moldings as shown. Nail the chair rail to the wall's level, between 33 in. and 35 in. from the floor.

DOOR SURROUND

The trick to reproducing the gently curving S

BASEBOARD   CHAIR RAIL   DOOR SURROUND   CORNICE

Reproduce period moldings from stock items available at lumberyards and home centers.

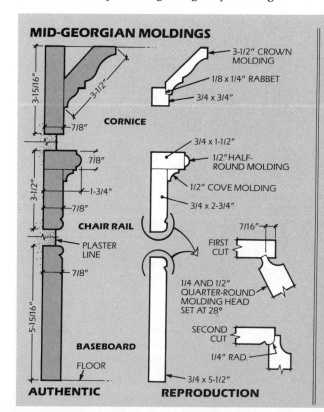

This homemade jig makes it easy to cut compound angles on the radial-arm saw. Note that molding is positioned upside down.

This simple jig is used in conjunction with a miter gauge, set at 45°, for cutting compound angles on the table saw.

shape of the authentic door surround is to cut out the center of 2½-in. crown molding. Three cuts on a table saw are required to produce this piece. For the final cut, tack the center section temporarily to a scrap-wood guide. Rip remaining members for ¾-in. stock.

Make the jamb by first cutting a 45° bevel on one edge and then a shallow rabbet as shown. Finally, nail ¾-in. half-round molding to the bevel face.

CORNICE

Make the cornice from 3½-in. crown molding and a ¾ x ¾-in. piece. Rabbet the piece to fit molding. Nail the cornice where ceiling and walls meet. Butt top of the molding to ceiling.

MID-GEORGIAN MOLDINGS

CORNICE
3-1/2" CROWN MOLDING
1/8 x 1/4" RABBET
3/4 x 3/4"
3-15/16"
3-1/2"
7/8"

CHAIR RAIL
7/8"
1-3/4"
7/8"
3/4 x 1-1/2"
1/2" HALF-ROUND MOLDING
1/2" COVE MOLDING
3/4 x 2-3/4"

PLASTER LINE
7/8"
5-15/16"
3-1/2"

BASEBOARD
FLOOR

AUTHENTIC

REPRODUCTION
7/16"
FIRST CUT
1/4 AND 1/2" QUARTER-ROUND MOLDING HEAD SET AT 28°
SECOND CUT
1/4" RAD.
3/4 x 5-1/2"

AUTHENTIC DOOR SURROUND
7/8"
3-9/16"
1/2"   7/8"
DOOR
DOOR JAMB
3/8" RAD.
PLASTER
2"

REPRODUCTION

DOOR SURROUND
5/8 x 3/4"
3/4 x 3-3/8"
1/8" x 45° BEVEL

DOOR JAMB
3/4" STOCK
1/8"
45°
5/8"
3/4" HALF-ROUND MOLDING

FIRST CUT
SECOND CUT
1"
TILT BLADE 13°
2-1/2" CROWN MOLDING

THIRD CUT
WASTE
NAIL TEMPORARILY
SCRAP-WOOD GUIDE

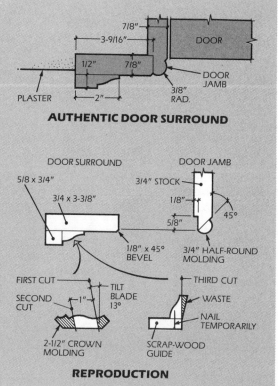

PANTRY ON WHEELS

Easy-to-roll-out racks increase pantry storage space.

After repeatedly digging into a deep, dark pantry to retrieve a bottle of soy sauce or a can of tomato paste, you may want to look at these roll-out racks of shelves. The racks stand side by side and are mounted on rollers. When one of the racks is pulled out, all items on its shelves are visible and accessible.

The racks are easy-to-build, ¾-in. plywood frames, assembled using butt joints. Cleats at the joints serve as strengtheners. The ½-in. plywood shelves provide further rigidity.

The racks move on appliance rollers. These multiwheeled plastic or aluminum supports are used for moving refrigerators and stoves. You can purchase them at hardware and discount stores or by mail from Sears. You'll need one set for each rack.

You can roll out the racks easily with a brass pull, positioned slightly above waist height on the side of the rack facing out.

To assemble and finish the racks, you'll need a hammer, drill, screwdriver, nailset, paint brush and some 80- and 120-grit sandpaper. A corner clamp is also handy. Use the clamp at each shelf corner to hold the parts in place while you attach them with nails or screws.

To determine the number and size of racks your pantry can accommodate, measure the depth of the pantry or closet and the height and width of the opening. Allow ½ to 1 in. clearance at the sides and between racks. Racks at least 8 in. wide accept the rollers best, since both mates of a set can be extended to the same length. Subtract the height of the appliance rollers from the height of the opening to get the maximum height of the rack sides.

Next, decide upon the number of shelves you would like per rack. Either draw a rough sketch to scale for each rack, including the shelves, or use the dimensions on the drawing below, if your pantry can hold this size rack. From the drawing, make a materials list you'll need when purchasing lumber and hardware.

ASSEMBLY AND PAINTING
Cut the parts to size, then sand them smooth, dusting with a clean brush between steps.

Before building the pantry on wheels, the 30-in.-deep pantry was too cavernous to display its contents. You had to take everything off the front of a shelf to locate items pushed to the back.

Nearly every size package is visible and readily accessible in this pantry on wheels. Labeling each rack with its contents makes locating items even easier. On racks 8 in. or wider, appliance roller mates can be extended to the same length and fastened to a rack. On narrower racks, stagger rollers.

Lay out the rack sides. Prebore the cleats and, using a corner clamp, fasten them to the sides with glue and screws. Fasten the top and bottom pieces to the cleats with glue and nails. Then hammer finishing nails through the rack sides into the ends of the top and bottom. Set nails and fill holes with wood putty.

Prime and paint the shelves with a semigloss plastic or acrylic latex paint before installing. You can hang each shelf to dry by a string fastened to a small nail driven partway into one end. Then prime and paint the rack.

After the paint is dry, lay the rack on its front edge and measure and mark shelf placement. Then, stand each shelf on edge within the rack,

secure it with a corner clamp and drive nails to fasten it in place. Set the nails and fill the holes.

Make retainers of venetian blind slats nailed to rack sides and shelf bottoms or use ¼-in.-thick lattice.

If possible, snap out the rollers and shafts from their housings. Position the housing on the bottom of the racks so they're within ¼ in. of the edge. Bore a small hole in each end and secure with screws. Snap the rollers and shafts back in and stand the rack upright.

Touch up nail holes with paint and attach the brass pulls. If there is a saddle on the floor below the closet door, remove it so it won't interfere with the rack's mobility.

Each unit is a ¾-in. plywood frame with butt joints. Shelves are ½-in. plywood. Appliance rollers allow unit to move easily and the retainers keep items from falling off pantry shelf. A brass pull lets you pull the unit out of the pantry and return it when you are finished.

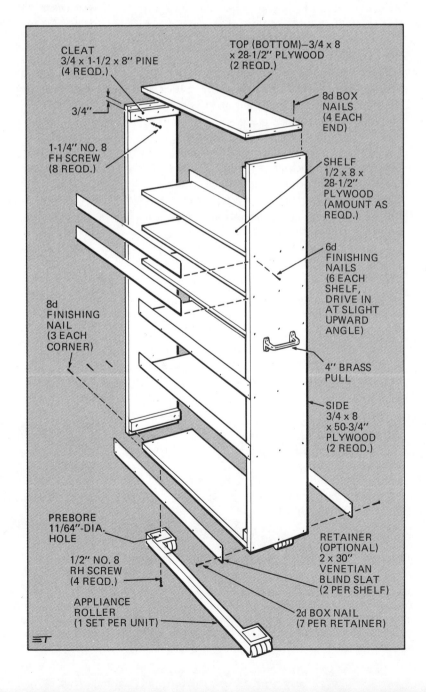

HOME WIRING

Electrical repairs *must* be done by the book. But they can be easy and will save you money.

The secret of successful electrical work is to respect electricity. If you add a circuit or install new wiring, you may need a permit from the building inspector in your town. After the work is done, but before you close the walls, you may have to get the job inspected.

PREPARATIONS

Always shut off the power before you start. Pull the fuse, flip the circuit breaker or open the master switch at the service entry panel where the current comes into your house.

Some older houses may have more than one service entry if circuits have been added, so double check to see that the power is really *off.* How? By using a circuit tester—insert its probes into the outlet—or by plugging in a table lamp. No light and you know the circuit is dead. Double check by touching a circuit tester to the black (hot) and white (neutral) wires after removing the wall plate. Many pros hang a sign on the main service entry warning not to turn on the power while they're working.

Common household tools can handle most wiring jobs, but a circuit tester and wire stripper will help.

REPLACING A PLUG

Even though the cord of a lamp or appliance lasts practically forever, rough handling can break the connections inside the plug. To repair it, you can either cut the plug off the cord and put on a new one or junk the old cord and make up a new one.

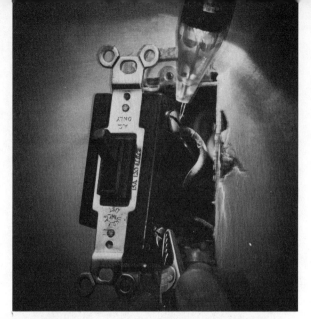

Battery-powered continuity tester is used to check out a wall switch. With power shut off at the service entry, remove the switch plate and mounting screws so you can bring the switch out of its box with the wires attached. With the switch turned on (and the power off), the tester should light when you touch its leads to the brass (black wire) and silver (white wire) terminals. Tester should go out when the switch is turned off. If the tester does not light, the switch is bad.

Always unplug any lamp or appliance before inspecting, cleaning or working on it. Tie an Underwriter's Lab (UL) knot to keep the wires from pulling off screw terminals in plugs and lamps.

To repair clamp plugs, raise the lever, insert the wires and lower the lever to lock them in place. Specialized plugs come with instructions. Appliance cords, like those on electric irons, often have welded connections and must be replaced.

Be sure the replacement plug is for the same size wire. Some appliance cords use heavier wire to carry the current without overheating. Standard plugs will not fit on this heavier wire.

REWIRING LAMP SOCKETS

Changing a lamp socket with a failed switch or

Junction boxes, also called GEM boxes, must enclose and protect all splices, connections switches, outlets and other in-wall wiring fixtures. Surface wiring boxes are slightly different. This in-wall wiring junction box has removable ends so two or more boxes can be ganged to make one larger box.

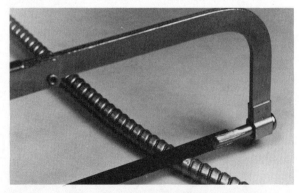

Cut metal-armored BX cable by hacksawing through the two coil wraps at an angle. Break the sawed cable to expose the wires, which are then cut with snips. Insulators protect conductors from sharp cable end.

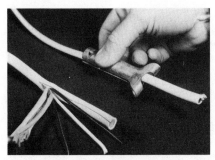

Cut back BX or plastic sheathing about 6 inches with a utility knife or special plastic sheathing cutter (left). This will free the wires for stripping with a hand tool (right) that also cuts wires and screws, in addition to crimping solderless terminals.

The round junction-box knockouts can be pried out with a screwdriver to admit plastic-sheathed cable (small size) or armored BX (large). Inside the box, clamp plastic cable (left) or secure BX with special fittings (right) over the red insulation protector.

A solderless connector joins two wires inside a GEM or other junction box. Twist the stripped wires together (left) and screw the connector down tightly to make the splice. Wrap the connector and wires with insulating tape (some codes require friction tape).

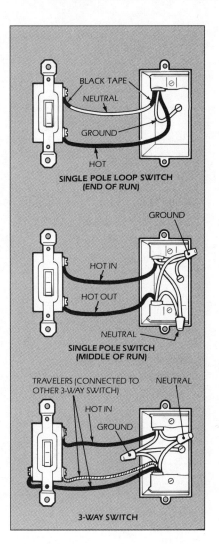

SINGLE POLE LOOP SWITCH (END OF RUN)

SINGLE POLE SWITCH (MIDDLE OF RUN)

3-WAY SWITCH

burned insulation is almost the same as rewiring the lamp. Take the lamp apart and run a new wire through it before connecting the socket. Replacing the socket is a straight swap.

If the insulation sleeve is the only defective part, check the terminals for tightness and replace the sleeve.

Two-socket lamps should have both sockets replaced even if only one is bad. Parts come as an assembly. But two-socket lamps wired independently, so each bulb turns on and off with the same switch, can have either socket replaced separately.

Three-socket lights have their sockets replaced one at a time. Follow the wiring as installed originally. Lamp switches that are not

part of a bulb socket come prewired. Install them by cutting out the bad switch and hooking up the new one with solderless connectors and tape.

CHANGING WALL SWITCHES

Wall switches, like all other house wiring junctions and controls, are mounted inside protective boxes. Before removing the switch cover plate, shut off power to the circuit.

Get an identical switch for the one you must replace. Single pole switches have only two terminals and control a light from one point. Three-way switches let you turn a light on or off from either of two points. They have four terminals: two for the switch, one for a traveler wire

BASIC WIRING HOOKUPS

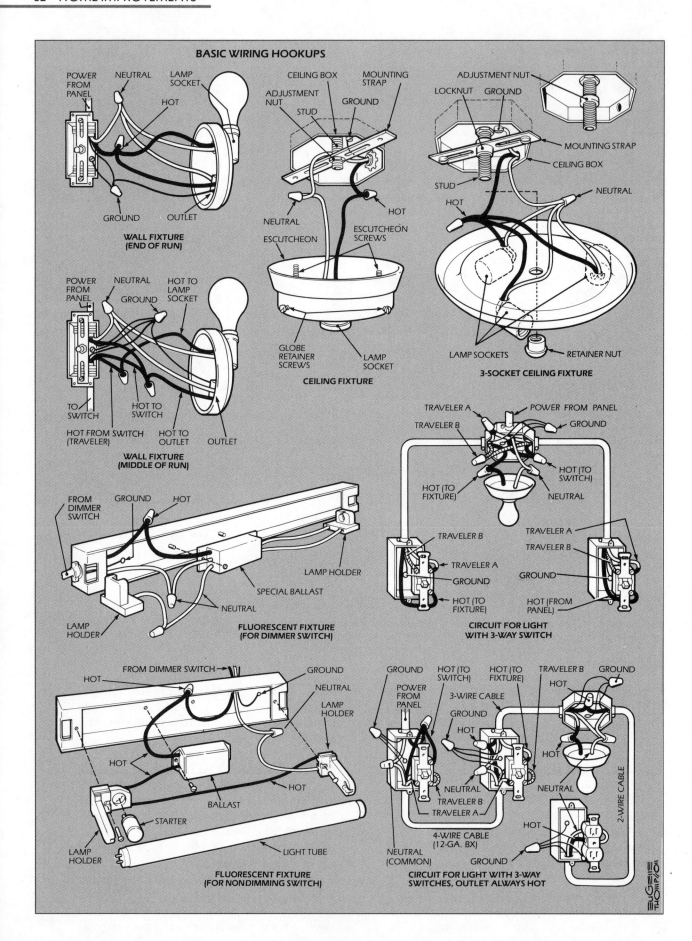

WALL FIXTURE (END OF RUN)

POWER FROM PANEL · NEUTRAL · LAMP SOCKET · HOT · GROUND · OUTLET

CEILING FIXTURE

CEILING BOX · MOUNTING STRAP · ADJUSTMENT NUT · STUD · GROUND · NEUTRAL · HOT · ESCUTCHEON · ESCUTCHEON SCREWS · GLOBE RETAINER SCREWS · LAMP SOCKET

3-SOCKET CEILING FIXTURE

ADJUSTMENT NUT · LOCKNUT · GROUND · MOUNTING STRAP · CEILING BOX · STUD · HOT · NEUTRAL · LAMP SOCKETS · RETAINER NUT

WALL FIXTURE (MIDDLE OF RUN)

POWER FROM PANEL · NEUTRAL · GROUND · HOT TO LAMP SOCKET · TO SWITCH · HOT TO SWITCH · HOT FROM SWITCH (TRAVELER) · HOT TO OUTLET · OUTLET

FLUORESCENT FIXTURE (FOR DIMMER SWITCH)

FROM DIMMER SWITCH · GROUND · HOT · LAMP HOLDER · SPECIAL BALLAST · NEUTRAL · LAMP HOLDER

CIRCUIT FOR LIGHT WITH 3-WAY SWITCH

TRAVELER A · POWER FROM PANEL · TRAVELER B · GROUND · HOT (TO SWITCH) · HOT (TO FIXTURE) · NEUTRAL · TRAVELER B · TRAVELER A · TRAVELER A · TRAVELER B · GROUND · GROUND · HOT (TO FIXTURE) · HOT (FROM PANEL)

FLUORESCENT FIXTURE (FOR NONDIMMING SWITCH)

FROM DIMMER SWITCH · GROUND · HOT · NEUTRAL · LAMP HOLDER · HOT · HOT · BALLAST · STARTER · LIGHT TUBE · LAMP HOLDER

CIRCUIT FOR LIGHT WITH 3-WAY SWITCHES, OUTLET ALWAYS HOT

GROUND · HOT (TO SWITCH) · HOT (TO FIXTURE) · TRAVELER B · GROUND · HOT · POWER FROM PANEL · 3-WIRE CABLE · GROUND · HOT · HOT · NEUTRAL · TRAVELER B · TRAVELER A · NEUTRAL · 4-WIRE CABLE (12-GA. BX) · NEUTRAL (COMMON) · GROUND · HOT · 2-WIRE CABLE

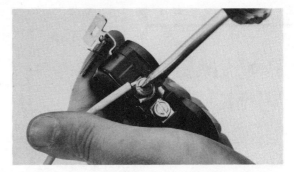

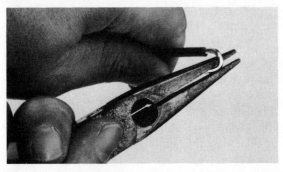

Bend the stripped-wire end into a hook (left) by gripping it with long-nose pliers and twisting. Hook the wire around the terminal screw (right) so that as the screw is tightened in a clockwise direction, wire will wrap tighter around terminal.

Wrap the switch or other fixture in insulating tape after connecting wires to prevent shorts when inserting in box.

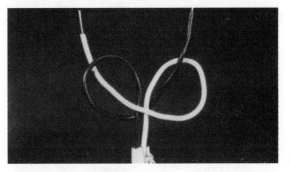

Tie a UL knot in lamp and wall plug cords to keep the wires from pulling off terminals.

taking power to the other switch, and a metallic ground.

A four-way switch controls a light from a third location working with two three-way switches. It has four brass terminals, all of which accept traveler wires to the two three-way switches and a ground.

Front-, side- and back-wired switches are the same except for terminal location. Some back-wired switches have spring slots (you poke the wire into the slot to make the connection) instead of screw terminals. These are only for use with copper wires. Do not use them with aluminum wires.

CHANGING RECEPTACLES
Like wall switches, outlets and receptacles are in wall boxes protected by cover plates. Replacing one is almost the same as replacing a switch.

A single outlet usually has three terminals: brass (hot), silver-colored (neutral) and green (ground). A double outlet has five terminals: Four power the outlets, and the fifth is a ground wire (green).

THREE-WAY SWITCHES
You can't simply replace two single pole switches with three-way switches to get two control points for the same light. You need a third wire, called a traveler or messenger, to carry power between the switches. But, if the traveler is not in the wall cable, installing one can be more trouble than the job is worth.

Changing an existing three–pole switch is a straight swap. If you put the hot lead on a traveler terminal, the switch won't turn off. Cure this by moving the hot wire to the hot terminal.

CHANGING A CEILING FIXTURE
A ceiling fixture is simply an overhead wall box, except it has a support bar. To work on the fixture, shut off the power, remove the decorative nut at the bottom of the escutcheon and lower the fixture from the ceiling. Support it on a wire hook made from a coat hanger to keep the strain off the wires. Disconnect the wires, remove the old fixture, connect the new one and remount it on the stud with the escutcheon nut.

GROUND FAULT INTERRUPTER
Many modern houses have ground fault circuit interrupters to reduce shock hazard in the kitchen and bathroom. A GFCI detects current leakage in a hot wire and instantly trips a circuit breaker to prevent electrical shock. Should an appliance short out and charge the housing, a GFCI protects you if you touch it.

Installation in an existing line should be made near the main service entry. The GFCI protects only downstream outlets. After killing the power, cut into the line and install a standard box. The GFCI has four wires that splice onto the conductors. Follow the instructions supplied with the unit. Push the RESET button to set the GFCI. Then press the TEST button to be sure it's working. If the appliances on the line have no power, first reset the GFCI, then check the fuse or circuit breaker.

BASEMENT WINDOWS

Here's an easy-to-build extension jamb for covering basement utility windows and some tips on replacing broken glass.

FRAME AND FINISH A BASEMENT WINDOW

A common problem is encountered by many homeowners when remodeling a basement: How to frame and finish a window that is recessed back from the foundation wall. The answer: Install an extension window jamb made of 1 x 6 or 1 x 8 No. 2 pine ripped to the appropriate width.

First, frame out a rough opening around each window with 2 x 3s. Cut the header and sill 2 in. longer than the window width. Nail the header 1 in. above the window opening and the sill 1 in. below the window.

Next, determine the width of the jamb. Measure the distance from the window frame to the *finished* wall, then rip the pine stock accordingly.

Cut and assemble the jamb so its inside dimensions clear the window opening by at least ¼ in. on all sides. Assemble the jamb using 2-in. finishing nails and butt-joined corners. Next, hold the jamb in the rough window opening and use cedar shingles to shim it into position. Be certain the bottom of the jamb is level with the window opening and that the jamb sides align with the window frame.

Check the jamb for square and then drive 2½-in. casing nails through the jamb and shims and partially into the 2 x 3 framing. Once again, check the jamb for square before driving the nails all the way in. Then, toenail the back of the jamb into the window frame using 1½-in. finishing nails. Apply caulking where the jamb meets the frame.

Finish the wall with plasterboard or paneling. The finished wall should be flush with the jamb. Finally, trim the window opening with casing molding. Paint or stain the jamb and trim as desired.

REGLAZING WINDOWS

Replacing a broken pane of glass is a relatively straightforward task, but it can be dangerous. To begin with, always wear tough work gloves when handling the broken shards and the new glass. Also, because the glass is installed on the exterior side of the window, it's best to remove the sash and make the repair on a bench.

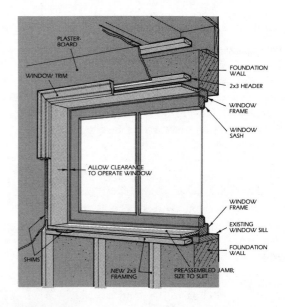

PLASTER-BOARD

WINDOW TRIM

FOUNDATION WALL

2x3 HEADER

WINDOW FRAME

WINDOW SASH

ALLOW CLEARANCE TO OPERATE WINDOW

WINDOW FRAME

EXISTING WINDOW SILL

FOUNDATION WALL

SHIMS

NEW 2x3 FRAMING

PREASSEMBLED JAMB; SIZE TO SUIT

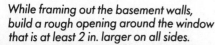

While framing out the basement walls, build a rough opening around the window that is at least 2 in. larger on all sides.

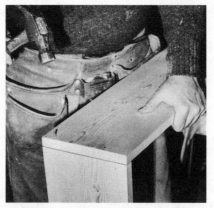

Preassemble the jamb before you nail it into the rough opening. You should use 2-in. finishing nails and simple butt joints.

Use shims to hold the jamb in position for nailing. Be sure to check the jamb for square before you drive in the nails.

The steps shown apply to wood frame windows. On older metal frames the procedure is basically the same, but spring clips instead of glazier's points are used to secure the glass. If you have a newer aluminum sash, replacement usually involves a rubber or plastic retaining gasket, not glazing compound. For all types, cut the glass ⅛ in. shorter—in both dimensions—than the opening.

Remove loose glass pieces; then use an old but sharp chisel to chip off the hardened glazing compound. Do not gouge the frame.

If the compound is too hard to chip away easily, use a hair dryer or flameless heat gun to soften it first. Be careful not to char the sash when using the heat gun.

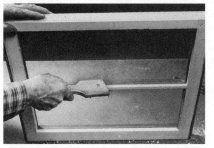

Once the bulk of the compound and all the glass have been removed, use a paint scraper to clean the muntin and frame rabbets. For best results scrape down to bare wood.

Apply a light coat of linseed oil to the bare wood so it will not absorb oil in the fresh compound. Otherwise, new compound will dry, lose flexibility and crack sooner.

Score glass in one quick stroke using a glass cutter and metal square. Butt glass and square to stop board as shown, and lubricate cut line with touch of kerosene.

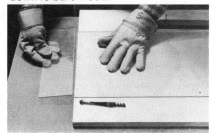

Move score line over the edge of the cutting surface and snap the glass with a quick downward motion. Wear gloves when handling the glass to prevent cuts.

Apply a ⅛-in. bead of compound across all rabbets to form a tight interior seal and to act as a cushion for the glass. Lay the glass in place; press evenly into compound.

Secure glass with glazier's points pushed into the muntin and sash frame every 4 in. The push-type points shown are much easier to use than the flat triangular points.

Roll fresh compound between your hands to form an approximate ⅜-in.-dia. "rope." Lay the rope into the corner formed by the glass and frame, then press it into place.

Draw a flexible putty knife over compound to form a neat bevel. Allow compound to dry one week before painting, then let paint overlap glass ⅛ in. for a good seal.

HOW TO BEAM A CEILING

Here's how to buy, build and install decorative beams to create a custom country ceiling.

In spite of the countless hours spent making painstaking decisions on redecorating a room, the largest visible surface, the ceiling, is often overlooked. But, install decorative beams and that ceiling is suddenly an attractive detail that enhances the room.

MATERIALS AVAILABLE

Prefabricated ceiling beams come in polyurethane foam and real wood. Both are designed for do-it-yourself installation. In addition, you can make your own by following our plans for building and installing beams.

Lightweight polyurethane foam beams have been popular with homeowners since about 1967. Although many purists shy away from synthetic products, polyurethane beams provide a means for anyone, regardless of woodworking skills, to install a ceiling to be proud to show off.

INSTALLING FOAM BEAMS

Cut foam beams using a crosscut handsaw. Then, attach the beams to the ceiling with panel adhesive dispensed from a caulking gun. First, hold the beam against the ceiling and draw a light pencil line along each edge of the beam. Next, apply an adhesive bead on the *inner* edge of both underside rails, where the beam makes contact with the ceiling. Now here's the secret for a lasting bond: Press the beam firmly against the ceiling. Then, pull it away for at least one minute, but not more than five. Finally, reposition the beam, using the pencil lines as guides, and apply pressure for two minutes.

INSTALLING WOOD BEAMS

For those who prefer real wood, Rusticated Beams Inc. of West Warwick, R.I., manufactures prefabricated pine beams. These three-sided beams come in sizes from 4 x 6 in. to 18 x 18 in.

To install these beams, first screw a ¾-in.-thick mounting strip to the ceiling. Cut the strip width equal to the inside opening of the beam. Be certain the screws are long enough to go through the ceiling material and into the joist to

Decorative ceiling beams capture the warmth and charm of authentic structural timbers. Here, a cathedral ceiling is accented with prefabricated wood beams.

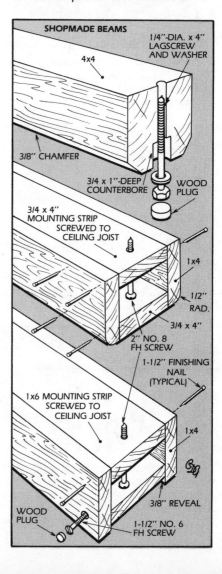

SHOPMADE BEAMS

1/4"-DIA. x 4" LAGSCREW AND WASHER

4x4

3/8" CHAMFER

3/4 x 1"-DEEP COUNTERBORE

WOOD PLUG

3/4 x 4" MOUNTING STRIP SCREWED TO CEILING JOIST

1x4

1/2" RAD.

3/4 x 4"

2" NO. 8 FH SCREW

1-1/2" FINISHING NAIL (TYPICAL)

1x6 MOUNTING STRIP SCREWED TO CEILING JOIST

1x4

WOOD PLUG

3/8" REVEAL

1-1/2" NO. 6 FH SCREW

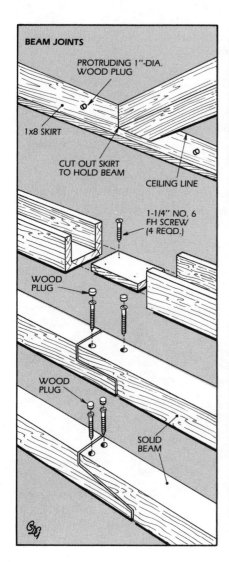

hold the beam securely. Hold the beam over the mounting strip and nail through the beam side into the strip.

MAKE YOUR OWN BEAMS

As an alternative to buying ready-made beams, use these plans to build them. The two basic beam designs are the solid and three-sided box beams.

To install a solid beam such as 4 x 4, 4 x 6 or larger timber, lagscrew it directly to the ceiling with screws long enough to catch the ceiling joist.

Install a box beam over a mounting strip fastened to the ceiling. Again, be sure to screw into the joists. Then, nail through the beam side into the strip.

At times, the desired beam location may fall between the joists, leaving nothing solid to screw into. In this situation, you must get above the ceiling, via an attic or crawlspace, and toe-nail 2 x 4 bridging between the joists. Then,

mount the beam to the bridging.

When installing any type of ceiling beam, always start and end with half-beams against opposite walls. For example, if 4 x 6 beams are used, space them between 2 x 6 beams at each end of the room. This is in keeping with authentic beam construction.

FINISHING THE BEAMS

Finishes that resemble hand-hewn and rough-sawn timbers are the most popular for shop-made beams. Use a broad ax, hatchet and spokeshave to produce a hand-hewn texture. Chop and scallop the beam to create the desired effect. Distressing is then added, if desired, to produce a weathered look by striking the beam with a heavy chain, hatchet and hammer.

To create a rough-sawn texture, first use a chain saw to roughen the beam's surface. Work the saw back and forth along the beam, scoring but not cutting into the surface. Then, use a wire wheel in a drill motor to brush out the wood's soft grain. *Caution:* Wear eye protection during these operations.

Another way to achieve a rough-sawn look is with a band saw fitted with a rough-cutting wood blade or a 3-tpi resawing blade. To roughen the surface, start the saw and move the beam slowly across the saw blade, perpendicular to the teeth. Allow the blade to roughen the beam, but not cut into it.

Next, use a rasp, drawknife, spokeshave and/or belt sander to take off the sharp edges from the beam's two bottom corners. The more hand tools used, the more authentic the look.

Finally, the beam is ready for staining. A

hand-rubbed oil finish (be sure to wear gloves to avoid splinters) is an alternative to stain.

ADD WOOD BEAMS TO A SUSPENDED CEILING

A suspended ceiling can incorporate wood beams instead of the usual metal T-bars. The 4-in.-wide beams consist of two hardwood oak rails joined by a ¼-in. oak veneer plywood panel. The beams are locked together and hung from the existing ceiling using an assortment of metal clips. The ceiling accepts standard ceiling panels and lighting fixtures.

You can install this ceiling as easily as a con-

Snap a level chalkline to indicate ceiling height. Then, nail oak side rail in place. Prebore rail to prevent chance of splitting.

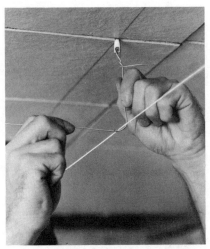

Bend hanger wire 90° at dry line that's stretched to show main beam location. Acoustical lag anchors wire to ceiling.

Attach the main beam to the side rail using a rail clip (insert). Then, screw through the clip and into the rail to secure the beam.

Check main beams for level after installation. Hanger wire passes through a hanger clip. Prebent wires aid positioning.

Install divider beams after main beams are in place. Snap on interlocking clips to secure divider beams. Wire only main beams.

Finally, maneuver the ceiling panels gently into place. Cut the panels with a crosscut handsaw to fit around room perimeter.

ventional T-bar suspended ceiling. Begin by determining the new ceiling height. Be certain to allow clearance for all obstructions. Next, mark the height in one corner of the room. Using a dry line with a line level, transfer the height to the next corner. Continue transferring until each corner is marked. Then, snap a chalkline from one mark to the next on each wall.

Install the L-shaped oak side rails that hold the main beams and divider beams at the wall. First, line up the side rail bottom edge with the chalkline. Then, nail the rail to the wall studs with 2-in. common nails. Prebore the rail to prevent splitting.

Next, insert acoustical lags (see photo) or screw into the ceiling joists every 4 ft. along the main beam positions. Then, attach lengths of 16-ga. steel wire to the lags or eyes for hanging the main beams. If the room is more than 8 ft. long, join two main beams with an extension clip. Also, place one hanger clip onto the beam for each wire and thread the wire through the eyelet in each clip to hold the beam.

Install the divider beams perpendicular to the main beams. Then, check the beams for level. Hire a licensed electrician to wire in the lights. Finally, tilt the ceiling panels through the beams and gently into position.

DECORATOR'S GUIDE TO BEAM INSTALLATION

Here are some tips from a professional New York decorator about using decorative beams correctly. By following these guidelines, you can decorate with a flair.

Create an Early American country kitchen by adding beams to hold baskets, pots and pans, or lighting fixtures. Lighting on beams can illuminate counters and bars at right angles to the wall.

Beams can lend individuality to a tract house or can be used to balance a ceiling where a structural change has replaced a bearing wall with a structural beam. For style continuity, frame the door opening into the room with the new beams.

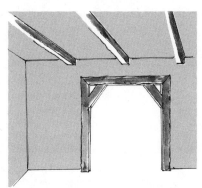

Install track lighting on beams in a room that has a cathedral ceiling. The area between the beams can be finished with plaster, paint or planks.

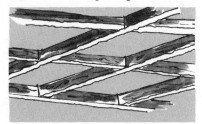

To reproduce an English Tudor look, hang beams in two directions to form squares or rectangles. Trowel on plaster to the area between the beams. Use dark beams, French antiques or reproductions and a mix of small provincial prints to transform an ordinary room into one of charm.

INSTALL YOUR OWN PHONE

It's easy to install your own extension telephone or convert to modular equipment.

Now that you can buy and install your own telephone, how do you go about it? Here are answers to some of the most asked questions about phones and their installation.

GOING MODULAR

You can modernize your home to accept the new modular plug phones. The phone company and many electronics and department stores sell conversion covers for the standard type 42A terminal block. A converter consists of a new cover with a modular outlet and four color-coded snap-on clips. These are snapped onto the terminal screws in the back, according to color, and the conversion cover is tightened down.

The type 42A terminal block is the old type of baseboard connector to connect a telephone. When you take off the cover, you will see four terminals with four different color wires attached. The placement of these colored wires is crucial because they are the key to proper phone hookup. For many years, the phone system has used color coding as a way to simplify and speed installation. When you are installing any conversion device, you must match the colors of the wires to the proper terminals.

A modular plug is little more than a snap-in plug with four conductors in the tip. It mates with a connector inside a modular jack or converter. The telephone company made the change to the modular plug as a result of an FCC ruling that mandated standardization between the many phones on the market. The result is an easier plug to use.

You may find two different kinds of terminal blocks in your home: One type is a four-pronged jack, the other is a flush-mounted terminal block. It's easy to convert a four-pronged jack by using a modular converter. For the flush-mounted terminal, you'll need a flush-

INSTALLING A MODULAR JACK

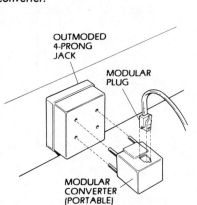

To convert a four-pronged jack to one that will be able to accept a modular plug, it's necessary to buy a modular converter. The modular plug from the telephone can then be plugged into the converter.

A terminal block is found in some older homes. It must be replaced with a modular jack. Once replacement has been made, it's relatively easy to add your own phones.

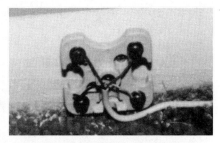

Taking the top off the terminal block reveals color-coded wires. Carefully unscrew the terminals enough to loosen wires, and then remove unit from your baseboard or wall.

OUTMODED 4-PRONG JACK

MODULAR PLUG

MODULAR CONVERTER (PORTABLE)

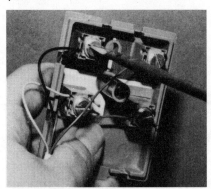

Attach the modular jack's base to the wall and then attach the wires in the same color-coded manner as before. Tighten screws and see that wires do not short against each other.

Snap-fit the connections from the jack cover to the base terminals by simply following the color code. All you have to do next is to attach the jack cover, and you're finished with the job.

mounted modular jack converter. Simply remove the old jack, leaving the wires hanging free, and then install the new bracket and snap-on clips. When this is done, insert and fasten the new modular jack and reinstall the faceplate.

Converting a wall phone outlet to modular involves removing the old phone by sliding it up and away and then removing the old base plate. When this is done, simply remove the old outlet, leaving the wires hanging. Next, install the new bracket and attach the wires to the converter plate by their color code. When this is done, tighten the converter into the bracket and attach the new base plate. Then slide the new wall phone over the clips.

The phone company supplies a modular plug converter to turn your nonmodular phone cable into a modular one. It requires that a four-wire cable be spliced according to instructions into the converter, which is then closed permanently.

EXTENDING THE WIRING

When installing new, or extending existing, telephone wiring in your house, it's best to use color-coded, four-conductor wire, similar to what the phone company uses. This way, it's easy to be sure the wiring is correct. Running this wire behind the walls ensures maximum protection and prevents an unsightly tangle. Running it under a rug, on the other hand, means there's more chance for damage as people walk on it. Further, it can leave a ridge in the rug. Baseboard mounting is acceptable, provided you run the wire out of any potential walkways and it is secured to the baseboard with *insulated* staples.

Many phone companies install a network interface in homes. This is a tiny integrated circuit that protects the phone network from any harm by user-installed equipment. Older homes may simply have a terminal block instead of a network interface. Either is the demarcation point between the phone company's equipment and

Adding a phone is easy if you use the right equipment. The portable, modular converter just plugs into one of the older-style, four-pronged jacks, and it can be moved from room to room. The permanent modular connector has four snap-on connections to attach to an existing base. Or you can install a completely new modular jack in place of your old four-pronged jack.

Once you've gone modular, it's simple to connect extra wiring for extensions. The modular wire junction will plug into a modular jack and allow you to run two additional phone lines. Wall phones can be hung on just about any surface using special baseplates. And you can even get modular jacks with built-in covers that keep the dust out of the connection points.

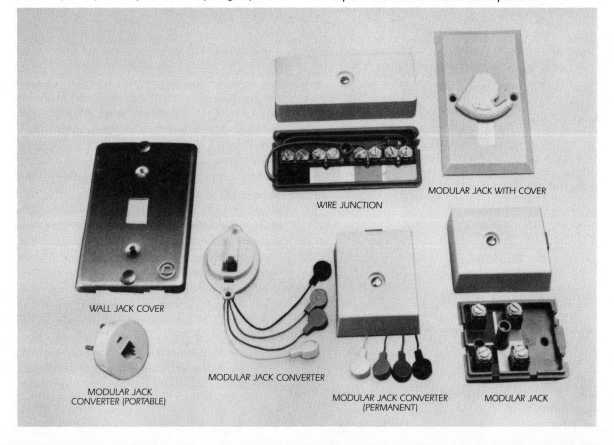

WIRE JUNCTION

MODULAR JACK WITH COVER

WALL JACK COVER

MODULAR JACK CONVERTER (PORTABLE)

MODULAR JACK CONVERTER

MODULAR JACK CONVERTER (PERMANENT)

MODULAR JACK

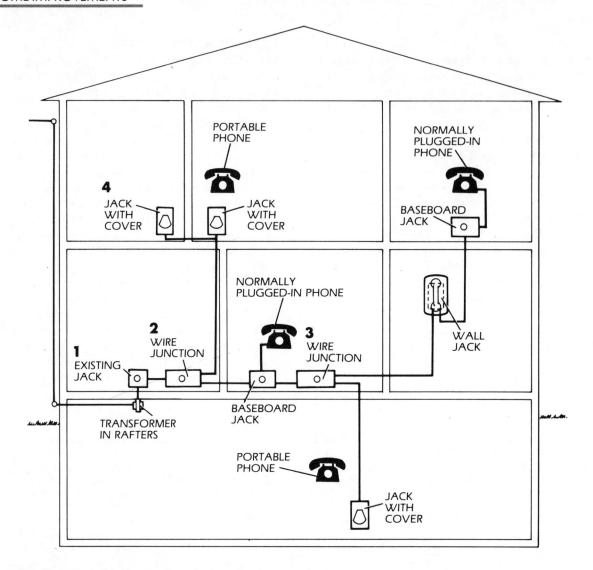

Here's how to install extra extension telephone lines in your home. The incoming telephone line goes to the phone company's transformer and then to an existing jack or network interface [1]. At this point you may have to convert the jack to a modular one. Then connect a modular wire junction [2]. One line from the junction may connect to a new jack and from there to another junction [3]. The junctions simplify the wiring. Some jacks will have phones normally plugged in. Other jacks [4] may have a phone carried between them. These jacks should be the covered type.

Color-coded wires and matching colors on wire junction make it easy to install.

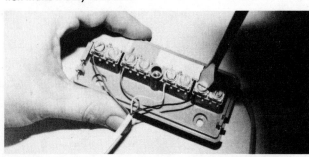

private home wiring. It's easy to install wiring beyond this point with a wire junction. Put this device near the interface, so they can be connected by the short modular plug cord attached to the wire junction.

When this is done, determine the wiring paths for your home's new wiring, and then run this wiring to the areas where you are installing new phone outlets. After the wires are run, strip the outer covering off the ends of the cables to expose the four conductors inside. Install these thin wires in the wire junction according to their color coding. After you replace the cover, your house will be all wired for phones.

According to the American Telephone & Telegraph Co., the maximum distance you can run a wire from the network interface or junction box is about 250 ft. This is the limit before line resistance and voltage loss become too great to run the phone.

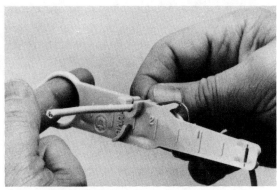

A wire stripper tool, available from the phone company, is a handy device. The tool, with a built-in measuring scale, allows you to strip a multiconductor cable without damaging the wires. Afterward, you can use it for other wiring jobs.

There are some other precautions you should take. According to the phone company, a person installing a phone should be sure the installation complies with local building regulations and the National Electrical Code. Avoid placing telephone wires in pipes, conduits or compartments containing other electrical wiring. Never place telephone wiring near bare power wires or lightning rods, antennas, transformers, steam and hot water pipes, or heating ducts.

Before you fasten any wire to metal surfaces—siding, recreational vehicles or mobile homes—be sure no hazardous voltages are present on the siding or other conducting surfaces. And, you must never run wiring between structures where it may be exposed to lightning. Further, avoid damp locations or any place where wiring would allow a person to use a telephone while in a bathtub, shower or swimming pool.

Never use telephone wire to support objects. Be sure the wire is enclosed in electrical tape to protect it when it runs across gratings or other rough metal objects.

When drilling through walls or floors be careful to avoid contact with concealed pipes, other electrical wiring or similar items. You should also avoid running wire to temporary structures or to any locations not easily accessible, or anywhere the wire will be subject to mechanical stress or pinching, such as through door jambs or window sills.

Finally, keep the wire runs as short as possible to avoid interference with your phone system, and never splice one length of wire directly to another, because it can cause interference on your line. Instead, use wire junctions or modular jacks for multiple connections.

The phone company uses a system that supplies 48 volts and between 20 and 35 milliamperes of current. This provides excellent service on one phone. As you add extra phones to the line, you are dividing this current and voltage further, and the quality of the service deteriorates. Usually, no more than six to seven phones should be in a house and plugged in at once.

BUYING YOUR OWN PHONES

According to law, you must give the phone company (your local business office) the ringer equivalency number and FCC registration code of any new phone you buy to install. The ringer equivalency number indicates the type of ringer circuit in the phone. For operation of its lines, the phone company must know the type and number of phones you're using.

Some phone company systems use pulse dialing. This is a type of service associated with rotary phones. Inside a dial-type phone (called a rotary) there is a set of electromechanical contacts that turns the number dialed into a precisely timed sequence of electrical pulses. They are sent through the phone line to the central office, where they are decoded.

Sometimes a pushbutton phone can be used on a pulse system. If you have a unit from the phone company (any Bell-brand unit) it will work correctly. And, if you have a phone that has a pulse/DTMF switch it, too, will work correctly in the pulse mode.

DTMF stands for Dual-Tone, Multi-Frequency phone service. With it, two tones are generated every time the buttons are pushed. These tones are translated into electronic equivalents and sent through the system, where they are decoded at the phone company's central office. A rotary phone will work on such a system because the system still recognizes pulse dialing. You can mix dial and Touch-Tone phones in your home if you have this service.

With the wide variety of telephones available today, the choice of which type of phone to buy is up to you, but a phone capable of DTMF is best from a long-range reliability standpoint. Advanced-capability phones contain other features such as memory dialing, "hold," automatic dialing, redialing of a busy number and display of the time, date and cost of a call. The phone company also offers phones with features such as "speed" dialing a list of phone numbers, or services such as call-waiting and call-forwarding, but these are extra-cost options on your monthly bill.

These cabinets accommodate a wide variety of entertainment equipment, including a slide projector on a center pull-out shelf.

MULTIPURPOSE WALL CABINETS

The clean, modern design of these built-in cabinets satisfies a host of storage and entertainment needs.

These cabinets were designed with both form and function in mind. They give a clean, contemporary appearance *and* plenty of room to accommodate a generous sampling of today's popular home entertainment equipment.

Included are two tape decks, a stereo receiver and speakers, a turntable on a sliding shelf, a television, and a slide projector on a pullout section of the countertop that allows for convenient image projection on an adjacent wall. All this—and there is still room left over for storing records, tapes, books and other items.

CONSTRUCTION STEPS

Begin by making the base for the lower cabinets. Cut the plywood and the supports to size, then screw the front plywood rail to the face of the front support. Next, screw the plywood base to the top of the front support as shown in the drawing. If your base is over 8 ft. long, the platform must be built from two pieces of plywood, spliced in the middle.

Cover the base top and front with plastic laminate, using contact cement. Carefully follow the directions on the container of the cement you use.

Next, attach the rear base support to the room wall by driving 3½-in. No. 10 flathead screws through the support and into the wall studs. Make sure this support is installed level.

Place the finished base over the rear support and attach it with screws driven down through the base and into the support. Position these screws so they'll be covered by the cabinets later.

BUILDING IN A SHADOW LINE

Cut all base cabinet sides, bottoms, tops and backs to size. Be sure to cut the ½ x 1-in.-deep notch at the bottom front corner of all the sides. This "recess," and the ½-in.-wide space between the three middle cabinets and the countertop, are design features. They give a shadow line between all the units that makes the cabinets appear to float.

Apply laminate to the inside surfaces of all the cabinet parts and to the front edges exposed to view. Assemble with countersunk 1¼-in. No. 10 flathead screws driven through the sides into the edges of the tops and bottoms. Be sure each cabinet is square before installing the back. Determine the number and position of the shelves you want. Then, cut the shelves to size and apply laminate to the top and front edge of each. Install with countersunk screws through the sides and into the shelf edges.

Once the shelves are installed, cover the outside cabinet surfaces with laminate as indicated on the drawing.

The cabinets bordering the open speaker areas should have laminate over the entire exposed side. On the cabinets joined directly to each other, all that's required is a 2-in. strip on the sides to cover the plywood that's visible in front of the recessed spacer cleats. A 2-in.-wide strip is also applied to the cabinet tops, except on the center cabinet. It should be covered entirely with laminate so when the slide projector shelf is pulled out, the plywood will not be seen.

Build the drawer cabinets and drawers as shown, then install the drawers, using full extension slides. These cabinets were designed so the drawer side edges would be set in ⅜ in. from the perimeter of the cabinet *and* with a ⅜-in. space between each drawer front. It's not necessary to cover the inside surfaces of the drawer cabinets with laminate.

Determine the best position for your cabinets along the platform base—or use the positions indicated—and install the cleats (parts D and E

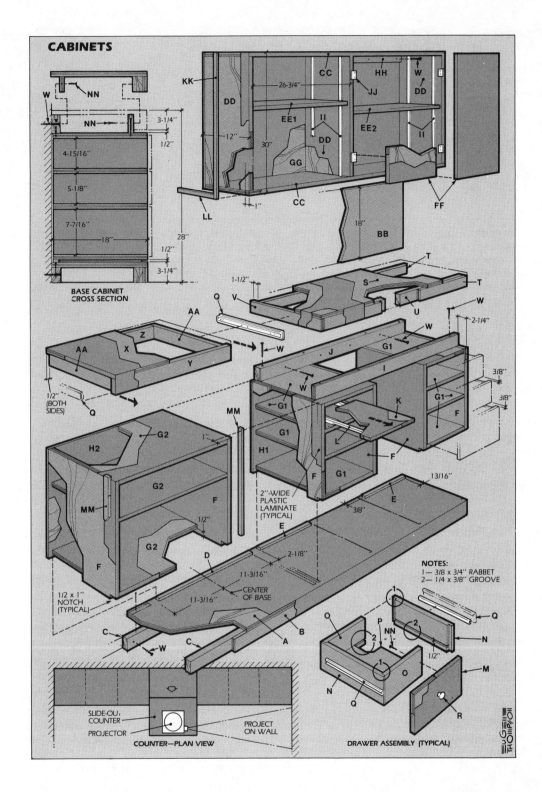

on the drawing). These cleats keep the individual cabinets from shifting side to side without the need for actually joining them to the base.

Cut a panel from ¼-in.-thick plywood to back up the open speaker areas, and cover it with laminate. Make it slightly wider than the opening so that when the cabinets are attached to the wall it will be held in place. If you want to avoid

the expense of making these panels, simply paint the rear wall with a color to match the laminate.

Place the lower cabinets on the base, starting with the end cabinets. Then position the middle cabinet. Cut the spacers (part M) to size, cover their front edges with laminate and screw to the side of the middle cabinet as shown. Place the

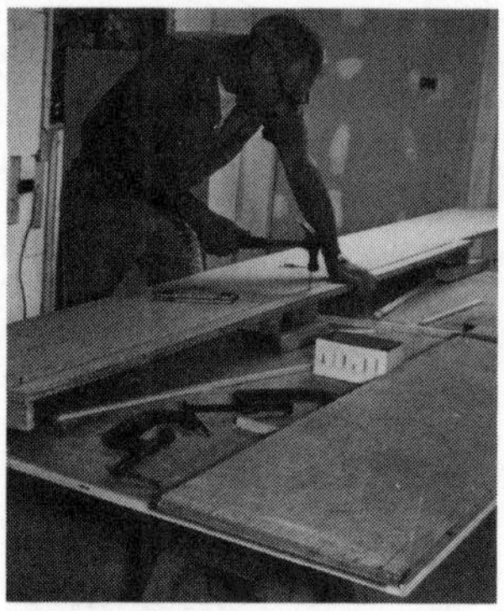

Because cabinet base is longer than one plywood sheet, it must be assembled from two pieces. Join halves together with a splice block installed below the plywood.

Assemble cabinet "box," then cut shelf and cover with laminate. Position shelf with scrap blocks clamped as shown; attach with screws driven through sides into shelf edge.

Assemble countertop parts and position on cabinets to check for fit and operation of sliding shelf. Do not attach. When you're satisfied, remove and cover with laminate.

Assemble drawer parts and install with drawer slides. Cover drawer front with laminate, then attach with screws driven through inside face of false drawer front.

last two cabinets on the base.

Install the countertop cleats (parts J and I) across the cabinet tops. Then attach the rear cleat to the wall, making sure to hit at least two studs per cleat. Build and laminate the stationary countertops as shown. Be sure to cover the ends of these tops with laminate, too, so that when the slide projector section is pulled out, all the edges will be finished. Install the counters by screwing the rear rail (part T) to the rear cleat (part J). Do this in the open speaker area where both boards are accessible from underneath.

Take the measurement between these two tops to determine the actual size needed for the slide-out top. You should plan on having two 1/16-in.-wide gaps between the three tops *after* the laminate is installed. Build the sliding top and install it with full extension slides hung on the sliding top and the ends of both fixed tops.

ADDING THE UPPER CABINETS

When the upper cabinets are complete, install one, using the hanging cleat (part HH). Be sure to hit at least two studs in the length of the cleat. Position the other cabinet on the countertop or brace it in position and at the proper height, and measure the distance between the cabinets.

Cut the spacer cleats (parts KK and LL) to match this dimension, cover the front edge with laminate, then remove the second cabinet and attach the strips to the installed cabinet. This method will give you a tight, professional fit.

Install the second upper cabinet and hang all the cabinet doors. Instead of using door pulls, rout out a ⅜-in.-deep by 3-in.-long section of the bottom back door edge to use as a finger grip.

To finish the job, just paint the wall behind the cabinets and countertop, or install panels of burlap-cover fiberboard as illustrated.

Upper cabinets were designed to fit flush to side walls and ceiling. Install one unit, then position the other on the countertop to find width of spacer cleats KK and LL.

MATERIALS LIST

MULTIPURPOSE WALL CABINETS

Key	No.	Size and description (use)
A	1	¾ x 18 x 121″ plywood (base)
B	1	¾ x 2½ x 121″ fir (rail)
C	2	1½ x 2½ x 121″ fir (supports)
D	1	½ x ¾ x 22⅜″ fir (cleat)
E	4	½ x ¾ x 14⅜″ fir (cleats)
F	10	¾ x 17¾ x 21″ plywood (cabinet sides)
G1	15	¾ x 14½ x 17¾″ plywood (small cabinet top, bottom, shelf)
G2	3	¾ x 17¾ x 22½″ plywood (large cabinet top, bottom, shelf)
H1	4	¼ x 16 x 21″ plywood (small cabinet back)
H2	1	¼ x 21 x 24″ plywood (large cabinet back)
I	2	¾ x 3 x 47¼″ fir (cleats)
J	2	¾ x 3 x 47¼″ fir (cleats)
K	1	½ x 14¼ x 16″ plywood (turntable base)
L	1 pr.	14½″ Grant Model A Record Player Slide
M1	4	¾ x 5⅜ x 15⅛″ plywood (small drawer front)
M2	2	¾ x 7⅞ x 15⅛″ plywood (large drawer front)
N1	8	¾ x 4½ x 17½″ plywood (small drawer sides)
N2	4	¾ x 7 x 17½″ plywood (large drawer sides)
O1	8	¾ x 4½ x 12¾″ plywood (small drawer false front, back)
O2	4	¾ x 7 x 12¾″ plywood (large drawer false front, back)
P	6	¼ x 12¾ x 16¾″ plywood (bottom)
Q	7 pr.	16″ Grant No. 328 drawer slide
R	6	Stanley No. 4482 drawer pull
S	2	¾ x 18 x 48½″ plywood (countertop)
T	4	¾ x 2½ x 47¾″ plywood (front, rear rails)
U	2	1½ x 2½ x 47¾″ fir (cleats)
V	2	¾ x 2½ x 18″ plywood (end rails)
W	*	3½″ No. 10 flathead screws
X	1	¾ x 18 x 23⅝″ plywood (countertop)
Y	1	¾ x 2½ x 23⅝″ fir (front rail)
Z	1	¾ x 2½ x 21¼″ fir (back rail)
AA	2	¾ x 2½ x 17¼″ fir (side rails)
BB	1	18 x 121″ burlap-covered fiberboard
CC	4	¾ x 11¾ x 60¼″ plywood (cabinet top, bottom)
DD	6	¾ x 11¾ x 28½″ plywood (cabinet end, divider)
EE1	3	¾ x 11½ x 26¼″ plywood (open cabinet shelf)
EE2	2	¾ x 11½ x 30¾″ plywood (closed cabinet shelf)
FF	4	¾ x 15¾ x 29¼″ plywood (doors)
GG	2	¼ x 30 x 60¼″ plywood (back)
HH	2	¾ x 1½ x 31¼ fir (cleats)
II	16	28½″ shelf standards, with 32 support clips
JJ	4 pr.	Hinge-A-Matic No. 591-26 self-closing overlay door hinges
KK	1	½ x ¾ x 30″ fir (spacer)
LL	1	½ x ¾ x 10¼″ fir (spacer)
MM	2	½ x ¾ x 21½″ fir (spacer)
NN	*	1¼″ No. 10 flathead screws

(*) As required.

TIPS FOR HOME IMPROVEMENT

Some of the more common problems a homeowner encounters have to do with moisture, mold, mildew, condensation and a lack of a vapor barrier.

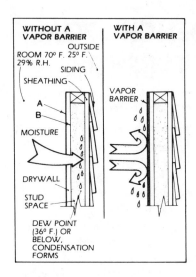

For good airflow from the attic, a combination of vents, such as the soffit and ridge vents shown, is recommended.

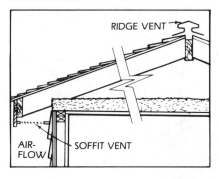

MOISTURE, MOLD AND MILDEW

The drawings and dew point chart help explain when and why condensation occurs and moisture problems develop. Dewpoint is the temperature at which dew starts to form or vapor to condense into liquid.

DEW POINT CHART
(Outside Temperature at 25° F)

Room Temperature	Room Relative Humidity (%)	Dew Point Temperature (°F)
70° F	79	63
	68	59
	57	54
	48	49
	38	43
	29	**36**
	19	26
	9	11
75° F	79	68
	68	64
	57	60
	48	55
	38	47
	29	**40**
	19	30
	9	15

In winter, temperatures outside the home are below the dewpoint of the air inside. Unless there is a vapor barrier (at points A and B in the drawing), the moisture will migrate through the drywall or plaster, across the insulation and through the siding. For example, if the temperature outside is 25°F, and the inside air temperature is 70°F, at 29% humidity, a surface within the wall will be at or below the dewpoint (36°F). Moisture will condense—usually on the sheathing—causing it and the siding to become saturated. Moisture cannot pass through a vapor barrier.

ATTIC AIRFLOW AND MILDEW

Filling in roof deck spaces can alter the ventilation pattern of a house. The attic no longer breathes as easily as it did before the deck spaces were filled. This causes a moisture buildup, which results in mildew.

Gable vents are helpful, but only if they are adequately sized. The effective opening for louvers is not the same as the actual opening cut out for those louvers.

The gross area of the actual opening can be reduced by as much as 65 percent because of the resistance introduced by the louvers. If you have a gable vent with outside dimensions of 2 x 2 ft., depending on the type of louvers and insect screen used, you may only have an equivalent opening of about 1 x 1 ft.

At attic should have effective openings, equivalent to 1/300 of the attic floor area. A single vent opening in an attic, even though it satisfied the total area requirement, is not considered adequate. The best method for ventilating an attic is to use a combination of vents, such as soffit (fascia) and gable vents, or soffit vents and a ridge vent.

WORKBENCH FROM PM'S SUPERSHOP

Creating a dream shop centers on the workbench, with a handy auxiliary worktable.

The solid maple workbench measures 32 in. wide x 80 in. long to provide almost 18 sq. ft. of work surface. The 20-in.-wide shoulder vise and full-width tail end vise each have an 8½-in. jaw capacity. A series of bench dog slots and flush-mounted bench stops work in conjunction with the vises for clamping large workpieces. Other features include a large utility drawer, an auxiliary worktable, a C-clamp storage rack and four rubber casters—two of which lock—for moving the workbench easily to suit your shop space.

Begin by edge-gluing five 1⅜-in. maple boards together to form the workbench top. First, cut the boards about 2 in. longer than needed to permit final trimming with a portable

circular saw. Then join the board edges to form tight-fitting joints. Use a doweling jig to bore holes in the edges of each board to accept ⅜-in.-dia. dowel pins. Glue and clamp the boards into a large slab using long bar or pipe clamps.

Next, cut the 2¾-in.-thick x 5½-in.-wide maple pieces that frame the workbench top. Screw the frame together temporarily using two lagscrews in each corner. Then make each leg, as shown, from four pieces of maple assembled in two L-shaped, offset parts. The offset at the top forms a strong shoulder, which supports the heavy workbench top. The leg bottoms are offset to accept the workbench shelf. Clamp one leg into each corner of the workbench frame. Bore four pilot screw holes through the legs and into the frame. Remove the legs, plane and sand each smooth and rout the edges with a ½-in. rounding-over bit.

Disassemble the frame to permit cutting the bench dog slots and to bore holes for installing the vise hardware. First, cut the bench dog slots in the frame front and back on a radial-arm saw. The slots angle 2° toward the tail end vise to compensate for the small amount of play built into the dogs. Also, the bench dog slots opposite

The auxiliary worktable stows under the bench and slides on tracks routed in workbench shelf. Shoulder vise (right) houses a mortised bench stop for clamping large workpieces.

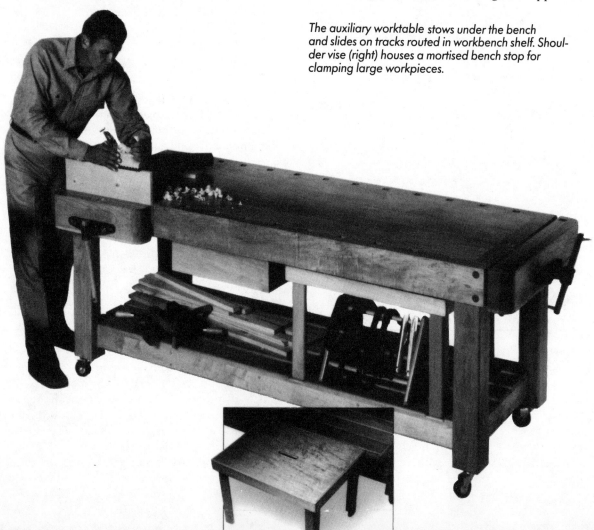

Form the workbench top by edge-gluing five maple boards together. Reinforce the joints with 3/8-in.-dia. hardwood dowel pins.

Clamp the workbench frame together temporarily to counterbore 1-in.-dia. dowel plugs and to bore the lagscrew pilot holes.

Make each workbench leg from two L-shaped assemblies. Be sure the offsets at the leg tops are identical for each leg.

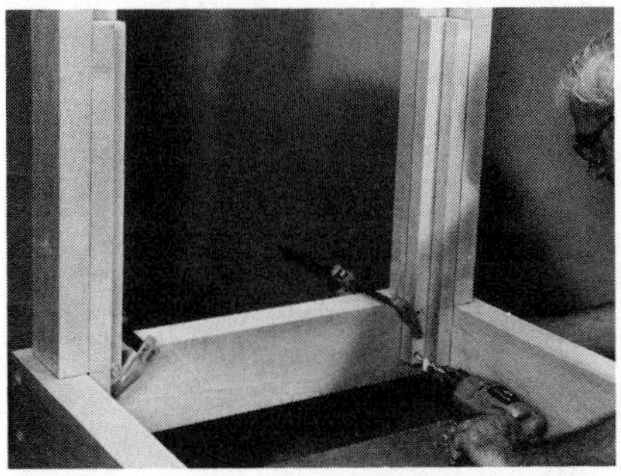

Clamp the legs to the workbench frame and bore lagscrew pilot holes. Stagger screw locations so screwheads clear each other.

Cut bench dog slots in bench frame front and back with radial arm set at 2° angle. Use kerf cut in tail saw fence to align each cut.

Establish the vise rod collar mortises using a hole saw. Then bore a rod clearance hole. Clear the mortise using a router freehand.

the shoulder vise are spaced differently from the others in order to clear the vise guide rods. Cut the 1 1/16-in.-deep x 1⅛-in.-wide slots using a ¼-in.-wide dado blade. Make the shoulder in each slot by gluing a ⅛-in.-thick wood slat in place to prevent the dog from falling through the slot.

Bore holes in the front and end frame pieces for installing the vises. Both vises use the same piece of hardware: a Model B shoulder vise available from Garrett Wade. The vise guide rods ride on collars that must be recessed below the wood surface. There are two methods for cutting the recesses using a router and a straight

MATERIALS LIST

SUPERSHOP WORKBENCH

Key	No.	Size and description (use)
A1	4	1¾ x 4¼ x 24⅜" maple (leg parts)
A2	4	1¾ x 2½ x 24⅜" maple (leg parts)
A3	4	1¼ x 2½ x 22⅞" maple (leg parts)
A4	4	1¼ x 1¼ x 22⅞" maple (leg parts)
A5	4	1⅝ x 2½ x 2½" maple (support blocks)
B	2	2¾ x 5½ x 80" maple (frame front and back)
C	2	2¾ x 5½ x 26¾" maple (frame ends)
D	5	1⅜ x 5⅜* x 74⅝" maple (bench top pieces)
E	2	13/16 x 4⅛ x 69½" maple (crossbrace supports)
F	3	13/16 x 3 x 26¾" maple (crossbraces)
G	2	¾ x 3 x 25" maple plywood (spacers)
H	2	¾ x 10¼ x 25" maple plywood (drawer supports)
I	2	1¾ x 1¾ x 21" maple (end supports)
J	1	1¾ x 6 x 11" hardwood (shoulder vise support block)
K	1	1¾ x 5¼ x 7¾" hardwood (tail vise support block)
L	1	13/16 x 6 x 20" maple (drawer face)
M	2	¾ x 5¼ x 24" maple plywood (drawer sides)
N	2	¾ x 5¼ x 16⅝" maple plywood (drawer front and back)
O	1	¼ x 16¼ x 22⅜" maple plywood (drawer bottom)
P	2	1 1/16 x 3¼ x 74¾" maple (shelf frame)
Q	2	1 1/16 x 3¼ x 24⅝" maple (shelf frame)
Q1	3	13/16 x 3¼ x 24⅝" maple (stretchers)
R	5	13/16 x 4 15/16 x 74¾" maple (slats)
S	2	¼ x 2¾ x 26" maple plywood (tracks)
T	4	¼ x ⅜ x 26¾" maple (track sides)
U	4	¼ x ⅜ x 2¾" maple (trim)
V	1	3½ x 6 x 32" maple (tail vise) laminate two pieces of 1¾"-thick stock
W	1	3½ x 6 x 20" maple (shoulder vise) laminate two pieces of 1¾"-thick stock
X	24	⅜"-dia. x 2" hardwood dowel pins
Y		Maple veneer tape
Z	2	1"-dia. x 12" hardwood dowel (vise handles)
AA	4	½"-dia. x 1½" hardwood dowel (handle pins)
BB	2	3"-dia. caster with locking brake
CC	2	3"-dia. caster
DD	1 pr.	Grant No. 528 20" full-extension drawer slide
EE	4	Mortised bench stop
FF	4	Bench dog
GG	2	Shoulder vise hardware
HH	26	3/16 x 1 x 4 7/16" maple (dog shoulder slats)
HH1	2	3/16 x 1 x 2 7/16" maple (wedges)
II	8	⅜"-dia. x 5" lagscrew and washer
JJ	8	⅜"-dia. x 2½" lagscrew and washer
KK	16	5/16"-dia. x 1½" lagscrew
LL1	8	2½" No. 16 flathead screw
LL2		2" No. 12 flathead screw
LL3		2" No. 10 flathead screw
LL4		1½" No. 10 flathead screw
LL5	8	1¼" No. 10 flathead screw
MM	8	½"-dia. hardwood plug
NN		½"-dia. hardwood plug
OO	1	¾ x 21¼ x 27¼" maple plywood (worktable top)
PP	4	¾ x 2½ x 17¼" maple (leg parts)
QQ	4	¾ x 1¾ x 17¼" maple (leg parts)
RR	4	1 x 1 x 17¼" maple (corner blocks)
SS	2	¾ x 2½ x 28" maple (table skirt)
TT	2	¾ x 2½ x 21¼" maple (table skirt)
UU	2	¾ x 1⅝ x 21¼" maple (stretchers)
VV	2	¾ x 12 x 14" maple (clamp rack ends)
WW	3	¾"-dia. x 15¼" hardwood dowel

Misc.: Carpenter's glue, Deftoil Danish oil finish.
(*) Approximate width; trim to fit.

WHERE TO GET HARDWARE

The vise hardware, bench dogs and mortised bench stops are available from Garrett Wade, 161 Avenue of the Americas, New York, N.Y. 10013. The workbench casters are available from Armor Products, Box 290, Deer Park, N.Y. 11729. Write for latest prices and availability.

WORKBENCH

BENCH STOP MORTISE

3/8"
1/4"
1/2"
5/8"
3/4"
10"
1-1/2"
1-1/2"
11-5/8"
EE
3/4"-DIA. HOLE
7/8"
7/16"
8-1/4"

VISE DETAIL

4-1/8"
2-5/8"
4-1/8"
4-5/8"
7/8"-DIA. HOLE
1-3/8"-DIA. HOLE
1/2"
9/16"-DEEP x 2-1/2"-DIA. RECESS IN BENCH

VISE DOG SLOTS SLANT 2° TOWARD BENCH

ADD 2° WEDGE
HH1
℄
HH
V

TAIL VISE DETAIL

BENCH DOG SLOTS SLANT 2° TOWARD TAIL VISE
1-1/16"
1-1/8"
12-1/2"

2-3/8"
6-3/4"
6-5/8"
5-1/4"
6"
6"
6"
6"
6"
6"
6"
6"
5-5/8"
TAIL VISE—V

SHOULDER VISE—W

EE

BENCH TOP DETAILS—TOP VIEW

NN
LL3
D
FF
X
1"
1"
J, LL1
JJ
B
LL3
12"
12"
8"
1-1/8"
AA
C
I
G
HH
GG
Z
W
E
F
G
℄
LL3
LL4
H
F
K, LL1
C
Y
E
B
V
M
O
N
1
3
NN
L
N
2
LL4
24-1/2"
II
BB
DD
M
R
℄
Q1
17-1/2"
MM
T
S
U
P
CC
KK
4-1/4"
Q
P
LEG
P
LL2
Q

NOTES:
1. 1/4 x 1/4"-WIDE GROOVE
2. 3/8 x 3/4"-WIDE RABBET
3. 3/8 x 3/4"-WIDE DADO
4. 3/8 x 3-1/4"-WIDE DADO

Q1
P
④
SEE LEG ASSEMBLY
BB

A2
A3
A4
A1

LEG TOP VIEW

1/2"
5/8"
3"
4-1/8"
3/8"-DIA. HOLES
18-3/4"
A3
A4
A2
A1
4"
A5

LEG ASSEMBLY

3/8 x 3/4"-WIDE RABBET
3/8 x 3/4"-WIDE DADO
SS
TT
UU
SS
OO
TT
RR
LL5
1 x 5" HANDGRIP CUTOUT (CENTERED)
PP
QQ

AUXILIARY WORKTABLE

3/8"-DEEP x 3/4"-DIA. HOLE
1"
12"
60°
2-5/8"
VV
WW
1" RAD.
2"

C-CLAMP STORAGE RACK

The vise rod collar mortises can also be formed by using a template and a router with a straight bit and guide bushing.

Cut notches in the cross-brace support on the table saw. Screw a fence to the miter gauge to stabilize the workpiece.

The assembled workbench frame, with cross braces installed, is now ready to accept the legs and the glued-up workbench top.

Rout tracks for the auxiliary worktable in the bench shelf using a ¾-in.-dia. straight bit. A simple jig keeps router on course.

With vise rods in position, attach the vise base to the large wood support block which is glued and screwed to bench underside.

Rout the multilevel recesses for installing the mortised bench stops using a template. Insert various-width strips to control cuts.

bit. The first method requires using a hole saw to establish the diameter and depth of the recess. Then, use the router freehand to clear out the mortise. For the second technique, make a plywood template of the mortise and use it with a router fitted with a guide bushing to cut the recess.

Make the three crossbraces and two long brace support pieces that support the edge-glued top. Notch the support pieces on a table saw to accept the crossbraces. Then cut the two short braces that support the workbench top at each end. Reassemble the frame using glue and lagscrews. Attach the legs and screw the four perimeter support pieces to the inside of the frame. Finally, glue and screw the crossbraces into the notches cut in the support pieces.

Trim the workbench top to size using a circular saw and a straightedge guide clamped in place. Then plane and sand the top surface smooth. Drop the workbench top into the frame and counterbore all screw-hole locations to accept ½-in.-dia. dowel plugs. Continue boring

pilot holes through the top into the support pieces and crossbraces. Remove the top, apply glue to all contact surfaces and screw the top in place.

Construct the workbench shelf as a separate unit. Before installing the shelf, build the auxiliary worktable and rout tracks into the shelf for housing the table. Then line each track with ¼-in. maple plywood edged with a ¼ x ⅜-in. maple lip on each side for sliding the table in and out. Place the workbench upside down and screw the shelf to the legs. Add four corner blocks under the shelf for extra support.

Glue and screw wood support blocks to the workbench underside for the vise bases. Make the two vise jaws by gluing together two pieces of 1¾-in.-thick maple stock. Cut the bench dog slots on the tail end vise before laminating the maple. Build the utility drawer and make the C-clamp rack.

Finish-sand all surfaces and apply two coats of Deftoil Danish finish.

CAR CARE GUIDE

WAX, POLISH AND PAINT
See color illustration on page 86.

The shelves of auto parts stores are stocked with row upon row of waxes, polishes and similar products. They fall into four main categories: straight waxes, straight cleaners (sometimes called polishes), combination cleaner/waxes and compounds.

There are two ways to restore luster to a car's finish. One is to rub out weathered paint with a cleaner or compound which brings back gloss if it's there, and then apply a coat of wax to protect that gloss. This is referred to as a two-step process. The other way is to use a single product that combines a cleaner and wax—the one-step process.

A two-step process may provide more uniform results over the long run, but it's a lot more work. Many companies sell separate waxes and polishes only because there is still a demand for them from people who prefer to do it the old-fashioned way. Most experts agree that a one-step product is as good as a two-step.

CHECK PAINT CONDITIONS
Many people who buy new cars keep them looking good by waxing every few months with a one-step product. The silica or clay cleaning agents, although classified as "mild abrasives," do a good job of removing slightly oxidized paint called "chalk." Also contained in these products are hydrocarbon solvents (naptha or kerosene) and detergents that will dissolve stains.

But what about the older car? Can you use the easy one-step process or should you use an abrasive compound? The answer to this question lies with the condition of the paint. If it's

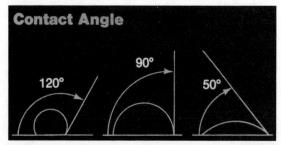

Contact Angle

120°   90°   50°

Shape of water beads determines when to wax car. When tangent line of beads slumps to 50°, it's time to rewax.

Here's how to sort through the confusing array of auto body care products on the market, and know what to use when.

merely dull and discolored, try a liquid cleaner. If you find yourself rubbing like crazy to make the cleaner work, move up to a paste-type compound.

ABOUT COMPOUNDS
Suppose the finish looks as if it's a goner—badly weathered, stained, scratched and covered with a road film. You may think a paint job is in order, but before spending hundreds of dollars, try compounding. It just may bring back the luster.

There are two types of compounds—moderate-duty (polishing compound) and heavy-duty (rubbing compound). Polishing compound, which is often white in color, removes moderately weathered paint, moderate film and light stains. Rubbing compound, usually red in color, is needed to remove badly weathered paint, heavy film and bad stains. Try a polishing compound first. If it doesn't do the job, use rubbing compound.

Put the car in a shaded area and follow the instructions printed on the compound can. Do not use a heavy hand and never use an electric buffer with rubbing compound. It is extremely abrasive and can rub off paint right down to the primer, at which a new paint job is unavoidable. Use light pressure and a back-and-forth motion. A circular motion leaves swirl marks on the car finish.

It will help to avoid overrubbing spots if you wash the car first and then get rid of stubborn stains like bug splatters, bird droppings, tree sap, tar and the like.

NEXT, WAX IT
After compounding the car, step back and take a critical look. If you like what you see, you've avoided the need for new paint. Then, apply wax.

Keep the vehicle out of direct sunlight, and start in the middle of a panel and work out toward the ends. Apply a little wax and use a circular, light-handed motion to spread it.

Don't assume two coats of wax are better than one. As you apply a second layer, you'll

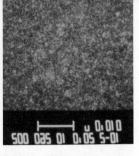

Electron microscope photos show a new metallic paint job and some paint after accelerated weathering equivalent to 2-3 years in Florida. Magnification is 2000x. Wax can slow damage.

remove wax that was previously applied. Spreading on a second coat is work for nothing.

BORDERLINE FINISHES

Suppose the paint on your car doesn't look all that bad. Is it advisable to use the one-step process to clean and wax at the same time? Experiment. Use a one-step product on the worst-looking area. If the results aren't good, turn to the two-step process.

TYPES OF ONE-STEP PRODUCTS

There are three general categories of one-step products: paste, liquid and spray. Results produced by paste and liquid one-step waxes are equally long-lasting, while some spray products may not be as long-lasting, since some of the active product has been given up to get more room for the fluid to permit sprayer application.

TIPS ABOUT WAXING

If you've ever waxed a car, you know the sides are the most difficult areas to do. You may want to tackle fenders and doors first, when you're fresh and have a full head of steam, before waxing the hood, trunk and roof.

Another trick is to know when your car needs waxing. What you do is to check how water beads on the surface. On a freshly waxed surface, beads will be almost round. As your wax protection wears down, beads will flatten out. When a line from the surface tangent to a bead gets to be 50°, it's time to wax the car again.

Besides restoring paint, here are other things you can do to make your car look sharp: Clean the engine with an engine cleaner/degreaser. Use a special cleaner to clean the wheels without marring the paint finish. A soft toothbrush is a good tool for getting into tight spots. Use chrome cleaner on bright work and a silicone-rich preservative to clean nonmetal moldings and bumper strips. Give tires a new look with tire black.

Auto body corrosion generally begins on the underside of the car where wax is never applied. Periodically hose down the underside of the car to get rid of dirt and road salt.

UNDERSTANDING PAINT

If compounding fails to bring paint luster to an acceptable level, it's time to consider repainting. On the surface, the task looks simple enough. Just turn it over to a body shop and have it "spritzed." In reality, it is not that simple.

You'll find the job can cost $100, $600, $700, $900 or more. The price depends on the type of paint "system" used. In the economic rank order, from lowest to highest, here are the systems you'll encounter:

Baked enamel. Enamel refers to the type of binder used in the paint. Baked enamel will begin to fade after one to three years if it isn't properly cared for. It has a tendency to fade rapidly because of the sun's ultraviolet rays. The cost to paint a full-size car is about $100 at cut-rate shops.

Acrylic enamel. This is the system most widely used by paint shops. The term *acrylic* refers to the type of polymer (plastic) used in the binder to hold pigment particles together. An acrylic enamel paint job on a full-size car costs about $600. Life expectancy of acrylic colors is approximately five years, with good care. Acrylic enamel has good resistance to ultraviolet rays and fades at a minimal rate.

Acrylic lacquer. This system uses lacquer as the binder. It has been widely used by General Motors for painting new cars. It requires intense heat that is difficult for body shops to duplicate. Those body shops that can provide an acrylic lacquer paint job generally charge about $100 more than for acrylic enamel.

One advantage of acrylic lacquer is that it gives a higher gloss. Its color will last about as long as acrylic enamel and has good resistance to ultraviolet rays, but it requires more frequent waxing to maintain its gloss.

Base coat/clear coat. At about $900 and up for a full-size car, this is the most expensive paint job you can buy. The paint is oversprayed with a super-tough urethane that protects the finish indefinitely. The urethane clear coat slows ultraviolet paint fading. If something scratches the car's surface, the urethane coat gets scratched—not the paint. Minor scratches are easily polished out. Once the clear coat is penetrated or degrades, however, the color coat fades rapidly, without the gradual dulling of traditional finishes. It is virtually impossible for the do-it-yourselfer to touch up chips and scratches on clear coat paints.

Clear coats were first introduced on imports, but they are showing up on more and more new domestic cars, too.

GETTING RID OF RUST AND DENTS

Car body repair can be dangerous. Wear a face mask when you're doing grinding, sanding or spraying paint. Also wear safety goggles when there's danger of flying debris.

1 Clean dented area. Working from behind, use a 2 x 4 and a sledge to bang out metal. Be careful—if you hammer a dent into a bump, rehammering may crack metal.

2 To remove wrinkles, use a hammer and dolly. Hold dolly behind and against metal and tap edge of dent. Dollies— flat, heel-and-toe, all purpose—fit different areas.

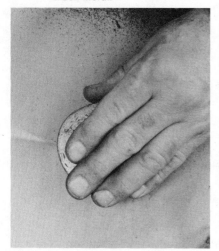

3 Tap out wrinkles by striking metal supported from behind with the dolly. Avoid hard banging. Touch spot to judge when metal is smooth enough for filler and sanding.

4 Use a slapper when wrinkles are spread over extended area. Hold a dolly in place and strike metal hard. Metal won't stretch because blow is spread over a wide area.

5 If you can't get dolly behind damaged area, drill ⅛-in. holes into dent 1 in. apart. Screw slide hammer into holes and slap slide toward you to pull out dents. Work in from edge.

REPAIRS YOU CAN MAKE YOURSELF

You should use a screwdriver, pliers or gentle taps of a hammer. By the time you finish preparation (step 2), the hole may be twice its original size.

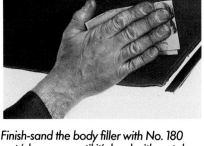

Use a squeegee to spread plastic or aluminum (shown here) body filler around the cavity. Press a piece of fiberglass cloth into the filler and let it dry in place.

Finish-sand the body filler with No. 180 wet/dry paper until it's level with metal. Spray on primer, let it dry, then sand lightly, as shown, with No. 400 waterproof sandpaper.

This type of damage can be repaired by a do-it-yourselfer, since the rust doesn't extend to the edge of the panel. Start by loosening and pulling away the decora-

Set your electric drill with a No. 36-grit sanding disk and grind off the finish surrounding rust. Don't overheat the metal— pull back disk for a second or two every so often.

Coat the area with plastic or aluminum body filler and let it dry. Then use the drill and No. 36-grit sanding disk to grind the filler smooth and to remove excess cloth.

Spot-paint the repair. We used the Preval Sprayer. Fill the 6-ounce jar with paint and screw on the aerosol bomb, then use a smooth and even motion. Mask surrounding parts.

tive chrome molding trim. Enlarge the hole by prying off rusty sections that are ready to fall off.

Use tin snips to cut away remaining rust-thinned metal. Then clean all debris from the cavity with a brush and by tapping around the hole with a hammer. Don't dent the metal.

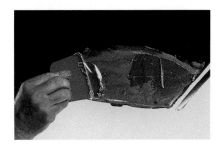

Apply more body filler, building it up in thin layers until it's about 1/4 in. above the surrounding surface. Let it dry for 20 minutes, then rough-sand with No. 100 waterproof sandpaper.

Protect the inside of the panel to keep rust from undermining the repair. The next best thing to welding on metal is to use undercoating—lots of it, built up in layers.

WHEN YOU NEED A PRO

This degree of rust damage is difficult for most do-it-yourselfers to handle. The rust has eaten away the fender metal right to the end of the panel, leaving no biting surface for body filler and fiberglass cloth.

The kind of do-it-yourself patch shown above would be unsupported along one edge, which would allow it to vibrate and crumble. New sheet metal must be welded in place for a proper repair.

Cross Section of Clear Coat/Color Coat Finish

Clear Coat
Top Coat
Primer

Substrate

Cross Section of Typical Finish

Top Coat
Primer

Substrate

Illustrations show cross-sections of conventional paint (FIG. 41-02) and new clear-coat paints. The substrate is the car body.

Paint Film Typical Metallic

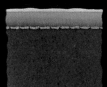

• Vehicle or Binder
• Pigment
• Metallic Flakes

Weathered Finish

Polishing and Wax Film Effects of Car Wax

Typical metallic paint consists of metal flakes between a tinted top coat and pigmented base. This paint is chalking.

As weathering continues, chalking gets worse and paint film begins to get uneven and crack.

Polishing with a mild abrasive removes some chalk and smoothes surface. A cleaner/wax removes stains and fills cracks.

WHAT IS WOOD?

Knowing how wood behaves could make your next project look better, build easier and last longer. See page 108 for the inside story.

1. Yellow birch
2. Cottonwood
3. Red oak
4. Spanish cedar
5. Ebony
6. Eastern hemlock
7. Elm

8. Teak
9. Sugar maple
10. Western red cedar
11. Concalo alves
12. Douglas fir
13. Staghorn sumac

14. Redwood
15. Black locust
16. Catalpa
17. Purpleheart
18. Ramin
19. White oak

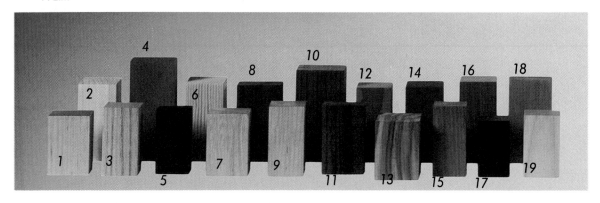

GARDEN BENCHES YOU CAN BUILD
Relax on an easy-to-build country bench. See page 95.

All of the blocks of wood below weigh the same despite their size difference. The smallest block, lignum vitae (left on scale), is the most dense. The largest block, balsa (right on scale), is the least dense. Density is an important guide to the workability of wood. The table (left) lists the density expressed as specific gravity for a number of species commonly used by woodworkers.

20. Mahogany (Bolivian)
21. Southern yellow pine
22. Red alder
23. Bubinga
24. Mahogany (Central America)
25. Yellow poplar
26. Eastern white pine
27. Barberry
28. Black walnut
29. Hickory
30. Tulipwood
31. Black cherry
32. Eastern spruce
33. Butternut
34. Obeche
35. Basswood
36. Eastern red cedar
37. Rosewood
38. Beech

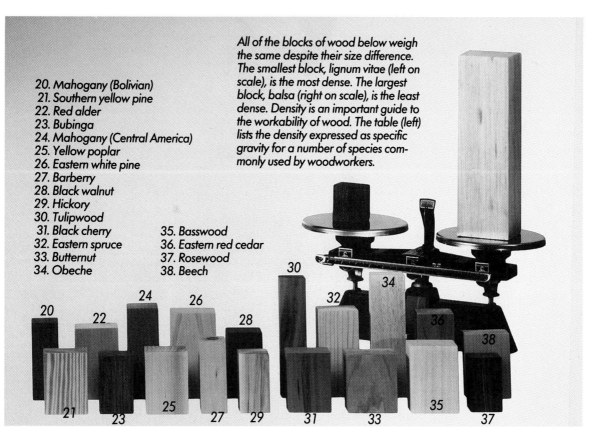

LAWN AND GARDEN PROJECTS

REDWOOD BARBECUE CART

An outdoor classic in redwood that's perfect for your back yard or patio.

This barbecue cart is designed to withstand exposure to heat and moisture and to fulfill specific outdoor living needs. To begin with, kiln-dried, clear, heartwood redwood was used throughout. This grade is very smooth and free of blemishes and warps. It's also lightweight, structurally stable and highly water-resistant.

SUBASSEMBLIES AND MATERIALS
The unit is constructed of two separate assemblies: a case that contains the drawers, storage bin, cutting board and broiler pan; and a framework that acts as the basic structural support for the case and for the top and shelf boards. When reviewing the materials list for this project, keep in mind that architectural-grade 2 x 4s were used for the legs. These measure 1⅝ x 3½ in. If you use construction-grade stock instead, adjust the materials list to reflect the narrower 1½-in. thickness.

Assembly is made with waterproof resorcinol glue and finished with three coats of UGL Imperial Zar satin finish to help withstand the elements.

Simple cup hooks mounted on one end rail (left), provide a convenient place to hang long barbecue utensils. The built-in ice chest (right) is lined with Styrofoam insulation and has a lift-out plastic bowl.

CONSTRUCTION DETAILS
Begin building the framework by cutting the legs and rails to size. Then cut the dadoes in the legs as shown on the drawing to receive the lower shelf rails. The end rails are let completely into the legs and the side rails are joined with half-lap joints. Also, cut to size the add-on wheel blocks that form the support for the wheel axles. Join these blocks to the inside of the wheel legs with glue and four 4d finishing nails per joint. Clamp and let dry.

Then, using a router with a ⅜-in.-rad. rounding-over bit, ease the upper half of each leg edge as shown in the photo. Stop approximately 3¼ in. below the leg top. This will leave the leg top square for maximum gluing surface later when the rails and cases are attached to the legs. Also, by starting the cuts halfway up the legs, the lower half of each remains square for joining the lower rails. Later, when the rails are glued in place, finish the round job by moving the router down the legs and across the rails in one continuous cut.

Bore the wheel axle holes in the wheel legs. Fabricate the wheels by gluing together two squares of 1 x 6 stock with the grain direction of each running at right angles to the other. Clamp until dry, then lay out a 4½-in.-dia. circle on each block. Bore a 1-in.-dia. blade entry hole on the waste side of the circumference line, then cut out the wheel using a sabre saw with a pivot guide as shown. Sand the wheels smooth and bore an axle hole through the center of each. Cut the aluminum rod for the axles, and test-fit both.

Next, glue and clamp the lower side rails to the legs. Let dry, then join the lower end rails to the legs using glue and screws. Cut the sliding shelf notch in one end rail, then clamp all upper rails onto the legs. Bore screw plug and shank holes into the rails and pilot holes into the legs. Separate, apply glue and attach the rails with screws.

Attach the shelf slat support cleats to the lower rails with glue and clamps. Then glue and clamp the cleats and the spacers to the upper rails.

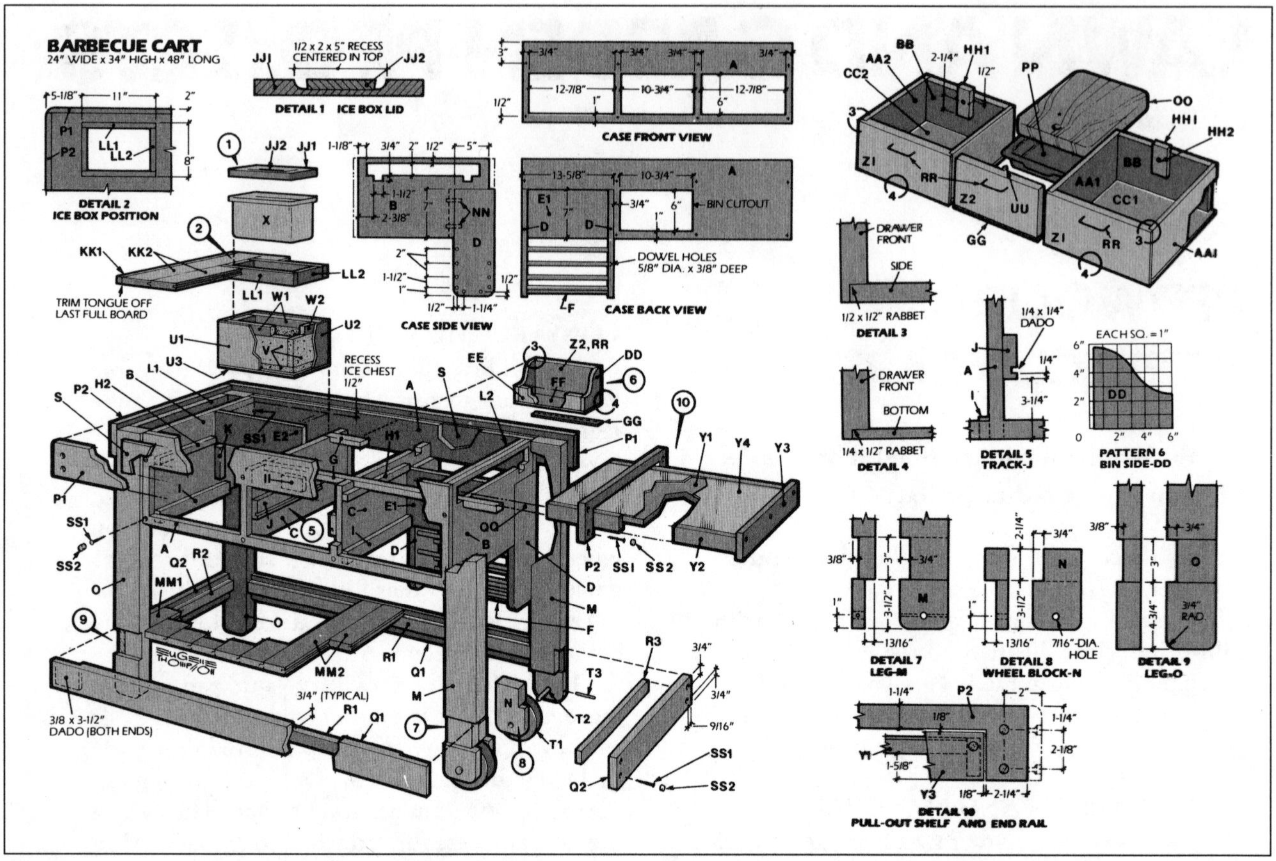

MATERIALS LIST
BARBECUE CART

Key	No.	Size and description (use)
A	2	¾ x 11¼ x 39½" redwood (case side)
B	2	¾ x 11¼ x 20¼" redwood (case end)
C	2	¾ x 8¾ x 20¼" redwood (case partition)
D	2	¾ x 5¾ x 15" redwood (bottle rack side)
E1	1	¾ x 7 x 12⅞" redwood (bottle rack partition)
E2	1	¾ x 4 x 12⅞" redwood (ice-box partition)
F	9	⅝"-dia. x 12⅞" hardwood dowel
G	2	¾ x 1½ x 29⅜" redwood (side track)
H1	2	¾ x ¾ x 14½" redwood (upper drawer guide)
H2	2	¾ x ¾ x 11½" redwood (upper drawer guide)
I	4	¾ x 1⅛ x 14½" redwood (lower drawer guide)
J	2	¾ x 1½ x 14½" redwood (board, pan track)
K	2	¾ x ¾ x 5" redwood (drawer stop block)
L1	1	¾ x 2 x 19¼" redwood (top cleat)
L2	1	⅜ x ¾ x 19¼" redwood (top cleat)
M	2	1⅝ x 3½ x 32" redwood (wheel leg)
N	2	1⅝ x 3½ x 5¾" redwood (wheel block)
O	2	1⅝ x 3½ x 33¼" redwood (straight leg)
P1	2	¾ x 4 x 48" redwood (top side rail)
P2	2	¾ x 4 x 22½" redwood (top end rail)
Q1	2	¾ x 3 x 46½" redwood (shelf side rail)
Q2	2	¾ x 3 x 21¾" redwood (shelf end rail)
R1	2	¾ x 1¼ x 39½" redwood (shelf cleat)
R2	1	¾ x 1¼ x 19¼" redwood (shelf cleat)
R3	1	¾ x 1¼ x 16" redwood (shelf cleat)
S	2	⅜ x 3 x 39½" plywood (spacer)
T1	2	1½" x 4½"-dia. redwood (wheel)
T2	2	7/16"-dia. x 3½" aluminum rod (axle)
T3	2	3/32"-dia. x 2¼" brass rod (axle pin)
U1	2	¼ x 5⅞ x 11" plywood (ice-box front, back)
U2	2	¼ x 5⅞ x 7½" plywood (ice-box end)
U3	1	¼ x 8 x 11" plywood (ice-box bottom)
V	2 sq. ft.	¾"-thick Styrofoam insulation, cut to fit
W1	2	¾ x 1¼ x 10½" redwood (block)
W2	2	¾ x 1¼ x 6" redwood (block)
X	1	Freezette No. 336, 4½-qt. plastic bowl (ice bowl)
Y1	1	¾ x 16 x 29¼" plywood (shelf)
Y2	2	¾ x 1½ x 29¼" redwood (shelf side rail)
Y3	1	¾ x 2⅝ x 17¾" redwood (shelf end rail)
Y4	1	1/16 x 16 x 29¼" Wilsonart No. D30-6, Natural Almond plastic laminate
Z1	2	¾ x 5¾ x 12¾" redwood (drawer front)
Z2	2	¾ x 5¾ x 10⅝" redwood (door, bin front)
AA1	2	½ x 5½ x 15" plywood (drawer side)
AA2	2	½ x 5½ x 12" plywood (drawer side)
BB	2	½ x 5½ x 11¾" plywood (drawer back)
CC1	1	¼ x 12¾ x 15" plywood (drawer bottom)
CC2	1	¼ x 12¾ x 12" plywood (drawer bottom)
DD	2	½ x 5⅜ x 5¾" plywood (bin side)
EE	1	½ x 2¼ x 9⅝" plywood (bin back)
FF	1	¼ x 5¾ x 10⅝" plywood (bin bottom)
GG	2	1½ x 10½" aluminum continuous hinge
HH1	2	½ x 1½ x 3½" redwood (drawer stop)
HH2	2	¾" No. 8 flathead screw
II	1	¾ x 1½ x 3" redwood (door catch block)
JJ1	1	¾ x 6½ x 9½" redwood (ice-box top)
JJ2	1	½ x ¾ x 3¾" redwood (ice-box handle)
KK1	2	½ x ¾ x 22½" redwood (top end slat)
KK2	14	¾ x 3¼ x 22½" redwood (top slat)
LL1	2	¾ x 1¼ x 11" redwood (ice-box frame)
LL2	2	¾ x 1¼ x 6½" redwood (ice-box frame)
MM1	2	¾ x 3 x 21" redwood (shelf end slat)
MM2	13	¾ x 3¼ x 21" redwood (shelf slat)
NN	2	⅜"-dia. x 2" hardwood dowel
OO	1	13/16 x 10½ x 14½" maple (cutting board)
PP	1	Wearever broiler pan No. 2672
QQ	2	Grant 24" No. 308 full-extension drawer slide
RR	4	Stanley 3" No. 4483 aluminum pull with No. 4487 aluminum bases
SS1	51	1½" No. 8 flathead screw
SS2	43	½"-dia. x ¼" redwood plug
UU	1	Stanley No. SP34 cabinet catch

One side of the cart has a center drop-down door (left) that covers a slide-out cutting board and broiler pan. A built-in bottle rack (right) provides storage for wine, spirits and mixes close to the ice chest.

Use a dado head in a radial-arm saw to cut shelf rail dadoes in legs. By installing a higher fence in the table, the cut through it serves as a leg cut alignment guide.

The cut leg parts are ready for assembly. The two center legs, and blocks between, form the axle support for wheels. The others are single legs for cart front.

Join the wheel blocks to the rear legs using glue and four 4d finishing nails per joint. Set nailheads and let the assembly dry overnight before continuing.

Slide each rail completely into its proper leg dado. Then use a utility knife to mark the precise width of the half-lap joint on the inside surface of the rail.

Use a router to round corners on the upper section of each leg before top rails are attached. Nail a block in place to stop the cutter 3¼ in. below the leg top.

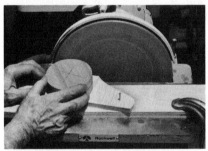

Glue up 1 x 6 stock for the wheels, let dry, then draw a 4½-in.-dia. circle on the block. Bore blade entry hole on waste side of the line and cut using a sabre saw with pivot guide.

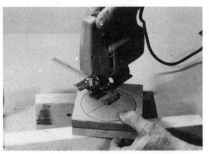

A simple disc-sander jig assures precise circular sanding. Place wheel onto projecting nail, then pivot jig until wheel touches disc. Rotate wheel until smooth.

Glue and clamp the long bottom rails to legs. Let dry, then clamp the other rails in place. Bore screw plug, shank and pilot holes through the rails and into the legs.

Here is the completed frame. Support cleats for the top shelf boards are on the inside surface of the rails, and the cutout on the end rail is for the sliding shelf.

Begin case construction by gluing up stock for the facing panels. Then, using a table saw, cut out drawer openings by holding board in place and raising handle.

Make vertical drawer cuts on a radial-arm saw. Use a square to align the blade center over opening center. Lock carriage in place, then lower blade into stock.

Install bottle rack handing dowels in case end, then join all parts with glue and screws. Test-fit extension slide tracks, then remove and finish-sand.

Attach case to frame by driving two screws through the inside of each case corner into the legs. Install slides, build shelf, then check shelf for proper fit.

Install lower drawer guides, then build drawers and check for fit. Install upper guides, cutting board and pan track, and the bin on the opposite cart side.

Cut top boards to size, then install with glue and 1-in. brads driven through the tongue into the support cleats at a 45° angle. Keep V-joint side of boards down.

When boards reach ice-box partition, install small frame boards as shown in drawing (parts LL1 and LL2). Cut remaining top boards to conform to opening.

Cut ice-box top to size, then hold it in jig frame shown, made of 1¼-in.-wide stock. Install ¾-in. core box bit in router and cut depression using jig as fence.

CASE ASSEMBLY

Cut the case sides and ends to size. Cut out the drawer, door and bin pockets in the case sides using a table saw and radial-arm saw. You can also use a sabre saw to make these cuts. Just clamp a guide fence in the proper position for each cut so they will be straight and square. Also, bore a small hole in the corner of each opening—on the waste side of the lines—for blade entry.

Cut out the notch in the case side for the bottle rack and cut the bottle rack partition (part E1) to size. Then cut the opening for the sliding shelf in one case end as shown on the drawing. Also cut the bottle rack notch in the same board. Bore two ⅜-in.-dia. dowel holes—for supporting the bottle rack—in this notch, then glue the dowels in place.

Assemble the case ends and sides with glue and screws, check for square and let dry. Then cut the case partitions to size and install with glue and screws driven through the face of the case sides. Use two screws for each partition end. Install the bottle rack partition, between the case end and the first partition, with glue and 6d finishing nails.

JOINING CASE TO FRAME

Slide the case into the frame assembly and attach by driving two screws through the inside of each case corner into the corner of each abutting leg. Next, glue and clamp the lower drawer guides, cutting board and pan track in place.

Cut the parts for and assemble the drawers, bin and ice box. Test-fit each. Remove the drawers and install the upper guides. Attach the bin and drop-down door with continuous hinges, then glue and clamp the bottle rack in place.

Install the ice-box partition with glue and 6d finishing nails. Then hang the box from this partition and the top side rail with ¾-in. No. 8 flathead screws driven through the inside of the box into these supports. Cut and fit the rigid insulation to the interior of the box. Make the fit tight so friction, instead of adhesive, holds the pieces in place.

Next, install the tracks for the pullout shelf extension slides. Then build the shelf and cover it with plastic laminate. Attach the slides to the bottom of the shelf and the top of the tracks with several mounting screws. Check for proper movement before installing the remaining screws.

Install the top and shelf boards with glue and 1-in. brads driven through the board tongues into the support cleats at a 45° angle. Set the heads. Be sure to install the boards with the V-joint face down so you end up with a smooth surface on the top.

Fill all screw holes with redwood plugs and all nail holes with redwood- or mahogany-colored wood filler. Then round over the outside corners of the top rails to a 1½-in. radius. Use a portable belt sander with an 80-grit abrasive belt to remove most of the stock, but stop short of the completed radius and finish the shaping by hand-sanding with 150-grit sandpaper.

Complete the router work by easing all exposed edges with a ⅜-in.-rad. rounding-over bit. Finish-sand the entire piece with 150-grit paper. Remove the dust and apply the finish.

Install the wheels, attach the pulls to the drawers, door and bin, and mount the magnetic catch for the door. Make the cutting board and finish with mineral oil. Then slide it and the broiler pan into their tracks. Finish up by boring a ½-in.-dia. hole in the bottom of the ice box to provide drainage, and by inserting the plastic bowl into the box.

GARDENING AIDS YOU CAN BUILD

The potting bench, lettuce shader and caterpillar cloche can turn an "all thumbs" gardener into a green thumb.

LETTUCE SHADER

The lettuce shader does a perfect job of partially shading lettuce from the sun. This minimizes leaf burn and produces a more bountiful crop. If you build it of No. 2 common pine and treat it with wood preservative, it will last for years.

Since the slat assembly is not attached to the legs, you can store it nearly flat against a wall.

The shader shown has 1 x 2 slats spaced 1½ to 2 in. apart. These are secured by 6d hot-dipped galvanized nails to a base of 2 x 3 rails and end pieces. You can also use 2 x 4s.

Cut stake joints on the legs as shown. Secure the legs to their cross members. Apply a wood preservative.

A pair of shading units can share a common (center) leg unit if each shader is set to occupy just half the crosspiece width. This leaves a lip upon which the next shader can rest.

POTTING BENCH

The potting bench is adapted from one used by Bob Thompson, host of the *Victory Garden* TV program, aired nationally on PBS. The simple but sturdy bench is built to withstand strenuous daily use. Plans are for a smaller version to suit a home gardener's needs and space limitations. A garden tool board and a top shelf for parking flowerpots during work sessions has been added.

The bench is framed with pressure-treated 2 x 4s; work and storage surfaces are 1 x 6s. Or you can use common pine for the frame and work surfaces. If you opt for the latter, coat all surfaces of these members with a wood preservative, such as Woodlife, several hours before you assemble the parts. Give the bench a second coat.

You can use exterior plywood for bench shelf, sides and back. The board to hold tools is perforated hardboard fitted with tool-holding hardware.

Cut frame members for the deck. Hold parts together temporarily with bar clamps. Check corners with a large square; adjust if needed. Then bore pilot holes for nails to prevent the wood from splitting. Use resorcinol glue and

nails to assemble parts.

Cut the 1 x 6s for the work surface and the lower storage shelf to length. Cut the notches for the legs in two shelf members. Bore pilot holes and nail the work top in place.

Cut the plywood sides and back. The sides taper in height from 21 in. in back to 7 in. in front. Glue and nail the back and sides to the bench top and to each other.

Cut the upper shelf to size and bore the optional flowerpot holes. You can make these using a fly cutter in the drill press, but clamp the shelf firmly to the press table on both sides of the cutter. Or you can make the circular cuts with a sabre saw.

The bench legs are cut to length and the notches are cut. You can make the internal notches with a sabre saw and chisel. Or use a radial-arm saw in this manner: Mark for notch width and depth on the face of the leg and align the notch (waste) area with the saw blade. Ad-

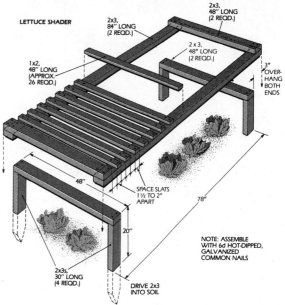

LETTUCE SHADER

2x3, 84" LONG (2 REQD.)

2x3, 48" LONG (2 REQD.)

2 x 3, 48" LONG (2 REQD.)

1 x 2, 48" LONG (APPROX. 26 REQD.)

3" OVER-HANG BOTH ENDS

48"

SPACE SLATS 1½ TO 2" APART

78"

20"

2x3s, 30" LONG (4 REQD.)

DRIVE 2x3 INTO SOIL

NOTE: ASSEMBLE WITH 6d HOT-DIPPED, GALVANIZED COMMON NAILS

just the blade to notch depth. Make successive overlapping passes with the blade. Clean using a chisel.

Rest the bench top bottom side up. Position the back legs; bore pilot holes, and glue and nail the legs in place.

Rotate the bench onto its front assembly and install the front legs in the same manner. Let the glue dry for 24 hours. Next, cut the lower frame members to length. Test-assemble using clamps, and bore pilot holes after checking that the frame is square. Then secure the parts with glue and nails.

Finally, cut out parts for the tool board. Glue and nail the frame together with 4d nails and set aside. Bore lead holes and fasten the cleats to

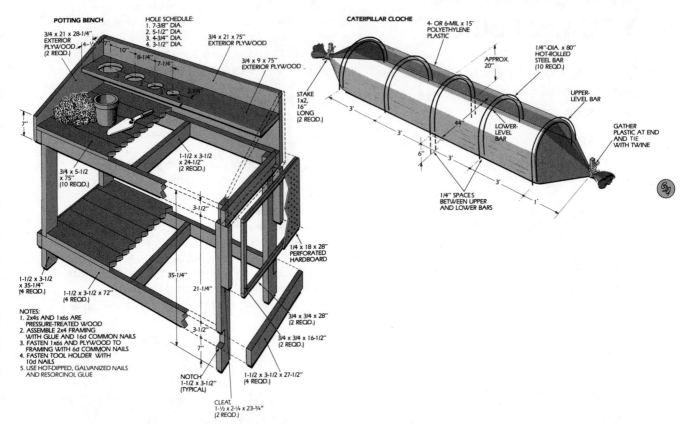

POTTING BENCH

3/4 x 21 x 28-1/4"
EXTERIOR
PLYWOOD
(2 REQD.)

HOLE SCHEDULE:
1. 7-3/8" DIA.
2. 5-1/2" DIA.
3. 4-3/4" DIA.
4. 3-1/2" DIA.

3/4 x 21 x 75"
EXTERIOR PLYWOOD

3/4 x 9 x 75"
EXTERIOR PLYWOOD

STAKE
1x2,
16"
LONG
(2 REQD.)

3/4 x 5-1/2"
x 75"
(10 REQD.)

1-1/2 x 3-1/2
x 24-1/2"
(2 REQD.)

3-1/2"

1-1/2 x 3-1/2
x 35-1/4"
(4 REQD.)

1-1/2 x 3-1/2 x 72"
(4 REQD.)

35-1/4"

21-1/4"

1/4 x 18 x 28"
PERFORATED
HARDBOARD

3/4 x 3/4 x 28"
(2 REQD.)

3/4 x 3/4 x 16-1/2"
(2 REQD.)

NOTES:
1. 2x4s AND 1x6s ARE
PRESSURE-TREATED WOOD
2. ASSEMBLE 2x4 FRAMING
WITH GLUE AND 16d COMMON NAILS
3. FASTEN 1x6s AND PLYWOOD TO
FRAMING WITH 6d COMMON NAILS
4. FASTEN TOOL HOLDER WITH
10d NAILS
5. USE HOT-DIPPED, GALVANIZED NAILS
AND RESORCINOL GLUE

3-1/2"

7"

NOTCH
1-1/2 x 3-1/2"
(TYPICAL)

1-1/2 x 3-1/2 x 27-1/2"
(4 REQD.)

CLEAT,
1-1/2 x 2-1/4 x 23-3/4"
(2 REQD.)

CATERPILLAR CLOCHE

4- OR 6-MIL x 15'
POLYETHYLENE
PLASTIC

1/4"-DIA. x 80"
HOT-ROLLED
STEEL BAR
(10 REQD.)

APPROX.
20"

UPPER-
LEVEL
BAR

LOWER-
LEVEL
BAR

44"

6"

GATHER
PLASTIC AT END
AND TIE
WITH TWINE

3'

1/4" SPACES
BETWEEN UPPER
AND LOWER BARS

the legs with 10d nails. Bore lead holes and fasten the perforated hardboard to the bench with 6d common nails. Apply veneer edge tape to exposed edges, if desired, using contact cement.

CATERPILLAR CLOCHE

The caterpillar cloche adds a season extender to your garden. You can assemble it in several hours with tape measure, hacksaw, paint brush, scissors or knife, and hammer.

Materials you'll need include ¼-in.-dia. hot-rolled steel bar, 4- or 6-mil polyethylene plastic, rustproof paint, two 16-in. wood stakes and twine. Steel bar is sold in 20-ft. lengths (check the classified directory under "Steel distributors and warehouses"). The cloche shown covers a 40-in.-wide x 12-ft. planting bed. You'll need four bars to cut ten 80-in. lengths. For beds of other dimensions, allow two arched bars for every 3 ft. of garden bed.

The cloche shown requires a 4 x 15-ft. piece of plastic. For other sizes, figure the amount of plastic by adding 3 ft. to the length of the growing bed. If your bed is wider than 4 ft., place two caterpillars side by side.

Use a hacksaw to cut the bars to 80-in. lengths. Clamp the bar stock in a vise to cut it. Apply two coats of rustproof paint to the bars using a paint brush or old rag. Set aside to dry.

Starting at one end of the bed, mark the ground at 3-ft. intervals; you'll insert the steel bars at these points. Mark along one side of the bed, then along the other.

Push a steel bar for the lower level of bars about 6 in. into the ground. If it doesn't stand by itself, push it deeper. Straddling the bed, grip the top of the bar and slowly bend it toward the marked spot on the opposite side of the bed. Then push the end 6 in. into the soil. Repeat on the lower-level bars.

Unroll and spread out the polyethylene plastic and cut it to size. Lay the plastic over the support bars. Gather the last 18 in. of plastic at one end and tie it with twine; repeat at the other end.

Cut the wood stakes to 16-in. lengths. Tie one end of the plastic around a stake and hammer the stake in place. Then tie the plastic to the other stake and pull the plastic tight before hammering the stake.

Insert the upper level of steel bars directly over the lower ones, leaving ¼-in. between them so the plastic slides freely for covering or uncovering.

The plastic skin should open roll-top-desk fashion. Pull the plastic up about 2 ft. at each support; then continue to pull it to reveal the entire bed.

The charming country design of the patio bench makes it a favorite for use in gardens or along paved walkway.

GARDEN BENCHES

Relax on one of these easy-to-build country benches—right in your yard.

Build one or both of these outdoor benches for wherever summertime relaxation is convenient: by a garden, at poolside, under a tree, in a breezeway or on a sun deck or porch.

The patio bench and park bench are easy to build, comfortable and weatherproof. Pressure-treated lumber should be used for both benches, but redwood heartwood (which is naturally decay-resistant) or wood treated with an exterior finish could be used as well.

PATIO BENCH

Start by cutting six 21-in.-long legs from 2 x 3 stock. Then cut a ½ x 2½ x 2½-in. tenon on one end of each leg using a radial-arm or table saw. Next, cut parts from 1 x 4s for the two frames that support the seat slats. Assemble the frames with 1½-in. galvanized finish nails and butt-joint corners. Screw the legs to the frame, as shown, using 1½-in. No. 14 flathead screws. Keep the legs square and flush with the front apron. Be sure to countersink and bore screw-shank clearance holes for every screw used in this bench.

Next, cut three aprons from 2 x 4 stock to fit snugly between the three pairs of legs. Attach the aprons to the 1 x 4 frame using 1½-in. No. 14 flathead screws and waterproof resorcinol glue. The aprons hold the legs square while stabilizing the bench. The center 2 x 4 apron fits between the two frames to stabilize the middle pair of legs.

Cut the three bench feet from 2 x 3 stock. Mark the mortise locations on the ends of each foot. Then use a ½-in. mortising chisel mounted in a drill press to cut the mortises. The mortises can also be made by first boring a series of overlapping ½-in.-dia. holes and then clearing the remaining waste with a sharp chisel. Round the ends of each foot as shown, using a wood rap or Surform tool, then sand smooth. Dry-fit the tenons into the mortises. The fit should be snug, but not too tight.

Bore a ½-in.-dia. x 1¼-in.-deep hole into the center of the mortise and tenon. Apply resorcinol glue to the end of a ½-in.-dia. hardwood dowel, then tap the dowel tightly into the hole to lock the foot onto the leg. Cut off the protruding dowel and sand smooth. Repeat this procedure for all six joints. Cut and install the eight corner braces as shown. Be sure to cut the braces square.

Next, cut six 1 x 4s for the seat slats. Round the top edges of the slats using a router and a ¼-in. rounding-over bit or a sanding block to prevent splintering. Sand the slats smooth before fastening them. Leave about a ¾-in. space between each slat. Finally, apply an exterior stain if desired.

PARK BENCH

Begin by cutting all the parts to the lengths shown. Use 2 x 3s for the seat slats and stretcher, 2 x 4s for the front legs, backrest, leg braces and seat frames, and 2 x 6s for the back legs. Then shape the eight frame pieces as shown in the cutting pattern using a band or sabre saw. The frame pieces are assembled with ¾-in.-deep half-lap joints. The stability of the bench depends upon tight-fitting joints. Loose, sloppy joints will allow the bench to rock.

An easy way to mark the half-lap joint locations is to first clamp together the four parts that form each bench frame: the back and front legs to the seat frame and leg brace. Be sure the two legs are on the outside of the other two parts. Then use a pencil to mark the seat frame and brace where they meet the legs.

Disassemble the frame and cut the half-lap joints where indicated by the pencil lines, using

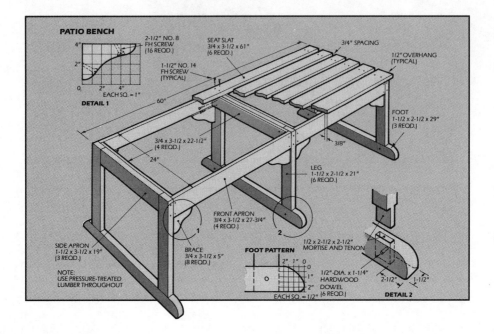

a radial-arm saw, table saw or router. Sand all the parts before assembly.

Next, reassemble the two bench frames using waterproof resorcinol glue and 1½-in. No. 14 flathead screws. Drive the screws in from the inside of the bench—that is, through the half-lap members and into the legs. You must be sure to countersink and bore screw-shank clearance holes for every screw used in this bench.

Bore the screw locations in all the seat slats and both backrest parts. Each part is attached by two 2½-in. No. 8 flathead screws on each end. The seat and the backrests should overhang the seat frame by about 8 in.

The backrest screw locations are ¾ in. closer to the board ends than are those of the seat slats because of the offset from the half-lap joint. For example, if the seat-slat screws are 8 in. from the end, bore the backrest screw locations 7¼ in. from the end to fall on center on the back leg.

Next, round the top edges of the seat slats and backrests using a router and a ¼-in. rounding-over bit. Sand all parts smooth, using first 80-grit abrasive paper and then 120-grit. Screw the slats and backrests to the frames, but make sure you leave about a ¼-in. space between each slat. Be certain all screwheads are below the wood surface.

Finally, cut a 2 x 3 stretcher to fit between the leg braces. Fasten the stretcher with four 3-in. No. 12 flathead screws. Complete the bench by applying two coats of exterior stain.

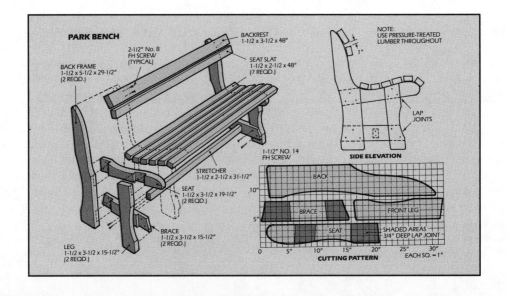

Place this redwood deck where you want it. It's independent of any other structures.

A DECK FOR ANYWHERE

This free-standing design allows for greater flexibility in positioning the deck on your property.

The deck shown here offers all the benefits of a house-attached deck with one unique difference—the freedom to be built independent of another structure. Its free-standing design means it can be placed near a garden or lake, at poolside, under shady trees, or on sloping, rocky or otherwise unmanageable terrain.

CONSTRUCTION AND MATERIALS NOTES

The deck's size and shape can be altered to suit your particular site, but the basic structural design can be used in any situation. Be sure to check the local building codes before you begin construction.

This deck was built to extend beyond an existing concrete patio to afford views of the picturesque canyon below. It's made of construction heart redwood that is used for outdoor applications.

Redwood was chosen for more than its looks. It's also dimensionally stable, so it resists warping, cupping and checking; it is lightweight and easy to work with; and redwood heartwood resists insects and decay. Redwood readily holds a finish and doesn't burn easily because it contains no volatile substances.

Use only redwood heartwood or pressure-treated lumber in or near the ground. Redwood sapwood is not decay-resistant.

GARDEN GRADES OF REDWOOD

Construction Heart: All heartwood, but does contain some knots. Suitable for posts, beams and structural framing near or on the ground.
Construction Common: Similar to construction heart, but contains sapwood. For use as deck boards, fences and other above-ground applications.
Merchantable Heart: Economical heartwood grade with larger knots and holes. Used for fences, garden structures and other applications at or near the ground.
Merchantable: Same as merchantable heart, but contains sapwood. Suitable for trellises, deck furnishings and other above-ground uses.

CHOOSING A LOCATION

The first step is to pick a spot on your property to build the deck. This decision is important because it's the key to the deck's usefulness. When choosing a site, consider the following: the path of the sun, water drainage patterns, the amount of available shade, privacy from neighbors and traffic, access to the house, and protection from wind and noise.

Next, to help you visualize the completed deck, lay out the deck's shape using wood stakes and nylon string. The deck size and shape are most often determined by the site's terrain and your budget. But remember, even a modest-size deck like the one shown provides over 250 sq. ft. of extra living space.

Time-saving galvanized metal fasteners are used throughout the deck construction to join structural wood members. Fasteners are available at lumberyards, home centers and hardwood stores. Refer to drawings for the specific model Teco fasteners used.

FOOTINGS AND PIERS

Footings, generally made of poured concrete, support the posts that transfer the weight of the entire deck to the ground. A concrete pier is often poured on top of the footing to raise the post off the ground (see drawing of typical footings). Generally, footings measure 8 in. deep x 16 x 16 in.

Pour the footings onto undisturbed or well-compacted soil or rock, not loose backfill. In colder regions, dig footings below the frost line to avoid heaving during freeze and thaw cycles. Check the local building code for specific footing size and depth in your area.

Lay out and dig the 12 footings as shown in the plan. Next, decide whether you want to use ready-mixed concrete or mix your own from cement, sand, gravel and water. Ready-mixed concrete costs more, but you only need to add water and mix.

If a pier is to be poured on top of the footing, be sure to leave three or four short reinforcing bars (rebars) protruding out of the footing about 6 in. to create a strong bond between the pier and the footing. After the footing has hardened, you can form up and pour the pier.

Build the pier's form using ¾-in. exterior plywood or an 8-in.-dia. spiral-wound fiber tube. The tube, commonly known by the trade name Sonotube, is a thick-walled paper tube designed for use as a concrete form. Piers should be at least 8 in. wide and project above the ground a minimum of 6 in. If a drift pin or metal post anchor is to be used, be sure to insert it into the pier before the concrete hardens. Cut the pin from a length of ⅝- or ¾-in.-dia. rebar. Then centerbore the bottom of the post to accept the pin.

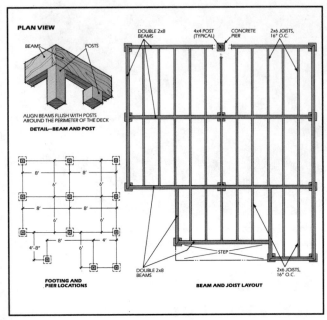

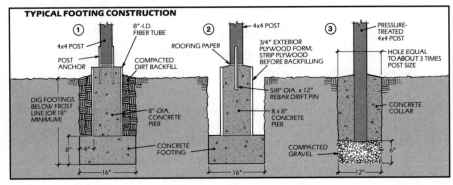

The back railing wraps around both sides of the deck to join a redwood yard fence.

POSTS AND BEAMS

First, cut the 4 x 4 posts slightly longer than needed, then position each post on its pier. If a drift pin is used, place a 4 x 4-in. square of heavy roofing paper over the pin to prevent the post from absorbing moisture. Brace each post temporarily with 1 x 3s. Use a carpenter's level to be sure each post is plumb.

Next, determine the posts' finished height by subtracting the decking thickness and the beam width from the desired finished deck height. For example, if the finished deck height is 30 in., subtract the 2 x 6 decking (1½ in. thick) and the 2 x 8 beam (7¼ in. wide) to arrive at a post height of 21¼ in.

Mark the post height onto the post that is sitting on the highest point of ground. From here, transfer the post height to the other posts using a nylon string and a line level. Then carefully mark and cut each post where indicated by the level string.

At this point, the posts may be different lengths because of sloping or uneven terrain,

but the tops of all the posts should be level with each other.

Nail together the double 2 x 8 beams using 3-in. (10d) top-quality, double hot-dipped galvanized nails. The beam ends that meet to form the outside corners are assembled with the inside 2 x 8 held back 1½ in. in order to form a strong interlocking corner joint.

Next, get the metal fasteners ready to use. Use two Ty-down rafter anchors on each of the 10 posts located around the deck perimeter (details 1 and 2). Fasten one angle-iron brace in each corner to further strengthen the joint.

On the two posts located in the center of the deck, use a Teco No. PC-4 post cap (detail 3). For the six places where a beam meets a beam, excluding the outside corners, use a 3-in.-wide double-joist hanger (detail 4).

With the aid of a helper, lift one of the perimeter deck beams onto the posts. Fasten the rafter anchors to the beam first. Then position the beam flush with the outside of the posts and nail the anchors to the posts. Continue nailing

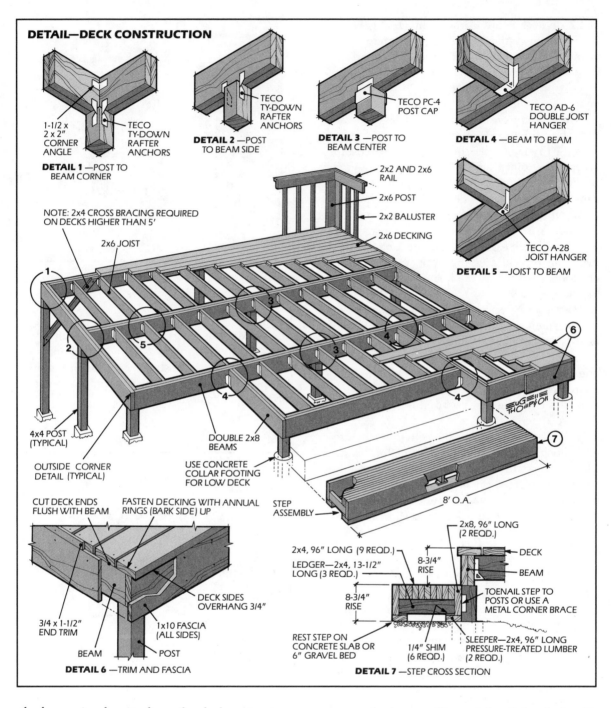

DETAIL—DECK CONSTRUCTION

1-1/2 x 2 x 2" CORNER ANGLE
TECO TY-DOWN RAFTER ANCHORS
DETAIL 1—POST TO BEAM CORNER

TECO TY-DOWN RAFTER ANCHORS
DETAIL 2—POST TO BEAM SIDE

TECO PC-4 POST CAP
DETAIL 3—POST TO BEAM CENTER

TECO AD-6 DOUBLE JOIST HANGER
DETAIL 4—BEAM TO BEAM

TECO A-28 JOIST HANGER
DETAIL 5—JOIST TO BEAM

2x2 AND 2x6 RAIL
2x6 POST
2x2 BALUSTER
2x6 DECKING

NOTE: 2x4 CROSS BRACING REQUIRED ON DECKS HIGHER THAN 5'

2x6 JOIST

4x4 POST (TYPICAL)

OUTSIDE CORNER DETAIL (TYPICAL)

DOUBLE 2x8 BEAMS

USE CONCRETE COLLAR FOOTING FOR LOW DECK

STEP ASSEMBLY

8' O.A.

CUT DECK ENDS FLUSH WITH BEAM
FASTEN DECKING WITH ANNUAL RINGS (BARK SIDE) UP

DECK SIDES OVERHANG 3/4"

3/4 x 1-1/2" END TRIM
1x10 FASCIA (ALL SIDES)
BEAM
POST
DETAIL 6—TRIM AND FASCIA

2x4, 96" LONG (9 REQD.)
LEDGER—2x4, 13-1/2" LONG (3 REQD.)

2x8, 96" LONG (2 REQD.)
DECK
BEAM
8-3/4" RISE
8-3/4" RISE

TOENAIL STEP TO POSTS OR USE A METAL CORNER BRACE

REST STEP ON CONCRETE SLAB OR 6" GRAVEL BED
1/4" SHIM (6 REQD.)
SLEEPER—2x4, 96" LONG PRESSURE-TREATED LUMBER (2 REQD.)
DETAIL 7—STEP CROSS SECTION

the beams in place to form the deck perimeter. Install the two beams that cross the center posts. Use a double-joist hanger (detail 4) where a center beam meets a perimeter beam.

JOISTS

Mark 16-in. on-center locations for all the 2 x 6 joist hangers (detail 5). Next, nail the hangers in place, but fasten only *one* side of each hanger. Then cut the joists and drop them into the hangers. Before nailing the joists in place, sight down the joist edge. If a noticeable crown (crook) exists, position the joist with the

crowned edge up. The weight of the deck will straighten the joist. Finish nailing the hangers. For single-joist hangers, use 3-in. (10d) nails. Use 4-in. (20d) nails for double-joist hangers.

BRACING

Braces are required on decks higher than 5 ft. to prevent lateral movement. Bolt the braces to the underside of the deck, as shown, using ¼-in.-dia. x 6-in. carriage bolts.

DECKING

Starting at the back of the deck, nail down the

first 2 x 6 deck board using 3½-in. (16d) galvanized nails. Let the board edge overhang the beam ¾ in. to conceal the fascia (see detail 6). Start with a straight board since measurements taken from here are used to keep subsequent boards straight.

If more than one board is used to span the deck, butt the boards over the center of a joist. Be sure to stagger the next row of boards to prevent the joint from falling on the same joist as the previous row. Also, leave space for expansion and drainage. The shank of a 16d nail is commonly used as a spacer. You can also use a block of ¼-in. plywood.

As you nail each row, let the board ends overhang the sides of the deck. Later, snap a chalkline and trim all the boards using a portable circular saw.

After every five or six rows, stop and take measurements from the starter board. If the boards are out of alignment, make several small adjustments to consecutive rows rather than one large adjustment. When you reach the final board, let it overhang the front edge of the deck ¾ in. As with the first board, this will conceal the fascia.

Next, snap a chalkline on both sides of the deck flush with the outside edge of the beam. Then trim off the board ends using a portable circular saw. *Caution:* Be certain to wear eye protection when operating any power tool.

Build the butcher block step as shown in detail 7. Fasten the step assembly to the posts using metal corner braces or by toenailing.

TRIM AND FASCIA
Since a free-standing deck is often visible from all sides, nail fascia board and trim around the deck perimeter to provide a finished look. Use 1 x 10 redwood for the fascia and 1 x 2 redwood for the end trim. Use rough-sawn cedar for a more rustic look. Keep the trim flush with the top of the decking, then nail the fascia under the trim and under the ¾-in. overhang in the front and back of the deck.

RAILING AND FENCE
Unless the deck sits directly on the ground, a railing is recommended. Make the railing from 2 x 2 and 2 x 6 redwood stock. Assemble the railing on the ground and bolt it to the deck using 6-in. carriage bolts, as shown in the drawing. Finally, plumb the balusters using a level, then secure each one with 2½-in. galvanized nails. Pre-drill the balusters to prevent them from splitting.

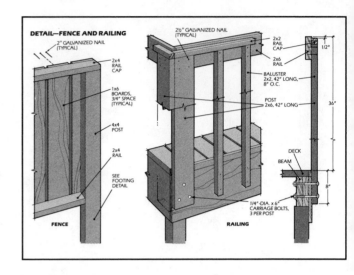

BENCH
The sturdy redwood butcher block bench consists of a 2 x 4 top with 2 x 6 legs. Cut and assemble the bench as shown. Although it's not necessary, the bench can be screwed to the deck for additional stability.

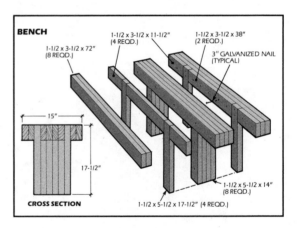

FINISHES
A clear water repellent containing a mildewcide should be applied to all garden-grade redwood. For best results, apply the water repellent directly to the lumber before construction, covering all surfaces. Then apply a second coat after the deck is completed.

If water repellent is applied every 12 to 18 months, it will eliminate the natural darkening process and help stabilize the color of the redwood to a buckskin tan. Water repellent also serves as a base for other finishes such as exterior oil-based decking stains.

KID–PLEASING PLAY STRUCTURES

Here are two wood designs, plus tips on planning, installing and maintaining them.

Design outdoor play equipment that's fun for kids, yet visually appealing to adults. That was the challenge given to Ira Grandberg, an architect with The American Institute of Architects and father of three. Ira returned with several ingenious creations. Two with modifications are shown here for you to duplicate.

MATERIALS AND CONSTRUCTION NOTES

For durability, use pressure-treated lumber. Select wood that carries the American Wood Preservers Bureau (AWPB) quality seal, is labeled "CCA" (chromated copper arsenate) or with another waterborne preservative and is dry after treatment so the preservative won't leach out of the wood. Posts and lumber that contact the soil should be labeled "LP-22 ground contact .40" Select No. 1 grade wood to minimize splintering. In addition, ease all edges and chamfer or round ends.

Use hot-dipped, galvanized or cadmium-plated hardware. In most situations, carriage

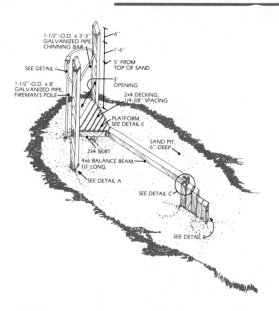

1 *Your child can balance on beam, chin or bar and slide down pole. It's a fun way to develop motor skills.*

bolts are recommended, pounded into prebored holes to admit the shoulders and secured with countersunk washers and nuts tightened from the back.

First, counterbore the nut hole, then clamp the two members together and bore through them. If the bolt ends protrude, mark, remove and cut them flush with a hacksaw.

PLANNING THE PLAY SITE

Carefully planning your child's outdoor play site will greatly reduce the possibility of accidents. Bruce Chivington of Site Specialties, Lithonia, Ga., planner of outdoor play areas, suggests the following:

Select a level space. Consider the location of underground power lines, sprinkler systems, water and telephone lines. To avoid placing a slide or swing too near a tree, for example, it helps to make a scaled diagram of the area with the proposed equipment. You'll also be able to plan an adequate safety apron, the ground around the equipment, which should be topped with semisoft material.

Chivington borders the play areas with sunken railroad ties "a safe distance" from the equipment. On equipment 4 ft. high, this means 4 to 5 ft. in all directions. The border for a swing suspended from a 10-ft.-high bar should be 10 ft. in front and back. After installation, Chivington fills the play area with bark or pine straw to a 6-in. depth. Sand is also good. Trees and bushes should be left nearby for shade.

All outdoor play equipment should have installation instructions made specifically for the equipment. It is important to follow these instructions.

2 *Balancing, rope climbing and swinging bar-to-bar are some of the activities offered by beam and ladder project.*

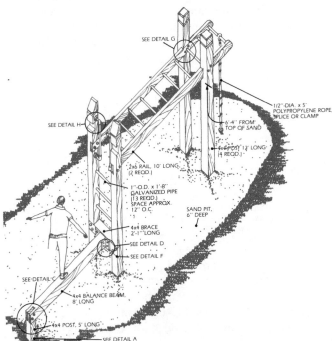

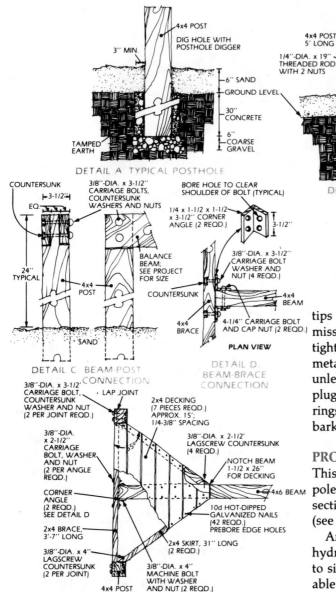

DETAIL A: TYPICAL POSTHOLE

4x4 POST
DIG HOLE WITH
POSTHOLE DIGGER
3" MIN
6" SAND
GROUND LEVEL
30" CONCRETE
6" COARSE GRAVEL
TAMPED EARTH

DETAIL B: BALANCE STEPS

4x4, 4'-6" LONG,
(2 REQD.);
BURY 2'-6" INTO
GROUND
1/4"-DIA. x 9-1/2"
THREADED ROD
WITH 2 NUTS
4x4 POST,
5' LONG
1/4"-DIA. x 19"
THREADED ROD
WITH 2 NUTS
1"-DIA. HOLE x 1"-DEEP
COUNTERBORE (TYPICAL)
4x4, 4' LONG (2 REQD.);
BURY 2'-6" INTO GROUND

DETAIL C: BEAM-POST CONNECTION

COUNTERSUNK
3-1/2"
EQ.
24" TYPICAL
4x4 POST
SAND
3/8"-DIA. x 3-1/2"
CARRIAGE BOLTS,
COUNTERSUNK
WASHERS AND NUTS
BALANCE BEAM;
SEE PROJECT
FOR SIZE
COUNTERSUNK

DETAIL D: BEAM-BRACE CONNECTION

BORE HOLE TO CLEAR
SHOULDER OF BOLT (TYPICAL)
1/4 x 1-1/2 x 1-1/2
x 3-1/2" CORNER
ANGLE (2 REQD.)
3-1/2"
3/8"-DIA. x 3-1/2"
CARRIAGE BOLT
WASHER AND
NUT (4 REQD.)
4x4 BEAM
4x4 BRACE
4-1/4" CARRIAGE BOLT
AND CAP NUT (2 REQD.)
PLAN VIEW

DETAIL E: PLATFORM, PLAN VIEW

3/8"-DIA. x 3-1/2"
CARRIAGE BOLT,
COUNTERSUNK
WASHER AND NUT
(2 PER JOINT REQD.)
LAP JOINT
2x4 DECKING
(7 PIECES REQD.)
APPROX. 15';
1/4-3/8" SPACING
3/8"-DIA.
x 2-1/2"
CARRIAGE
BOLT, WASHER
AND NUT
(2 PER ANGLE
REQD.)
3/8"-DIA. x 2-1/2'
LAGSCREW COUNTERSUNK
(4 REQD.)
NOTCH BEAM
1-1/2 x 26"
FOR DECKING
CORNER
ANGLE
(2 REQD.)
SEE DETAIL D
4x6 BEAM
10d HOT-DIPPED
GALVANIZED NAILS
(42 REQD.)
PREBORE EDGE HOLES
2x4 BRACE,
3'-7" LONG
2x4 SKIRT, 31" LONG
(2 REQD.)
3/8"-DIA. x 4"
LAGSCREW
COUNTERSUNK
(2 PER JOINT)
4x4 POST
3/8"-DIA. x 4"
MACHINE BOLT
WITH WASHER
AND NUT (2 REQD.)

INSTALLING OUTDOOR EQUIPMENT

Heavy wood equipment requires solid anchoring. There are three major concerns in determining adequate anchors: the *stress* to the equipment, the *soil* in which the equipment (posts) is installed and the *frost line* in your area.

A swing set that undergoes torque movement, for example, should be anchored deeper than a slide that doesn't receive this type of stress. A concrete collar in sandy soil should be deeper and wider than a collar in clay soil. Generally, wooden posts for home play equipment are installed 18 to 24 in. deep or to the frost line. Your local building codes can tell you the depth of the frost line in your area.

MAINTAINING PLAY EQUIPMENT

Following is a checklist of spring maintenance tips from the Consumer Product Safety Commission: Clear away debris, roots and rocks; tighten loose nuts, bolts and clamps; oil moving metal parts; sand rusted areas and paint with unleaded paint; replace rusted chains; cap or plug exposed ends of tubing; close S-hooks, rings and links; refill landing pits with sand or bark; and sand splintered areas.

PROJECT 1: BEAM AND POLE

This project incorporates a fireman's pole. The pole top is held in a tee-fitting, to which two sections of pipe curved 90° are also fastened (see detail I).

An electrical contractor with an electric or hydraulic bender can curve sections of pipe cut to size and threaded at the ends. You might be able to create the curved top of the pole with sections of straight pipe and cast 90° elbows.

The drawing gives dimensions of the wood parts. Details A, B, D, E and I give fastener tips.

Begin by cutting the steps (detail B) and posts (detail A) of 4 x 4s. Cut the 2 x 4 brace. Ease all edges, including those on the beam, and make decorative cuts and kerfs. Bore 1½-in.-deep holes for the chinning bar and cut notches for the brace connection on the two major posts. Notch the beam for the decking.

Mark and cut the post that connects to the beam (detail C) with a dado blade on a radial-arm saw. Set the blade to cut a 1⅛-in. depth and cut the post on both sides. Mark the notch to be cut on the beam and bore out both corners of the notch. Cut out the notch with a hand saw and use a sharp chisel to clear out waste.

Set the beam on the post and clamp or tack-nail it; counterbore for the washers and nuts.

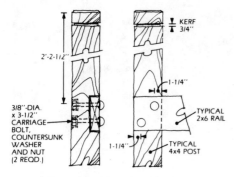

DETAIL G: POST-RAIL CONNECTION

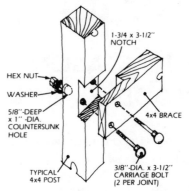

DETAIL F: POST-BRACE CONNECTION

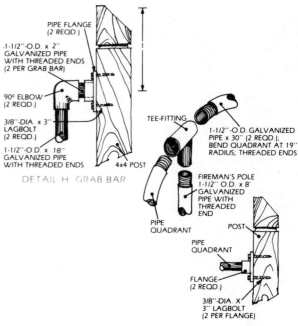

DETAIL H: GRAB BAR

DETAIL I: FIREMAN'S POLE

Then bore through-holes for the carriage bolts. Don't assemble the parts yet.

Counterbore holes in the short post (at the other end) and steps for nuts that hold connecting rods (detail B). Bore holes for the attachment rods. Join the steps with the rods and nuts. Secure the beam to the short post.

Install the chinning bar and platform brace (detail E) on the major posts. Secure the beam to the brace with a corner angle cut to size.

At this point, test-position the assembly. Then dig postholes (detail A) with a clamshell posthole digger. You can use a shovel to dig holes for the steps. Pour gravel into the holes. Position the structure and rock it slightly to seat it on the gravel. Plumb and level, brace if needed, and pour concrete collars.

Next, install the deck skirts and the rough-cut deck members with ¼- to ⅜-in. spaces between them. After installation, snap a chalkline and trim with a combination blade in a circular saw so it just cuts through the decking.

Thread the tee-fitting on to the fireman's pole (detail I). Thread both pipe quadrants onto the tee and into flanges on the other ends. Test-position the pole and dig its hole with a clamshell posthole digger. Install the pole; tamp the backfilled earth. Secure the flanges to the posts. Finally, add 6 in. of sand around the area.

PROJECT 2: BEAM AND LADDER

A number of children can enjoy this design at the same time. The drawing gives dimensions of the wood parts. Details A, C, D, F, G and H give fastening information.

Cut the posts, balance beam, rails and braces to size if needed. Ease the edges and round or chamfer the ends. Make decorative kerfs and cuts in the posts. Cut notches in the posts for the rails (detail G) and brace (detail F). Carefully mark aligned holes for the pipe bars in the rails and posts; bore holes 1 in. deep.

Mark and cut the post that connects to the beam (detail C) and notch the beam (see explanation for making this joint in Project No. 1). Secure the pieces.

Install the pipe bars in the rails and temporarily tack crossbraces on both ends to keep the rails together. Next, install pipe bars in the posts. Temporarily tack a crossbrace near the top pipe and secure the brace that connects to the beam (detail F).

Install the rail assembly onto the posts (detail G), leaving a 7-ft., 8½-in. space between posts. The rail assembly will extend 1 ft., 8½ in. beyond the posts at one end. Join the balance beam to its brace with two corner angles (detail D).

Dig postholes for the footings with a clamshell posthole digger (detail A). Pour gravel into the holes and position the unit, rocking the posts to seat them on the gravel. Plumb and level; brace if needed. Pour in concrete.

Install grab bars (detail H) and secure the polypropylene rope. The rope, which is meant for climbing, can be anchored at the free end or omitted for safety if the play area isn't supervised. Fill the area with 6 in. of sand.

HOW TO SEASON FIREWOOD

To achieve maximum efficiency when burning firewood, it must be properly seasoned.

Researchers at the U.S. Department of Agriculture's Forestry Sciences Lab conducted a study to find the best way of seasoning wood to the ideal 20 percent moisture content. Freshly cut hardwoods have a moisture content ranging from 30 to 55 percent. The researchers tested eight factors that might affect drying time: cutting season, tree species, log length, splitting, stacking method, exposure (in the woods or open), cover and solar assistance. This is what they found out:

Wood cut in the spring, then dried for six months, was only 1 percent wetter than autumn-cut wood seasoned for 12 months. In other words, wood cut around the first of June will be ready for October burning. Dense woods, such as hickory, dried more slowly than light woods. Sugar and red maple were the driest species after 12 months (see chart). Shorter pieces dried slightly faster. Splitting wood was a definite help, yielding 2 to 3 percent more dryness.

Log-stacking formation—parallel versus crisscross—made no difference. On the other hand, wood that was covered usually seasoned

Solar dryer with fiberglass top, particleboard base costs about $40 to build and holds one cord of wood.

better than uncovered wood. Tarpaper-covered wood dried equally well in the woods and in the open.

Two solar drying devices were also tested. A simple cover of clear fiberglass with a black particleboard base (above) produced firewood up to 3 percent drier than wood covered with tarpaper. Another unit (below) dried wood twice as fast. Two summer months in the unit were enough to dry firewood to 19 percent moisture content.

PERCENT OF MOISTURE—FIREWOOD

Species	Fresh Cut	12"	Seasoned* 18"	24"
Ash	31	20	21	24
Beech	42	25	23	23
Birch	40	26	22	23
Black cherry	35	26	22	24
Hickory	32	25	26	26
Red maple	35	13	14	15
Red oak	39	20	22	24
Sugar maple	36	20	19	19
White oak	38	19	23	26
Avg. for all	36	22	21	23

* After 12 months of drying

Logs being seasoned rest on 4 x 4 skids in 2 x 4 framed, plywood-sheathed dryer (above). Interior is flat black and top exterior is white. The front is covered by clear plastic (right). Materials cost $80.

SHOP PROJECTS AND EXPERT KNOW-HOW

PICKING LUMBER

The wood you work determines the result you get—buying wrong can ruin the best craftsmanship.

Do you judge lumber by looks? Walk up to a bin of 1 x 8s and pick out the two or three that please your eye? If you do, you are in the majority. Most people pick out boards by surface appearance, grain and color. They don't know or care whether it is B&H, Sterling or Clear. It doesn't matter whether it is western pine, eastern hemlock or cedar. Appearance should be important in any lumber-buying decision. Yet, knowing how wood is graded, how different species perform, what's commonly stocked in what sizes, and the way lumberyards will or won't serve you could save money—and still get you great wood for your project.

GRADES OF WOOD

Rough lumber is wood as it comes out of the saw. It has loose fibers and saw-tooth marks. Rough wood costs a little less than lumber that is dressed.

Dressed wood is the rough lumber that's been run through a planer. All four of the long sides are smooth.

Worked lumber is any wood shaped for a specific purpose. Tongue-and-groove floorboards are examples, as are grooved paneling and ogee base moldings.

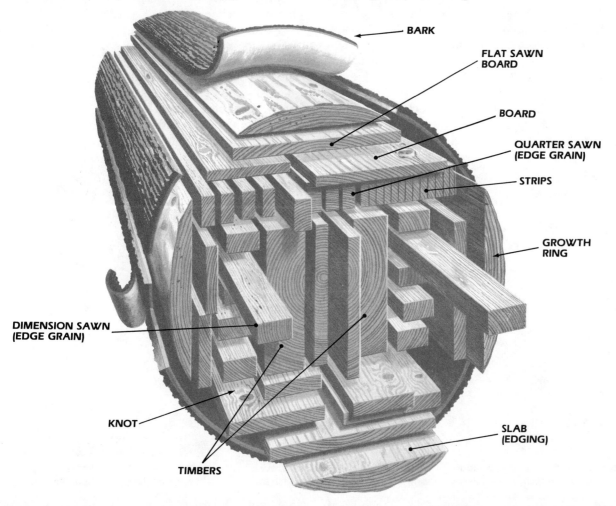

BARK

FLAT SAWN BOARD

BOARD

QUARTER SAWN (EDGE GRAIN)

STRIPS

GROWTH RING

DIMENSION SAWN (EDGE GRAIN)

KNOT

TIMBERS

SLAB (EDGING)

KINDS OF WOOD

There are only two basic kinds of wood: softwood and hardwood. Easily 90 percent of the wood sold is softwood. Cut from conifers (pine, spruce, hemlock and so on), it's the backbone of construction, most projects, home repairs and improvements.

Hardwoods cut from deciduous (leaf-dropping) trees like oak, maple and walnut go into fine furniture, knife handles and cabinetry. As more craftsmen take on these kinds of projects, more yards will stock hardwood. There are also many wood specialty mail-order sources.

SIZES OF WOOD

Actual softwood sizes refer to the dimensions of dressed lumber. A nominal 2 x 4 is very close to 2 in. thick and 4 in. wide when cut from the log. Planed smooth, the numbers come down to 1½ x 3½ in. When you plan a specific project, always work with the actual dimensions of the lumber you'll be using. At that stage, it doesn't matter what the standard sizes are; you care about what you've got.

Measurements for redwood are different, but not by much. Clear, All-Heart and B grades are planed to the same dimensions as other softwoods, but there are two exceptions: A ¾-in.-thick redwood board is surfaced to ¹¹⁄₁₆ in., and an 8-in.-wide board measures 7½ in. instead of 7¼ in. A garden-grade redwood 2 x 4 actually measures 1⁹⁄₁₆ x 3⁹⁄₁₆ in. because it's shaped green and shrinks as it dries.

Hardwood usually is not stocked in easily identifiable sizes at the yards, but check the mail-order houses. If local yards stocked ½-in.

boards, two buyers a year might ask for them. A standard 1-in. board can be planed to satisfy any customers requiring differing thicknesses.

BUYING LUMBER

Lumber is offered in even-numbered widths and lengths. If you want a 1 x 7, the yard will rip a 1 x 8, charge you for the 1 x 8, add a cutting charge and give you the sliced-off strip—or you can take home the 1 x 8 and rip it yourself.

Charges for cutting and planing are not consistent. Some yards tack on a small charge for each pass through the saw or planer. Others give you the first few cuts free, and some may cut to length free. Suburban and rural yards rarely cut lumber to project specs. Some city yards, catering to apartment-dwellers who often have no space for power tools, saw to a fraction of an inch.

LUMBER LANGUAGE

A *board* describes any lumber less than 2 in. thick and 1 in. or more wide. A board less than 6 in. wide is called a *strip. Dimension lumber*, the backbone of house construction, includes pieces from 2 in. thick up to but not including 5 in. thick, and 2 in. wide or more. *Timbers* are heavy structural members. Their smallest dimension in any direction is 5 in.

Reduced to essentials, a good-looking piece of wood *grades* high, a scruffy one, low. Top grades are clear, showing few tiny knots or none at all. High grades have no checks, splits or blemishes. As boards come lower on the grade scale, allowable knots become progressively larger, and other imperfections increase in size, number and importance.

Intergrown knot, also called tight or red, was a branch that grew into trunk.

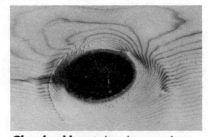

Checked knot shrank unevenly as wood dried, creating cracks along its grain.

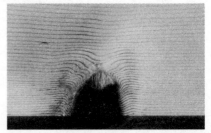

Spike knot was cut nearly parallel to the grain of the branch, weakening board.

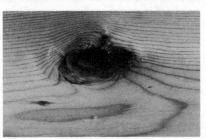

Unsound knot has surface damage, but it's tight and weakens timbers very little.

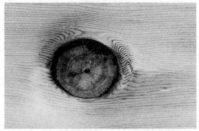

Encased knot is not firmly fixed. It's formed by an embedded branch stub.

Sloughed knot was outer section of spike knot that separated near the edge.

Machine burn leaves a black, charred mark that can usually be sanded out.

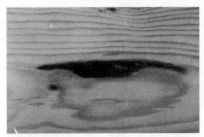

Pitch pocket is a seam or streak that holds or once held solid or liquid resin.

Wane is bark or missing wood along the edge of a board cut too near log surface.

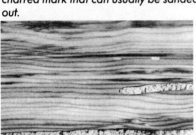

Grub holes bored by insects while tree was alive weaken and mar finished board.

Peck are pockets of dry rot in living trees. They are mostly in cedar and cypress.

Compressed wood is on low side of leaning softwood tree. It can be brittle.

WHEN GRAIN IS IMPORTANT

Graining counts if you're buying wood for a fancy project. Boards for an edge-glued tabletop must be perfect. First, you want good looks. Second, you need a *straight-grained* board cut at right angles to the growth rings in the log. These *quarter-sawn* boards are more dimensionally sta-ble as humidity changes. A *face-grain* board, displaying long loops of grain on the widest wood surface, is *plain*-sawn, cut near the edge of the log on a tangent with the growth rings. It may show pretty grain patterns, but it's more apt to warp or change size as humidity changes.

WOOD SELECTION CHART

A = High   B = Medium   C = Low

Species	Ease Of Working	Freedom From Warpage	Heartwood Resists Decay	Bending Strength	Stiffness	Strength As A Post	No. Of Knots	No. Of Other Defects
White Ash	C	B	C	A	A	A	C	B
Western Red Cedar	A	A	A	C	C	B	C	C
Eastern Red Cedar	B	A	A	B	C	A	A	C
Cherry	C	A	A	A	A	A	C	*
Cypress	B	B	A	B	B	B	C	B
Douglas Fir	C	B	B	A	A	A	B	B
Eastern Hemlock	B	B	C	B	B	B	B	A
Western Hemlock	B	B	C	B	B	B	B	B
Hickory	C	B	C	A	A	A	B	B
Western Larch	C	B	B	A	A	A	A	A
Hard Maple	C	B	C	A	A	A	B	B
Soft Maple	C	B	C	C	C	C	C	C
Red Oak	C	B	C	A	A	B	C	B
White Oak	C	B	A	A	A	B	C	B
Ponderosa Pine	A	A	C	C	C	C	B	B
Southern Yellow Pine	C	B	C	A	A	A	C	B
Northern White Pine	A	A	C	C	C	C	A	B
Sugar Pine	A	A	C	C	C	C	A	B
Idaho White Pine	A	A	C	B	B	B	A	A
Redwood	B	A	A	B	B	A	C	C
Eastern Spruce	B	A	C	B	B	B	A	B
Sitka Spruce	B	A	C	B	A	B	B	B
Engelmann Spruce	B	A	C	C	C	C	A	B
Walnut	B	A	A	A	A	A	C	C

*Depends on use

WHAT IS WOOD?

Knowing how wood behaves could make your next project look better, build easier and last longer. Here's the inside story.

Wood is common and familiar, yet it is a very complex substance. Although wood has been a basic necessity of the human race from the beginning of time, we have come to use wood routinely each day without much awareness of its intricate nature, and its complicated and sometimes troublesome properties.

But for those of us who work with wood, success requires a fundamental familiarity with its physical structure. This helps us understand its basic working properties and characteristics— why some woods are hard and others soft, which woods can be nailed easily and which woods split, or why some woods have striking patterns while others are plain.

GROWTH PATTERN OF WOOD

Most of the lumber and veneer we use comes from the stem or trunk of the tree, where over many years the wood has formed concentric layers, or growth rings, or permanent cells. In the temperate zones, where the growing season is interrupted annually by winter dormancy, each annual ring of wood is evident when the inner, first-formed cell mass called the *early-wood* is visibly distinct from the outer, last-

This block of Douglas fir shows how differently growth rings appear on radial (R), tangential (T) and cross-sectional (X) surfaces.

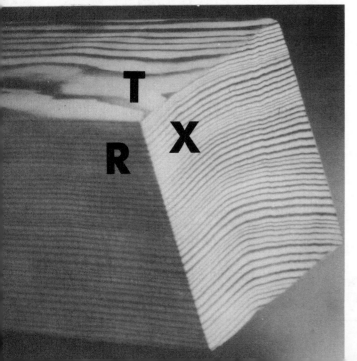

formed *latewood.* Woods like basswood that have little or no contrast between earlywood and latewood are said to be *even-grained.* Woods such as Douglas fir having a pronounced earlywood/latewood contrast are *uneven-grained* woods.

As the tree matures and increases in girth, the cells at the central region of the stem cease to conduct sap and become permanently inactive. The outer *sapwood* of this central core is transformed into *heartwood.*

In some species, the transition to heartwood is accompanied by the formation of materials called *extractives* in the cell walls. These extractives are sometimes pigmented, giving heartwood a distinctive color, such as the deep purple of eastern red cedar or the rich brown of black walnut. When extractives are toxic to fungi, the heartwood may have significant decay resistance, as does redwood and chestnut.

It is important to remember that wood is an aggregate of countless cells, as many as several million per cubic inch. Each cell is a cylindrical unit, up to 100 times longer than its diameter. In the standing tree, more than 90 percent of the cells run vertically. Sometimes, *longitudinal cells* are large enough to be seen with the unaided eye.

The orientation of the longitudinal cells gives wood its very important *grain direction.* Wood is many times stronger parallel to the grain direction than perpendicular to it. Therefore, wood splits along the grain by fracturing the longitudinal cells lengthwise or tearing them apart laterally. Similarly, nail splits or seasoning checks run parallel to the grain.

A small percentage of the cells in wood are elongated horizontally in the tree, arranged in narrow ribbon-like bands called *rays* extending radially from the bark inward toward the pith. All woods have rays, but in most they are too tiny to see without magnification. Because of the structure of the horizontal cellular rays and the growth rings, the properties of wood may be different in the tangential (parallel to rings) and the radial (perpendicular to rings) directions. For example, wood shrinks and swells about twice as much tangentially as radially.

DENSITY OF WOOD

Density (weight per unit volume) is the single most important indicator of the strength of wood. By knowing its density you can predict such characteristics as hardness, ease of machining and nailing resistance of a particular species. Dense woods generally shrink and swell more and present greater problems in drying. The densest woods also have the greatest fuel value.

The table lists the density expressed as specific gravity—the ratio of the weight of a body to the weight of an equal volume of water—for a number of species commonly used by woodworkers. There is a 12-fold range in density from less dense balsa to very dense lignum vitae. This gives you a good idea of the wide range of properties among the various woods.

SELECTING WOOD FOR SHOP WORK

Functional requirements of a finished project may influence the selection of wood on the basis of its density and related properties. Woods as soft as balsa are limited to uses such as model-making, pinning boards and novelties, where the surface hardness is not a factor. Low-density hardwoods such as basswood, aspen and cottonwood are worked easily with hand tools and can be nailed without splitting, yet they lack the minimal surface hardness for routine furniture uses. Slightly denser woods, such as yellow poplar and chestnut, are sometimes used for furniture, but more often as an interior or secondary wood.

It is easy to understand why mahogany, teak, black walnut and black cherry have been traditional favorites of the cabinetmaker. In addition to their rich color and pleasing figure, the density range of these woods is a happy compromise suited to most woodcrafting—hard enough to serve the needs of most furniture uses, yet not so hard that the wood can't be worked with hand tools. Woods in this range cannot be fastened with nails or screws without preboring holes, but tradition has devised joinery methods such as mortise-and-tenons, doweled joints and dovetailed joints.

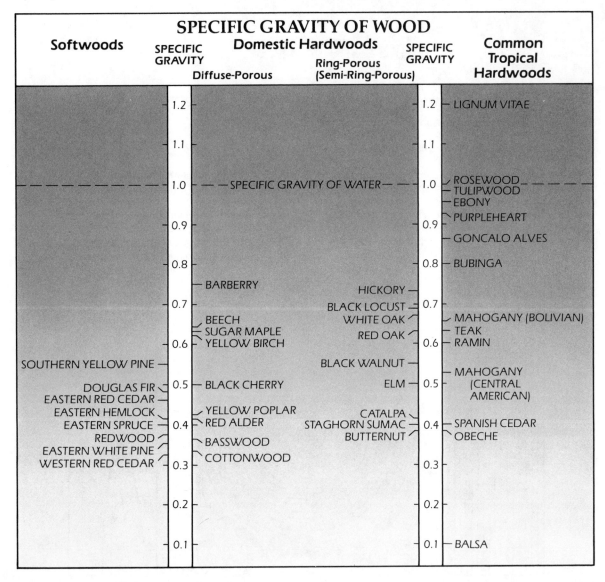

SPECIFIC GRAVITY OF WOOD

Softwoods	SPECIFIC GRAVITY	Domestic Hardwoods Diffuse-Porous	Ring-Porous (Semi-Ring-Porous)	SPECIFIC GRAVITY	Common Tropical Hardwoods
	1.2			1.2	LIGNUM VITAE
	1.1			1.1	
	1.0	— SPECIFIC GRAVITY OF WATER —		1.0	ROSEWOOD / TULIPWOOD / EBONY
	0.9			0.9	PURPLEHEART / GONCALO ALVES
	0.8			0.8	BUBINGA
	0.7	BARBERRY	HICKORY / BLACK LOCUST / WHITE OAK / RED OAK	0.7	MAHOGANY (BOLIVIAN) / TEAK
	0.6	BEECH / SUGAR MAPLE / YELLOW BIRCH		0.6	RAMIN
SOUTHERN YELLOW PINE			BLACK WALNUT		MAHOGANY (CENTRAL AMERICAN)
DOUGLAS FIR / EASTERN RED CEDAR	0.5	BLACK CHERRY	ELM	0.5	
EASTERN HEMLOCK / EASTERN SPRUCE / REDWOOD / EASTERN WHITE PINE / WESTERN RED CEDAR	0.4	YELLOW POPLAR / RED ALDER / BASSWOOD / COTTONWOOD	CATALPA / STAGHORN SUMAC / BUTTERNUT	0.4	SPANISH CEDAR / OBECHE
	0.3			0.3	
	0.2			0.2	
	0.1			0.1	BALSA

SOFTWOOD CELL STRUCTURE

Eastern White Pine

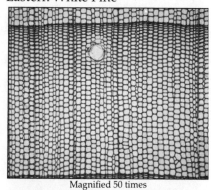

Magnified 50 times

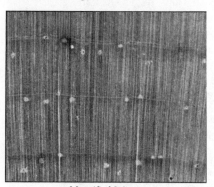

Magnified 8 times

Southern Yellow Pine

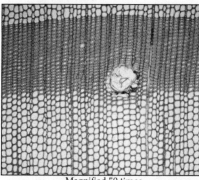

Magnified 50 times

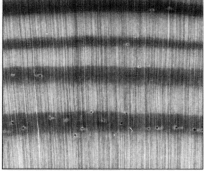

Magnified 8 times

Even-grained eastern white pine shows little contrast from earlywood to latewood. Uneven-grained southern yellow pine, however, shows dramatic cellular contrast.

The pattern on the surface of a board varies according to the orientation of the growth rings and the degree of earlywood/latewood contrast within the growths. For example, a board which is cut radially across the growth rings, or edge-grained (left), is characterized by parallel ring lines. The board presents a uniform surface for working. It wears relatively evenly when used as stair treads or as flooring. On the other hand, a board which is cut tangentially to the growth rings, or flat-sawn (right), typically has ellipses, V- or U-shaped markings on its surface. In a flat-sawn board having significant earlywood/latewood contrast, the surface might wear unevenly. It is more difficult to smooth a flat-sawn board without scouring out the softer earlywood than it is to smooth an edge-grained board.

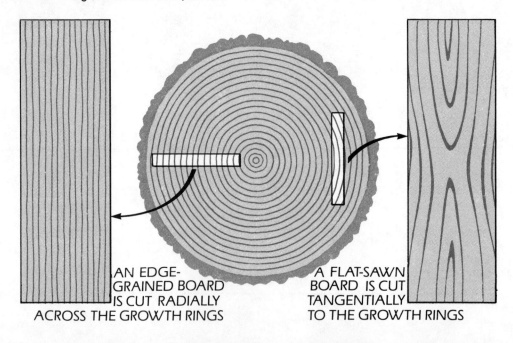

AN EDGE-
GRAINED BOARD
IS CUT RADIALLY
ACROSS THE GROWTH RINGS

A FLAT-SAWN
BOARD IS CUT
TANGENTIALLY
TO THE GROWTH RINGS

HARDWOOD CELL STRUCTURE

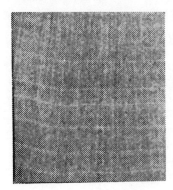  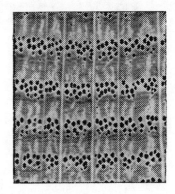

Magnified 8 times

Red Oak   Butternut   Basswood

A ring-porous wood (left) typically is uneven-grained and uneven in its working properties. A diffuse-porous wood (right) typically is even-grained and uniform. The pore distribution in semi-ring-porous wood such as butternut (center) may produce a striking figure, but usually the wood will not have uneven properties.

The highest-density groups of our native hardwoods—including birch, beech, sugar maple, ash, oak and hickory—are well suited to the most demanding uses. They are ideal for production woodworking with machine tools where a strong and durable product must result, as in the posts, legs, stretchers and backs of chairs.

An important message conveyed by the density chart is how misleading the familiar terms *hardwood* and *softwood* really are—the range of hardwood density extends below as well as above the densities of softwoods.

SOFTWOOD AND HARDWOOD

Trees designated as softwoods are within the *gymnosperm* group of seed plants, in the order *Coniferales.* That is why softwood trees are broadly termed *conifers.* These trees are characterized by needlelike or scale-like foliage which usually is evergreen.

The wood of the higher-density softwood species is strong for its weight, yet soft enough to be nailed and worked easily with hand tools. The large tree size and straight stem form yield the desired long lengths needed for structural lumber in buildings.

Some hardwoods have appropriate density and stem form to yield structural material. As examples, yellow poplar and chestnut were commonly used for building components. We usually associate hardwoods, however, with cabinetry, joinery and other uses where the shorter pieces of clear wood can be used, and where the more attractive colors and higher density provide desired beauty and functional properties to the finished items.

The relative earlywood/latewood contrast—or unevenness of the grain—is the most impor-tant factor in producing figure in softwoods. The darker latewood stands out against the lighter earlywood. When a softwood surface is wiped with a dark pigment stain, however, the stain will be taken up more heavily by the earlywood cells. Then the earlywood may become darker than latewood.

In some hardwoods such as oak, ash, elm and chestnut, large pores are concentrated in the earlywood, with distinctly smaller pores in the latewood. Such woods are said to be *ring-porous.* Ring-porous woods are usually uneven-grained. Depending on the function of the item, this can be an asset or a disadvantage.

Most of the volume of wood in typical conifers is the result of a single longitudinal cell type called a *tracheid.* In the earlywood, the tracheids are largest in diameter and very thin-walled. In the latewood, the tracheids are flattened and have thicker walls, resulting in denser wood. Tracheids determine both the unevenness of density and overall density of the wood. Hardwoods have a more complex cell structure than conifers. Through evolution, more highly specialized cell types have developed: On the one extreme there are large, thin-walled *vessel cells* for conduction; on the other extreme there are minute thick-walled *fibers* to provide mechanical strength to the tree. Among hardwoods, the overall density of a species depends on the relative numbers and sizes of the vessels and of the relative cell-wall thickness of the fibers. The uniformity of density is largely determined by the size and distribution of the vessels within each growth ring.

The vessel openings are called *pores* (see cross-sectional views). A wide range of pore sizes is represented among hardwoods. (Softwoods are said to be nonporous.)

PLYWOOD AND OTHER BUILDING PANELS

Examine the broad range of building panels so you can select the right type for your needs.

The original plywood design of cross-laminated wood veneers (plies) has changed little since 1905 when plywood was created in St. John,

Ore. But the plywood industry itself has grown into a large, diversified family of specialty building products, including reconstituted wood panels made from wood chips, wafers and strands.

This is a discussion of the wide variety of building panels and an explanation of their uses. Because of the many panels, it's important to select the right one for the job. The plywood and building panels discussed here are products you're most likely to find at local lumberyards and home centers. These are the most common products for typical home construction and furniture-making. In addition to using the infor-

Construction of a typical home, as shown here, requires several different plywoods and reconstituted wood panels. These panels are used in nearly every phase of construction, from roof and wall sheathing to furniture and cabinetry.

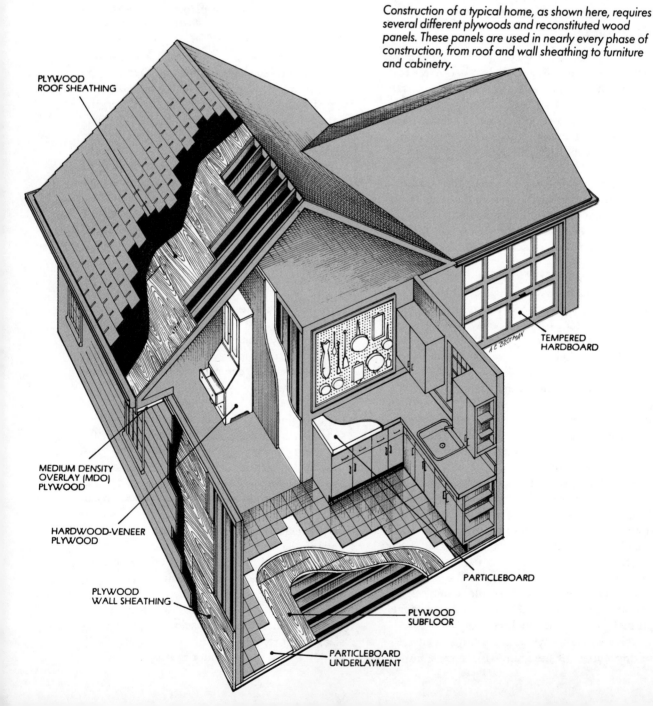

PLYWOOD ROOF SHEATHING

MEDIUM DENSITY OVERLAY (MDO) PLYWOOD

HARDWOOD-VENEER PLYWOOD

PLYWOOD WALL SHEATHING

PARTICLEBOARD UNDERLAYMENT

PLYWOOD SUBFLOOR

PARTICLEBOARD

TEMPERED HARDBOARD

TYPICAL PLYWOOD CONSTRUCTION

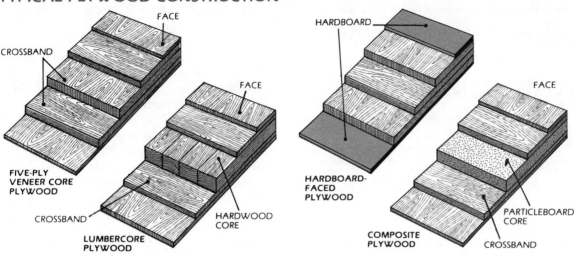

FACE

CROSSBAND

FACE

FIVE-PLY
VENEER CORE
PLYWOOD

CROSSBAND

HARDWOOD
CORE

LUMBERCORE
PLYWOOD

HARDBOARD

HARDBOARD-
FACED
PLYWOOD

FACE

COMPOSITE
PLYWOOD

PARTICLEBOARD
CORE

CROSSBAND

Cross lamination of veneers gives plywood its strength. The grain of the crossband runs at right angles to the adjacent plies.

mation here, contact the manufacturers in the source list for product specifications.

PLYWOODS

Softwood-veneer plywood is the panel most widely used for construction and industrial applications. It's made with an odd number of cross-laminated softwood veneers such as pine, fir, spruce and hemlock. The cross-lamination of veneers—wood grains running at right angles to each other—gives plywood its strength.

Plywood is graded by the quality of the veneer used for the face and back surfaces, and by the type of adhesive used to bond the veneers into panels. The highest-quality veneer grades are N and A. These veneers provide smooth, defect-free surfaces. The minimum grade veneers are C and D (see veneer grade marking chart).

During manufacture, wood veneers are bonded together with an adhesive under a hot press. Depending on the adhesive used, the plywood is graded either interior or exterior. Interior-grade plywood is made with a moisture-resistant glue for use indoors. Exterior plywood is manufactured with a 100 percent waterproof glue.

Certain structural plywoods (and reconstituted panels) are categorized by the American Plywood Association (APA) as performance-rated panels. Such panels carry a stamp indicating the maximum center-to-center spacing of supports, such as wall studs or floor joists, over which the panel should be placed. For example, a panel rated 24/16 can be used as roof or wall sheathing over rafters or studs spaced 24 in. apart. The same panel can also be used for floor

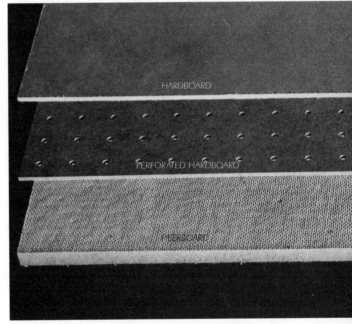

Here are three nonveneered, reconstituted wood panels. The two hardboards have smooth, hard faces. Fiberboard has a soft, screened face, but is strong enough for wall sheathing.

decking over joists 16 in. on center.

Standard size for softwood-veneer plywood is 4 x 8 ft., as for most building panels. Common thicknesses are ¼, ⅜, ½, ⅝ and ¾ in.

Hardwood-veneer plywood is a high-quality interior panel used typically in furniture and cabinet construction. The face and back plies are made of hardwood veneer. The inner plies, or core, are softwood. The most popular hardwood-veneer plywoods are birch, oak, lauan mahogany, walnut and ash. Standard thick-

PLYWOOD GRADE GUIDE

Veneer Grade

Grade Marking	Face	Inner piles	Back	Typical Uses
A-A Interior	A	D	A	Interior cabinet and furniture construction. Applications where both sides are visible.
A-B Interior	A	D	B	Same uses as A-A except that the back side is somewhat less attractive.
A-D Interior	A	D	D	Interior furniture construction and paneling where one side is not visible.
Under-layment	C plugged	D	D	Often called PTS (plugged and touch-sanded). Used as an underlayment for carpet, tile and other finished flooring.
A-A Exterior	A	C	A	Top quality exterior panel for storage sheds, patio furniture and boat interiors.
A-C Exterior	A	C	C	Good quality exterior panel for cabinets and shelters when one side is not visible.
B-C Exterior	B	C	C	Moderately priced rough work panel. Used for storage racks and pet shelters.
C-D Plugged/ exterior	C plugged	D	D	Commonly known as CDX. Rough exterior panel used for roof and wall sheathing.
Marine	A or B	B	A or B	High quality panel used for boats and fine crafted exterior shelters and cabinets.

nesses are the same as softwood-veneer plywood.

Lumbercore plywood is the highest-quality panel. Its face and back are hardwood veneers laminated to a core of solid hardwood strips. It's used in furniture and cabinet construction, mostly for desks and tabletops. Lumbercore plywood is available in standard and 4 x 10-ft. panels. Common thicknesses are ½, ¾ and 1 in.

Medium-density overlay (MDO) is an exterior plywood veneered with an opaque resin-treated fiber overlay. The tough, supersmooth overlay surface is highly suited for painting. MDO is generally used for exterior signs and soffits. In addition, because of the smooth overlay surface and the high-quality veneer core, MDO is a popular choice for building both interior and exterior cabinets. An MDO exterior plywood siding is also available.

High-density overlay (HDO) is an exterior plywood manufactured with an abrasion-resistant, resin-impregnated fiber overlay that provides an extremely hard, smooth surface. HDO is similar to MDO in uses, but it's tougher.

HDO is most commonly used for concrete forms. The overlay allows HDO panels to strip from hardened concrete surfaces without coming apart. It's also an excellent panel for exterior signs, countertops and workbenches. Both HDO and MDO plywood are available in common thicknesses: ⅜, ½, ⅝ and ¾ in.

Plyron is a trade name for plywood panels manufactured with a hardboard face and back. The tough hardboard surface permits Plyron to be used as a workbench top and for utility cabinets, doors and underlayment. It's available in interior and exterior grade in common thicknesses: ½, ⅝ and ¾.

Plywood siding is used when the natural beauty of wood is desired. Sidings are available in a broad range of veneer face grades and in several surface patterns and texture combinations.

Many plywood sidings are rated as structural panels and can be applied directly over studs. But check with the local building code before using plywood siding as wall sheathing. Plywood siding comes in ¹¹⁄₃₂, ⅜, ½ ¹⁹⁄₃₂ and ⅝-in. thicknesses.

RECONSTITUTED WOOD PANELS

Particleboard is the most widely used reconstituted wood product. This nonveneered panel is made from wood chips bonded with resins under heat and pressure.

The two most common types of particleboard are industrial grade and underlayment. Industrial particleboard is a high-quality, fine-finish panel used in furniture and cabinets and as countertops under plastic laminate.

Use underlayment particleboard over a subfloor and under carpet or tile. It comes in ½-, ⅝- and ¾-in. thicknesses.

Waferboard is a nonveneered structural panel made from wood wafers as opposed to particles or strands. Common uses include wall and roof sheathing, subflooring and underlayment. The distinctive wafer pattern has made waferboard a popular choice for cabinets, storage bins, paneling and craft projects. Waferboard sheets are available in ⁷⁄₁₆-, ½-, ⅝- and ¾-in. thicknesses.

Oriented strand board (OSB) is similar to waferboard, with two exceptions: OSB is made from thin wood strands instead of wide wafers, and the strands are mechanically arranged, or oriented, in perpendicular layers. The strands are then bonded with a phenolic resin.

Use OSB in the same applications as waferboard. But, because of the oriented strands, OSB is considered to be one of the strongest reconstituted panel products. OSB is available in standard 4 x 8 sheets; larger panels up to 8 x 24 can be specially ordered. Common thicknesses are ¼, ⅜, ⁷⁄₁₆, ½, ¹⁹⁄₃₂, ⅝, ²³⁄₃₂ and ¾ in.

Hardwood is a stiff, high-impact panel manufactured from refined wood fibers. The fibers are interlocked into a mat and compressed by heavy rollers into thin, hard sheets.

Hardwood (a well-known brand is Masonite) is available in three basic types: service, standard and tempered. Service hardboard is an interior panel that is used where low weight is important and high strength is not necessary, such as for cabinet backs. Select standard hardboard when high strength and good finishing qualities are required. Use it in furniture and as interior paneling and door skins.

Tempered hardboard is standard hardboard in which chemicals and heat-treating processes have been added to improve stiffness, hardness and finishing properties. Use tempered hardboard for exterior applications such a soffits, shutters and garage door panels.

Perforated hardboard, such as Pegboard, is available with closely spaced holes punched through the panel for accepting small hooks and brackets.

Hardboard is commonly available in ¹⁄₁₆-, ⅛- and ¼-in. thicknesses.

Fiberboard is a nonveneered structural panel made of individual wood fibers molded into durable sheets. This versatile product, also known as grayboard, is used as carpet underlayment, sound deadening panel, exterior siding, wall sheathing and as a protective floor cover-up.

Standard fiberboard panels measure 4 x 8 ft. But the Homasote Co. also offers fiberboard in 4 x 10, 4 x 12 and 8 x 12-ft. sheets. Panel thicknesses are ½ and ⅝ in.

Composite plywood is a softwood-veneer-faced panel with a reconstituted wood core made of either particleboard or oriented strand board. Composite plywood, known by the trade name Comply, is used virtually anywhere softwood-veneer plywood is used. Standard panel size for composite plywood is the same as softwood-veneer plywood.

SOURCE LIST
PLYWOOD AND BUILDING PANELS

American Hardboard Assn., 887-B Wilmette Rd., Palatine, Ill. 60067.
American Plywood Assn., Box 11700, Tacoma, Wash. 98411.
Elmendorf Board Corp., RFD 2, River Rd., Claremont, N.H. 03743.
Georgia-Pacific Corp., 133 Peach Tree St. N.E., Atlantic, Ga. 30303.
Hardwood Plywood Manufacturers Assn., Box 2789, 1825 Michael Faraday Dr., Reston, Va. 22090.
Homasote Co., Box 7240, West Trenton, N.J. 08628.
Louisiana-Pacific Corp., 1300 Southwest Fifth Ave., Portland, Ore. 97201.
National Particleboard Assn., 2306 Perkins Pl., Silver Spring, Md. 20910.
Potlatch Corp., 1 Maritime Plaza, Alcoa Building, Clay and Front Sts., San Francisco, Calif. 94111.
Weyerhaeuser Co., Box B, Tacoma, Wash. 98477.

Here are five methods of constructing wood panels (from the top): all veneer plywood, veneer with particleboard core, compressed wafers, compressed or oriented strands, and small wood particles formed into large, flat sheets.

PLYWOOD EDGE TREATMENTS

Here are ways to hide the laminated edges of plywood. Some are simple, others a bit more involved, but all have worked well.

Hardwood-veneer plywood is a great construction material with many advantages over solid hardwood. Among them are ease of fabricating large projects, great dimensional stability, resistance to splitting and warping, and near equal strength in both directions. These advantages are the result of the makeup of the panels: thin layers of wood bonded together with their grains running at right angles to each other. It is just this structure, however, that causes plywood's one major drawback: The exposed edges are unsightly and must be concealed.

Adhesive-backed hardwood veneer tape is applied directly to edge with a few passes of a hot clothing iron.

For curved edges, where using an iron to apply adhesive backed veneer tape is impractical, use plain hardwood veneer tape instead. It is attached with contact cement.

If you want to cover the edge of a plywood piece that must be rabbeted, be sure to apply veneer tape before rabbeting. Otherwise, overall length dimension will be off.

Solid-wood edging is stronger than veneer tape, so it's better for edges that get heavy use. Glue and tack-nail in place with two brads, then "clamp" with masking tape.

Solid-wood bands can also be let into edge by first cutting a groove with dado blades. You can leave only the face veneer on both sides or double accent line as shown above.

Panels can be joined with deep rabbets and glue so face veneer covers matching edges. If only two pieces are joined, joint is weak; if third is added as shown, joint is okay.

For tabletops, cover edges with thick molded boards that have mitered corners and a deep rabbet cut in the top edge. The rabbet increases gluing surface for more strength.

A V-shaped solid-wood strip glued into a V-groove cut in the panel yields a well-concealed edge. Cut groove in two passes using a table or radial-arm saw with blade at 45°.

To conceal edges without adding anything to them, use a splined miter joint and glue. A good spline for ¾-in.-thick stock is a ½-in.-wide piece of ⅛-in.-thick plywood.

If edges will be painted, two coats of diluted yellow glue can conceal them. Ratio is 1 part water to 4 parts glue. Sand edges smooth beforehand and after glue dries.

DRY ROT AND WOOD

A great enemy of wood exposed to the elements is dry rot. Its onset often goes undetected until the wood is so badly damaged that large parts of the structure have to be rebuilt.

WHAT IS DRY ROT?

Rot (wood decay) is caused by microscopic, plantlike fungi that grow within the wood and attack the cell walls. The fungi thrive in a wet/damp environment and will grow and develop only when the moisture content of the wood is greater than 20 percent. Musty odors and white staining on wood are also the result of fungi, although not the type that causes rot. Since rot can develop only in wet wood, the term "dry rot" is a misnomer. It evolved because wood that is in an advanced stage of rot, when dry, will crumble and break into small cubes.

WOOD RESEARCH YIELDS SECRETS OF DRY ROT

New research in Britain, reported in the journal *New Scientist*, may provide some answers to dry rot. Dry rot is caused by a fungus called *Serpula lacrymans*. The British researchers say these spores multiply faster than rabbits—a reproducing sample of the fungus can produce 50 million serpulae per minute for several days. The offspring in turn multiply as fast. Once dry rot begins, it can spread at lightning speeds.

Preventive measures include applying generous helpings of laundry bleach to the wood several times a year—at least once each season.

Spraying fungicides around the edges and corners of wood will also stave off the fungus. Wood, the researchers say, should be inspected regularly. At the first sign of dry rot, the affected wood should be cut away and the entire structure sprayed with fungicide.

TREATING DRY ROT IN A CRAWL SPACE

To treat dry rot in a crawl space, you must dry out the crawl space, or at least minimize the moisture buildup. By controlling the moisture in the crawl space, you will eliminate further rot deterioration of the wood framing. If you can't penetrate the beams beyond a fingernail, they are still structurally adequate. If an ice pick or screw driver penetrates them easily, they should be replaced.

The dampness in the crawl space is the result of condensation and seepage. Normally, you can control condensation by installing ventilation openings on all sides of the crawl space and covering the dirt floor with plastic sheets, overlapping the joints.

A formula for determining the total square footage of needed vent openings is $T = (6L+A) / 300$, where L is the perimeter of the crawl space in linear feet and A is the area of the crawl space in square feet: T represents the total square footage of vent openings needed. A dehumidifier can also help control moisture.

If the crawl space gets wet because of water penetration, you must locate the source of the water and eliminate it. Faulty gutters and downspouts, a high water table and leakage through foundation walls are some causes. Correcting the problem requires regrading around the house, redirecting downspouts away from the foundation, installing a sump pump and perforated drain tiles, or sealing foundation walls. Sometimes, all four steps are needed to dry the crawl space.

CONVERT A MATERIALS LIST TO A BUYING LIST

Careful planning of your lumber purchases from a materials list can save you money.

Most project materials lists are not lumber shopping lists. You've got to translate the materials list into a certain number of 1 x 10s by so many feet long, and so on.

Converting the materials list taken directly from the plans into a lumber-buying list serves two purposes. It produces your shopping list and lets you figure out exactly how you're going to cut and assemble the project.

Keeping in mind that wood is sold in even-numbered lengths and widths, start making your list by writing the materials required for each part in one column and the standard stock measurements closest to these numbers in the second column. Leave room for a third column for your actual order.

Using the in-the-wall workshop project as an example, you see the first item calls for four boards ¾ x 11⅛ x 76 in. The closest standard lumberyard size is ¾ x 12 x 96 in. (8 ft. long). This goes in the second column.

The third column becomes your actual order. The first two items are for ¾ x 12-in. boards. You could order four 8-ft. lengths for the first entry and three more for the second. Or, you could cover both with four 12-ft. lengths. Compare prices. At one yard, seven 8-ft. ¾ x 12s cost $81.20 in clear, all-heart redwood KD (kiln dried). Four 12-footers are $75.20.

MATERIALS LIST
IN-THE-WALL-WORKSHOP

Key	No.	Size and description (use)
		CABINETS (2)
A	4	¾ x 11⅛ x 78″ redwood (cabinet side)
B	11	¾ x 11⅛ x 22¼″ redwood (top, bottom, shelves)
B1	1	¾ x 8 x 22¼″ redwood (hinge shelf)
C	1	½ x 3 x 21⅞″ hardwood (hinge cleat)
D	2	¾ x 23¼ x 76″ redwood, edge-joined (back panel)
E	1	1½ x 3 x 45″ redwood (base front)
E1	2	1½ x 3 x 8″ redwood (base sides)
F	2	¾ x 1¼ x 21⅞″ redwood (rail)
G	2	¼ x 20 x 37″ oak plywood (tabletop veneer)
G1	1	¾ x 20 x 37″ fir plywood (tabletop core)
G2	2	11/16 x 1¼ x 37⅛″ redwood (edging)
G3	1	11/16 x 1¼ x 20″ redwood (edging)
H	2	¾ x 3½ x 32⅛″ redwood (legs)
H1	4	¾ x 3½ x 21″ redwood (braces)
I	1	¾ x 3″-dia. redwood (gravity stay top)
I1	1	⅜″-dia. x 3″ hardwood dowel (gravity stay pin)
J	2	1½ (open) x 72¾″ continuous hinge (for doors)
J1	1	1½ (open) x 21″ continuous hinge (for tabletop)
		DOORS (2)
K	4	¾ x 5 5/16 x 76″ redwood (door side)
L	13	¾ x 5 5/16 x 22¼″ redwood (top, bottom, shelves)
M	2	¾ x 23¼ x 76″ redwood, edge-joined (door front)
N	2	¾ x 1¼ x 21⅞″ redwood (rail)
O	2	⅛ x 21⅝ x 28⅛″ Peg-Board
P	6	⅜ x 11/16 x 27⅝″ furring strip (Peg-Board frame)
P1	4	⅜ x 11/16 x 21⅞″ furring strip (Peg-Board frame)
Q	2	¾ x 1 x 2½″ redwood (catch plate block)
Q1	2	Heavy-duty magnetic catches
R	2	Brass door handles, Amerock No. BP 302BB

Misc.: Carpenter's glue, 8d common nails (to attach cabinet backs), 1½″ No. 8 fh screws (to attach shelves), 1″ No. 6 fh brass screws (to attach table hinge to shelf B1), 2″ No. 14 fh screws (4, to secure unit), ⅛ x ½″-dia. wood plugs, ⅛ x ½ x 76″ plywood splines, 1 standard electrical outlet box, ¼ x 3¼″ capscrew with washer and nut (for installing lamp bracket).

Note: Use nominal ¾″ clear all-heart KD redwood (actual dimension: 11/18″). Other lumber as noted.

No.	Materials List (in.)	Stock Lumber Nearest in Size	Lumber Order
4	¾ x 11⅛ x 78	¾ x 12″ x 8′	(4) ¾ x 12″ x 12′
11	¾ x 11⅛ x 22¼	¾ x 12″ x 2′	
1	¾ x 8 x 22¼	¾ x 10″ x 2′	(1) ¾ x 10″ x 2′
1	½ x 3 x 21⅞ (hardwood)	½ x 4″ x 2′	(1) ½ x 4″ x 2′ (hardwood)
2	¾ x 23¼ x 76	¾ x 10″ x 8′ ¾ x 10″ x 8′ ¾ x 6″ x 8′ (edge-glued)	(See order A below) (See order B below)
1	1½ x 3 x 45	1½ x 4″ x 4′	(1) 1½ x 4″ x 6′
2	1½ x 3 x 8	1½ x 4″ x 1′	
2 2 1 2 4	¾ x 1¼ x 21⅞ 11/16 x 1¼ x 37⅞ 11/16 x 1¼ x 20 ¾ x 3¼ x 32⅛ ¾ x 3½ x 21	¾ x 2″ x 2′ ¾ x 2″ x 4′ ¾ x 2″ x 2′ ¾ x 4″ x 3′ ¾ x 4″ x 2′	(1) ¾ x 4″ x 12′ (C) (1) ¾ x 4″ x 10′ (Rip in half after ¾ x 4″ lengths are taken)
1	¾ x 3 dia.	Cut from scrap	
1	⅜ = dia. x 3 dowel (hardwood)	⅜″ dia. x 3″	(1) ⅜″-dia. x 3″ dowel (hardwood)
4	¾ x 5 5/16 x 76	¾ x 6″ x 8′	(See order B below)
13	¾ x 5 5/16 x 22¼	¾ x 6″ x 2′	
2	¾ x 23¼ x 76	¾ x 10″ x 8′ ¾ x 10″ x 8′ ¾ x 6″ x 8′ (edge-glued)	(4) ¾ x 10″ x 14′ (A) (6) ¾ x 6″ x 14′ (B)
2	¾ x 1¼ x 21⅞	¾ x 2″ x 2′	(See order C above)
6	⅜ x 1 1/16 x 27⅝ (furring strip)	½ x 2″ x 5″	(1) ½ x 2″ x 12′ (to be ripped)
4	⅜ x 11/16 x 21⅞ (furring strip)	½ x 2″ x 2′	
2	¾ x 1 x 2½	Cut from scrap	

DRAW BETTER PLANS

Whether you're enlarging a plan someone else has drawn or designing a project yourself, these time-saving aids will help you do a better job.

DEVICE FOR DRAWING PERSPECTIVES

When you're planning a shop project, a perspective drawing will give you a good idea of the completed project's three-dimensional appearance. This simple guide helps maintain the correct perspective in a drawing, whether you're designing furniture or sketching a landscape.

The only materials you'll need are: two yardsticks or similarly sized pieces of wood, ¾ x 2½ x 54-in. main support of pine, two ¾-in. No. 8 wood screws to secure the yardsticks to the support, two small scraps of sheet steel or sheet aluminum and six thumbtacks. The last two materials fasten the device to the drawing board.

To use this device, secure it and drawing paper to the board. Use a T-square to draw horizontal lines, and a right-angle triangle to draw vertical lines. Use the yardsticks as guides in drawing lines that go back to the predetermined vanishing points—the far ends of the yardsticks.

To store the device, slip a rubber band around the yardsticks to hold them to the main support. Store it in a closet, or hang it on a nail from a hole bored in one end of the support.

PERMANENT GRID FOR ENLARGING

Project plans involving curves and unusual shapes are often placed on grids. When enlarging such a plan, you must first draw a full-size grid. Then you draw in the plan, using the placement of the lines on the original as a guide to line placement within the squares of the full-size grid.

You can save time by accurately drawing a permanent full-size grid on poster board. Then lay a sheet of tracing paper over the grid to enlarge a plan. Your work will be uncluttered by squares, and you can use the grid indefinitely. Two grids, one of ½-in. squares and one of 1-in. squares, will serve most needs.

You can also draw an original grid on 8½ x 14-in. paper and make extras on a duplicating machine if you prefer to draw directly on the grid. You should note, however, that the grid copied on a duplicating machine may be somewhat larger than the original. It may be necessary to change sizes of other parts slightly.

A perspective device, T-square, right-angle triangle and a sharp pencil can help you make accurate perspective drawings.

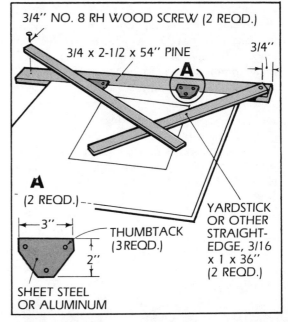

3/4" NO. 8 RH WOOD SCREW (2 REQD.)

3/4 x 2-1/2 x 54" PINE

3/4"

A

A
(2 REQD.)

3"

2"

THUMBTACK
(3 REQD.)

SHEET STEEL
OR ALUMINUM

YARDSTICK
OR OTHER
STRAIGHT-
EDGE, 3/16
x 1 x 36"
(2 REQD.)

A permanent grid will eliminate the need to redraw a grid each time you enlarge a plan. Draw the new plan on tracing paper that's placed over the permanent grid.

MEASURING AND MARKING

Good craftsmanship begins with careful measuring and marking. It doesn't matter how careful and consistent you are at cutting "right on the line."

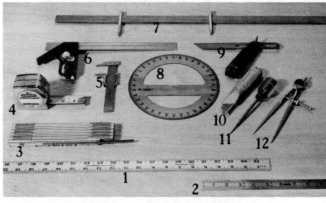

Most common tools for measuring and marking: 1, bench rule; 2, metal yardstock; 3, folding extension rule; 4, steel tape measure; 5, caliper rule; 6, combination square; 7, trammel points; 8, protractor; 9, T-bevel; 10, utility knife, 11, awl; 12, dividers.

Accuracy in measuring and marking is mostly a matter of using the right tool in the proper manner. The most common choices of marking and measuring tools are the ones you see here. When using any of these tools, be conscious of your angle of view, or you may err because of the parallax effect. This is the apparent displacement of two points (the desired point on the rule and the corresponding point you want to make on the workpiece) caused by different angles of view. This is why some rules have graduation marks on a bevel that runs down as close to the work surface as possible. Most sturdy metal rules don't have bevels, so turn these rules on edge to bring the graduation mark closer to the work surface.

To make your mark, use a medium-hard lead such as 2H. This produces a thin line that is much easier to work with than a bold, irregular line.

The way you hold most tools is also very important. Hold a pencil at about 80° to the work surface so the point rides in the corner formed by the rule edge and the work.

When marking a line with a square or T-bevel, place the pencil point on the measured mark and slide the other tool up to it.

Some jobs require greater accuracy than is possible with a pencil. Laying out lines for good-fitting joints requires the greater accuracy you get by using a utility knife or artist's blade. Blades produce very fine lines that also aid in starting the cutting tool and avoiding ragged edges. An awl does the same kind of job when you mark points.

Use a compass or trammel points to mark out circles or curved lines. Measure diameters with a caliper rule. Use a protractor for angles.

Hold a thick rule on edge to strike off a measurement for greatest accuracy. Distortion from viewing angle is minimized.

Hold your pencil so the lead point rides in the corner. Always use medium-hard lead pencils and keep the points sharp.

Avoid striking wide lines (left). These are usually caused by soft dull leads. A good lead to use is rated 2H (right).

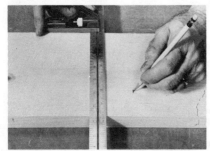

Hold the pencil point on the measured mark and carefully slide the square up to the point. Then strike your line.

Marking dovetails with a utility knife gives you greater accuracy than a pencil. Score also aids in beginning cutting work.

Use the caliper rule to measure diameters or thickness of stock. The stepped jaw projects are for inside measuring.

ADHESIVES

The number of glues and adhesives available these days makes it tougher than ever to choose the right one.

To show how the most common glues work, University of Florida engineers glued wood, then sliced off and photographed the joints with an electron microscope. The top row of photos from the University of Florida shows typical use for the glues; the center row is the magnified pictures (some blown up 480 times); the bottom row is an artist's rendering of how each of the glue processes shown works. See page 122.

WHY GLUE FAILS

There are few things more frustrating than carefully gluing a broken object or a wood joint, only to see the glue line fail hours or days later. Why does it happen? Perhaps the glue is too old, or the glue may have been exposed to too much heat. Heat and adhesives are bad companions. You should take to heart that old directive, "Store glue in a cool, dry location."

Another reason for glue failure: Perhaps you used the wrong glue for the job. As the chart "Adhesive Facts" shows, most adhesives are designed to perform best on certain materials, although many have secondary uses. Finally, perhaps you didn't follow instructions.

The idea of merely slapping some glue on a break, or joint, and sticking the pieces together is out of date. Adhesives today are highly sophisticated. Some, like the new family of cyanoacrylates, require no more than a tiny drop. Others, like water-base, contact-bond cements, must be applied liberally to both surfaces as if you were putting on paint.

If you buy the right glue in small quantities for a particular job, and label it with the purchase date, you'll minimize your chances of using old glue that might fail.

"While the bad news is that every product in our industry has a shelf life," says Jim Knauss, technical manager of Roberts Consolidated Industries (makers of Weldwood adhesives), "the good news is that you can nearly always tell when glue is too old to perform. It will be stringy or thick, dried out or lumpy. Dated plastic resin, for example, will drop like sand in water and will refuse to mix."

Shelf life is conservative for adhesives listed in the chart. Most makers are convinced their products will last a minimum of two years.

Some have successfully used adhesives stored for as long as 15 years—in a cool, dry spot. But remember, a two-year life includes the time from capping at the factory, to distributor shelf, to you—a period estimated at three months minimum and six maximum. Unfortunately, glue makers are not required to put the date of production on the glue container.

For anyone with a working knowledge of chemistry, glues aren't difficult to mix and package. Because of this, a good many "back yard" companies have sprung up. Their locally made and distributed products may be top rate, or they may give you nothing but problems. Sticking with known brand-name materials—and following directions—will help you avoid no-stick situations.

TYPES OF GLUE

Although some adhesives are still labeled for specific jobs such as "Glass and Ceramic Mender," the profusion of glue names is gradually subsiding. Taking their place are a dozen or so workhorse adhesives—essentially those listed in the chart.

Standing before a dealer's shelf that's loaded with adhesives, you'll have no trouble picking out the epoxies: They're clearly identified as such. The cyanoacrylates—usually tagged with such adjectives as Super or Wonder—will be identified by generic name somewhere on the label. But you'll have trouble finding neoprene adhesive (such as Weldwood Touch-N-Glue) or a urethane acrylic resin (Loctite's Crystal Clear Sunshine Glue, for example). The descriptions below will help.

Polyvinyl acetate (PVA), familiarly known as white glue, is the most universally sold all-purpose adhesive. But not all white glues are the same. Some are watered down for youngsters' use, while others can withstand nearly 3,000 lbs. per square inch (psi) when used to bond two blocks of hard maple. Since maple fails a stress test at about 2,600 psi, the glue line is stronger than the wood.

Superior PVAs can be used to repair a broken china figure, a vase or costume jewelry. At least one maker claims its PVA is dishwasher-safe, but warns that the glue line on a plate or cup must dry completely. Figure a week of drying when humidity is low and two to three weeks when it's high.

Aliphatic resin glues are sometimes labeled "aliphatic." Like PVAs, they're packaged in plastic squeeze bottles. They can be identified by their creamy yellow color. Aliphatic resins have virtually the same properties as PVAs. The big difference is their "grab" or wet tack. Aliphatics are stickier, which makes your gluing job somewhat simpler, since the parts being glued will not slip or slide around quite as easily.

Liquid hide glues are made from animal hides. These glues are being replaced on many dealers' shelves by the newer PVAs and aliphatics. Usually labeled "hide glue," they're characterized by a tan to brown color. Packaging and properties are nearly identical to PVAs and aliphatics, except for a slower grab and set time. Hide glues definitely need clamping. They also have more odor than the other types.

Solid hide glues are still heated in glue pots by old-time cabinetmakers. In either form, these adhesives make a strong wood joint.

Plastic resins, essentially urea formaldehyde resins, are powdery. They're sold in a can and mixed with water. This powerful wood glue is a standard in furniture factories and a favorite of cabinetmakers. Though a plastic resin joint requires clamping, it has many advantages: Once cured, it has high resistance to moisture and heat, and can withstand nearly any interior environment. Exclusively a woodworking glue, it has a comfortable four-hour pot life after mixing. That leaves plenty of time to match a couple dozen prepared joints in a large shop project.

Resorcinols are also easy to pick out. They're sold in two attached cans. One can contains a

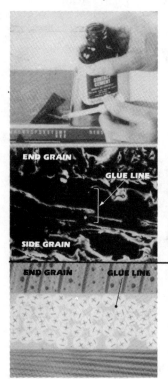

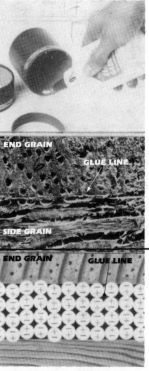

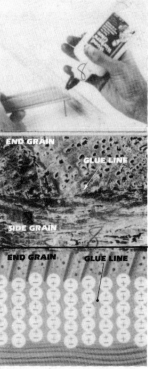

Contact cement is used for nonstructural bonding, such as laminating veneers. Glue molecules mix with a solvent which evaporates and causes bond shrinkage, as shown in the enlarged photo. Each molecule has positive and negative electric regions. Charges within change position constantly, creating dispersion, thus adhesion.

Super glues (cyanoacrylates) for porous materials like wood form a covalent chemical bond with the wood. The positively charged glue molecules and the negatively charged ionic salts at the wood surface link together to form a very strong bond. The chemical bond forms almost immediately as glue comes in contact with wood.

White glues (polyvinyl acetates) are the most universally sold, general-purpose adhesives. Molecules in the glue don't mix as thoroughly as they do in contact cement, but adhesion is somewhat stronger. The charges stay in the same place in each molecule. Still, in products using solvent, there will be some shrinkage of the bond.

Aliphatic resin glues, often used in furniture assembly, are diluted with water. These glues seep into the pores of the wood, adding a glue-to-wood link that gives extra strength. Since all glues exhibit various chemical properties under different circumstances, it's best to always follow package directions in use.

PREPARATION: THE KEY TO GLUING A STRONG JOINT

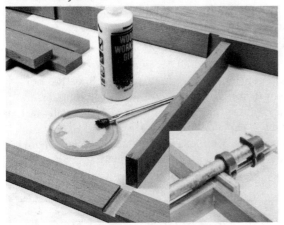

To achieve a strong, glued joint between two pieces of wood, the mating surfaces should be clean and an exact fit. Always test-fit parts before you apply glue. Use enough glue to just cover joint surface. There should be little glue squeeze-out (inset). Since end grain absorbs glue by capillary action, apply second coat.

Many glue failures result from too great a dependence on the glue's holding power and not enough on preparation. For example, all the fragments of this china cup handle must be glued back in place. You can't expect glue to bridge even a tiny gap, especially on a cup handle under constant stress when in use.

powdered catalyst; the other, a liquid resin. Once mixed, resorcinols, too, have a four-hour pot life.

This is the adhesive of choice for outdoor work—gluing on a boat, dock, lawn furniture or patio deck. Once cured, resorcinol makes a waterproof joint. Like plastic resin, this is exclusively a woodworking glue: wood, particleboard, plywood, hardboard. Moreover, resorcinol makes the strongest joint of any wood glue.

Epoxies were in great demand a decade ago. Now more mature, they continue to be popular. Makers have developed three variations on the standard two-tube, resin-and-hardener combination. One type uses the same 50:50 blend from the two tubes, but setting time has been reduced from hours to minutes. This reduces or eliminates the need for a tie or tape clamp. Curing time for both the regular slow-set epoxy and the fast-set epoxy, however, is still at least 12 hours—and 24 hours is better.

A second variation delivers the two clear liquids in a two-tube syringe. When you press the dispenser, the resin and hardener combine as they're forced through a single spout.

Finally, there are epoxy sticks of putty consistency. You slice equal portions of the two sticks, and knead them together to form a pliable mass. This type acts as much like a filler as an adhesive. It's ideal for patching metal pipe, gutters, metal toys, wrought-iron railings and cast-iron lawn furniture or for sealing broken masonry.

While its cost might deter you from using it

over a large area, it's still the glue of choice in many instances because of its versatility. It can attach almost any two surfaces to each other. After curing, clear epoxies will even permanently repair dinnerware that will be sent repeatedly through a dishwasher.

Cyanoacrylates are new, but not so new that they haven't had some bad press notices. Applied correctly, these so-called "super glues" will fasten any nonporous surface to a similar surface. Recently a new variation was developed for porous surfaces.

Cyanoacrylates set by reacting with vapor in the air: They don't need oxygen. That's why they can seal your fingers together very quickly. Your skin is constantly producing moisture. This reaction with vapor also explains why a tiny container of cyanoacrylate, left open, is soon useless.

You need only one drop of cyanoacrylate per square inch. When the patch covers less than a square inch—say, a diamond remounted in a platinum setting, or two halves of a decorative button—one drop is too much. A joint filled with too much of the stuff will fail faster than one touched with too little. So look for a package with a pin-like applicator that eases the application of amounts less than one drop.

On the market now is a blister pack that includes cyanoacrylate and acetone thinner. Use the acetone (or nail polish remover) to rebreak a bad bond or to unfasten glued fingers.

Acrylic resins are also newcomers to the field. They're sold in two-vial blister packs that

ADHESIVE FACTS

Most adhesives in this chart should be applied at room temperature. Aliphatics are an exception; they can be coated successfully on a surface at 40°F. Initial grab is also called wet tack. Setting time refers to the time an adhesive needs to solidify enough so clamps or other pressure can be removed. Curing time is a relative figure, indicating how soon the object can be put back safely into use. Adhesives generally don't attain full strength during this period. Most achieve about 75 percent of full strength and continue curing for days, reaching 100 percent in roughly one week. Shelf life is a conservative approximation. Glues may well last longer, especially if they are capped tightly immediately after use and then stored in a cool, dry spot.

Adhesive	Best use	Initial grab	Setting time	Curing time	Strength	Clamping needed?	Moisture resistance	Heat resistance	Color when dry	Package size/ price	Shelf life
Polyvinyl acetate (white glue)	Wood and wood products	½-2 min.	10-30 min.	24 hr.	High	Possible light taping	Poor	Poor	Clear	8 oz./$1.40-$1.75; 1 gal./$9-$12	1½ yr.
Aliphatic resin	See above	10-60 sec.	5-20 min.	24 hr.	High	See above	Fair	Good	Clear to pale amber	8 oz./$1.80-$2.25; 1 gal./$10-$14	1½ yr.
Liquid hide	See above	Slow	2-3 hr.	8-12 hr.	High	Yes	Poor	Excellent	Amber	8 oz./$3.25-$4; 1 gal./$18-$28	1 yr.
Urea formaldehyde (Plastic resin— two parts)	See above	Very slow; 4 hr. pot life	4 hr.	12-16 hr.	High	Yes	Excellent	Good	Light tan	8 oz./$2-$2.75	1 yr.
Resorcinol (two parts)	Wood, wood products, exterior	See above	10-12 hr.	24 hr.	Very high	Yes	Waterproof	Good	Brown	2 parts: 10 oz. powder; 32 fl. oz. resin/$10-$16	2 yr.
EPOXIES Fast set	Metal, glass, ceramics, china, hard plastics, marble, etc.	Slow	4-8 min.	12-24 hr.	Very high	Tie or tape during set	Good	Good	Clear, white or gray	½-oz. tube/$1-$2; 2½-oz. bar/$1.80-$2.50; 1-oz. liquid/$1-$2	2 yr.
EPOXIES Slow set			4-6 hr.								
Cyanoacrylates (Super glue)	Type for nonporous surfaces (see above); type for porous surfaces (wood, leather, etc.)	Very fast	10-30 sec.	24 hr.	Very high	No	Fair to good	Fair	Clear	.07 fl. oz./$1.50-$2	9 mo.- 1 yr.
Acrylic resins (two parts)	See epoxies; also bonds any two dissimilar materials	Fast	3-8 min.	5-20 min.	Very high	No	Good	Good	Amber to tan or clear	2 parts: 16-fl.-oz. adhesive; 12-fl.- oz. activator/$2-$3	1 yr.
Urethane acrylic resin (anaerobic)	See epoxies; requires tight fit	1-2 min.	2-5 min.	20 min.- 2 hr.	High	No	Good	Good	Pale amber to clear	.25 oz./$3.50-$6.50	2 yr. +
Neoprene	Metal and tile repair; metal to other surfaces	Fast	Set; pull away for 8 min.; press	24 hr.	Medium-high	No	Excellent	Good	Light tan	1 fl. oz./$1.80-$2.25	1 yr.
Silicone	Glass, metal, ceramic, tile	Slow	Fast	16-24 hr.	Fair	Light taping	Excellent	Excellent	Clear or color	2.8 fl. oz./$2.80-$3.75	1 yr.
CONTACT-BOND GLUES Flammable solvent	Laminates to plywood, particleboard, etc.	Tack-free; 15-30 min.	Bonds on contact; 3 hr. open time	24 hr.	Medium	Only to laminate bends	Good	Good	Amber	1 gal./$10-$18	1 yr.
CONTACT-BOND GLUES Nonflammable solvent	See above	See above	See above	24 hr.	Medium	See above	Good	Good	Amber	1 gal./$18-$23	1 yr.
CONTACT-BOND GLUES Water-based acrylic	See above	Tack-free; 30-60 min.	As above, but 5 hr. open time	24 hr.	Medium	See above	Fair to good	Good to excellent	Clear	1 gal./$15-$20	1 yr.
CONSTRUCTION GLUES Solvent-based	Paneling, tile-board, subfloor, gypsum board	8-12 min.	10-15 min.	24 hr.	Medium-high	Possible light bracing	Good to excellent	Fair to good	Light tan, black, others	11-oz. cartridge/ $1.50-$3.50	1 yr.
CONSTRUCTION GLUES Water-based	Paneling, subfloor, ceiling tile, etc.	Slow to medium	20-30 min.	24 hr.	Medium-high	Finishing nails on paneling	Fair to good	Good	White to off-white	11-oz. cartridge/ $2.25-$3.75	1 yr.

house a primer and an adhesive. You apply the primer to one surface and the adhesive to the other. When you press the surfaces together, setting action begins instantly. After 60 seconds you may be able to let go.

Urethane acrylic resins cure without oxygen, which is why they're called anaerobics. They're best used to glue nonporous surfaces in very tight gapless fits. Glass to glass, metal to metal, or metal to glass are typical applications: Anaerobics don't hold as well for broken pieces from which tiny particles may be missing.

Neoprenes are rarely labeled as such. You'll be able to identify them from their instructions for use. Apply the adhesive to one of the mating surfaces, and press on the part you want to glue. Then pull the surfaces apart as you would open a hinge. Wait the number of minutes noted in the instructions (usually about eight), and press the parts together again, this time for keeps. Use neoprenes for metal or tile repairs.

Silicones are sealants. They have some adhesive properties, but high strength is not one of them, since silicones tend to remain rubbery. When cured, however, they do form a dishwasher-safe bond on china. They're less effective on glass stemware.

Contact-bond cements, which are used almost exclusively for laminating and veneering, are available in three types: flammable, nonflammable and water-based acrylic. Before the Consumer Products Safety Commission required a change in 1978, the flammable types had a low flash point, making them dangerous to use in a poorly ventilated room. While you should never light a match or smoke in the pres-

USING THE RIGHT APPLICATOR TO APPLY THE RIGHT AMOUNT OF GLUE

A brush is an ideal tool for coating large surfaces, such as wallpaper, with a thin, even coat of adhesive. Brushes are also handy for large woodworking jobs.

Use a roller to apply contact-bond adhesive to plastic laminate. Apply a thin, even glue coat by rolling it on in overlapping passes, then evening out the glue.

The plunger on this epoxy-cement applicator forces out proper amounts of hardener and resin. Use this type of glue to join parts that can't be clamped.

This hide glue and many other woodworking glues come in plastic bottles with spouts. Apply zigzag glue bead and rub parts together to spread glue.

A notched trowel spreads adhesive for fastening ceramic tile and other material. Use a trowel with properly sized notches, as specified on the adhesive container.

Spray adhesive bonds paper, such as a print, to a backing without penetrating the front. To bond, spray both surfaces, dry 5 minutes and join them.

This panel adhesive and other construction glues are often packaged in cartridges. Apply them with a caulking gun, laying out beads in vertical zigzags.

A needle-nose glue injector puts glue in tight places. It can glue a chair rail, as here, or a veneer blister, for example.

Knead the two-part epoxy sticks together and mold them, like clay, into shape. Adhesive provides electrical insulation (left), repairs cracked handle (right).

ence of flammable cements, and should ventilate the room in which you're working, the flash point is now within levels considered safe by the CPSC. Both the flammable and nonflammable types are clearly labeled.

Despite its flammability, this first type of contact-bond cement is, by volume, the most popular for two reasons: It dries to a tack-free surface fast (the point at which panels can be laminated) and it's the cheapest of the three types.

The second variety is made nonflammable with additives. It also becomes tack-free quickly and requires ventilation during use. Its biggest drawback is its cost: This type is the most costly of the three. The last type, a water-based acrylic, takes longer to reach a tack-free state and is medium-priced. The water-based variety is also the safest to use.

Construction adhesives are usually packaged in cartridges designed for use in caulking guns. They fall into two general groups: solvent-based and water-based. The solvent-based category includes neoprenes and styrene butadienes. Neoprenes are more expensive, but many professional builders consider them to be the best.

Water-based adhesives also include two major types: acrylics and PVAs. Like other water-based glues, they set slowly, but their performance is high. It's unlikely you'll find any of these labeled by chemical category, but price is a guide. Construction adhesives secure wall paneling and subflooring.

Other varieties. Missing from the chart is an entire group of household adhesives, usually sold in quantities of a gallon or more. These glues are used for putting down carpet, resilient floor tile, ceramic tile, wall tile, acoustical ceiling tile and wood parquet flooring, among other things. While properties differ from brand to brand, performance of established brands (including those packaged by floor covering and tile makers) is uniformly high. None, except the

ceramic wall-tile adhesives, are unusually strong, since great strength isn't a particular requirement. In fact, a certain resiliency in these adhesives, often labeled "cements," is beneficial.

Also not on the chart are older materials, such as the caseins, rarely found today, and "hot glues," chalk-shaped sticks that are heated in glue guns. Improved PVAs and aliphatics—easier to use on wood projects—have stolen much of hot glue's thunder. But the hot glues often prove invaluable in special gluing situations when clamping is impossible.

MANUFACTURERS LIST

Below is a partial list of companies producing adhesives. "Household" refers to workshop and home-repair glues—white glue, epoxies and so on. "Construction" describes cartridge adhesives applied with a caulking gun on such surfaces as wall paneling and subflooring. "Surfaces" is the title given to cements for floor tile, wall tile, wall covering, plastic laminates and so on.

Full line: Household, construction, surfaces
Borden Inc., Box 16700, Columbus, Ohio 43215
Devcon Corp., Endicott St., Danvers, Mass. 01923
Dow Corning Corp., Midland, Mich. 48640
Franklin Chemical Industries, 2020 Bruck, Columbus, Ohio 43207
H.B. Fuller Co., 315 South Hicks Rd., Palatine, Ill. 60067
Leech Products, Box 2147, Hutchinson, Kan. 67501
Lucas Group (Tiger Grip adhesives), 1370 Ontario St., Cleveland, Ohio 44113
Macco Adhesives, SCM Corp., 900 Union Commerce Building, Cleveland, Ohio 44115
Miracle Adhesives Corp., 250 Petit Ave., Bellmore, N.Y. 11710
Roberts Consolidated Industries (Weldwood adhesives), 600 North Baldwin Park Blvd., City of Industry, Calif. 91749
Wilhold Glues, 8707 Millergrove Dr., Santa Fe Springs, Calif. 90670
Household construction
3M Co., Household and Hardware Div., 3M Center, St. Paul, Minn. 55101
Household
Krazy Glue Inc., 53 West 23rd St., New York, N.Y. 10010
Loctite Corp. (Duro adhesives), 4450 Cranwood Ct., Cleveland, Ohio 44128
Magic American Chemical Corp., 23700 Mercantile Ave., Detroit, Mich. 48209
Permabond International, 480 South Dean St., Englewood, N.J. 07631
Ross Chemical Co., 8485 Melville St., Detroit, Mich. 48209
Woodhill Permatex, Box 7183, Cleveland, Ohio 44128
Construction
Dap Inc., Box 277, Dayton, Ohio 45401
Gold Bond Building Products, 2001 Rexford Rd., Charlotte, N.C. 28211
Surfaces
Evans Adhesive Corp., 925 West Henderson, Columbus, Ohio 43214

GLUE TRICKS PROS USE

To avoid excess glue squeeze-out on hard-to-clean inside joints, run your finger along the inside edge after spreading the glue.

Cabinetmakers often use pinch dogs to pull joints together without clamping. Drive a dog in place straddling the joint.

To remove glue squeeze-out from a piece you plan to paint, wipe off excess glue with a rag. Don't do this on wood that will be given a stain finish. The wiping pressure will force some of the wet glue into the wood pores, preventing the stain from penetrating. Instead, let the glue set until it is dry. Then shave it off with a sharp chisel. This leaves a clean wood surface.

MASTER CRAFTSMAN TIPS

Time-tested shop secrets and techniques used by craftsmen to achieve professional-looking results in their workshop projects.

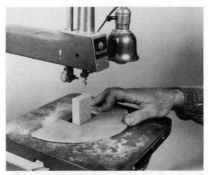

JIGSAW SANDING

You may be aware of the jigsaw's versatility as a cutting tool, but with this easy-to-make attachment, it can perform sanding operations as well.

Insert the wood-screw threads of a ¼-in.-dia. x 2-in. hanger bolt into the end of a ¾ x 1½ x 3-in. wood block. Then, use rubber cement to glue abrasive paper to both faces of the block. Glue coarse grit on one side, medium on the other. Or use adhesive-backed paper such as 3M's Press 'n Sand.

For sanding, place the protruding machine-screw threads in the saw's lower chuck. Use different-shaped blocks for specific sanding operations.

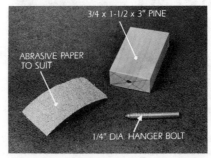

Mount the sanding block in the saw's lower chuck. Remove blade guide for easy access.

The sanding block is ready for assembly. Note the block's centerbored pilot hole.

DIMPLE-FREE NAILING

Prevent accidental hammer dimples on wood surfaces with this handy protective shield. Cut the shield from ⅟₁₆-in.-thick plastic laminate and bore a ⅛-in.-dia. centered hole as shown.

To use, start the nail, then place the shield over the nail. Hold the shield flat against the workpiece face and drive the nail until it's flush with the laminate.

Remove the shield and use a nailset to drive the projecting nailhead flush with or below the workpiece surface, as desired.

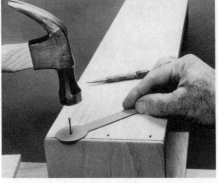
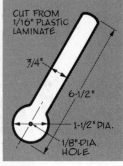

TRUING BOARD EDGES

To successfully edge-glue two boards, their mating edges must be perfectly true. Dressed lumber is rarely purchased with edges suitable for joining. Here is a quick and foolproof method you can use to true the edges of any two boards—simultaneously.

Clamp the boards with their mating edges butted together tightly. Then, using a straight-edge guide and a portable circular saw, cut straight through the center of the joint, removing stock from both boards.

If the gap between the boards is wider than the saw kerf, repeat the procedures as many times as necessary to close the gap. The result will be two straight and true mating edges that will produce an "invisible" joint.

Steer the saw along a straightedge guide. Arrows indicate unevenness in board edges.

PLANE GUIDE

This simple bench plane guide can aid you in planing perfectly square edges. Choose a square-edge piece of ¾-in. stock for the guide and cut it 3 in. longer than the plane. The guide's width often is determined by the job, but a 2½-in. width will be sufficient for most work. Cut a ⅛-in.-deep x ½-in. notch in the guide's top edge. The notch will allow the guide

to clear the protruding plane iron (blade) and sit flat against the plane's bottom. Next, bore two ³⁄₁₆-in.-dia. mounting holes through the plane's base. Attach the guide to the plane with two 1¼-in. No. 8 sheet-metal screws.

To use, simply keep the guide flat against the workpiece's face while planing. The plane will cut perpendicular to the guide, forming a square edge.

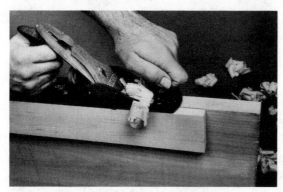

During planing, keep the guide flat against the work-piece's face.

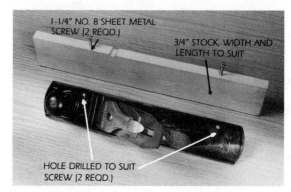

Here's the guide prior to mounting. Note the iron-clearing notch.

RADIAL SAWDUST SLOT

Sawdust that collects along a radial-arm saw fence can cause inaccurate cutting. The sawdust forms small mounds, preventing the workpiece from abutting the fence tightly. To eliminate this problem, provide a sawdust escape slot between the fence and the worktable.

Make the sawdust slot by nailing ⅛ x ¾ x 1-in. softwood spacer blocks along the fence. Place the blocks 6 in. apart, but don't put one directly under the saw-blade path. Position the fence on the saw with the spacer blocks facing forward. Tighten the fence lock knobs and be sure the spacer blocks are below the worktable's surface.

HINGING A PLYWOOD EDGE

Boring straight pilot holes into the edge of fir plywood for a continuous hinge can be tricky. The drill bit often is deflected off course when it hits a glued joint, a dense knot or a void in the plywood's edge.

To solve this problem, nail a ⅛-in.-thick pine reinforcement strip to the plywood's edge. Then tape the hinge in place over the pine strip. Punch screw-hole center marks and bore pilot holes through the strip and into the plywood edge. The pine strip will serve to support the drill bit and keep it straight. Remove the strip before installing the hinge.

This technique is also useful for installing other styles of hinges and hardware on delicate surfaces.

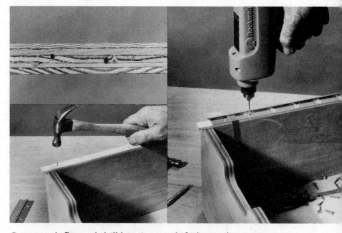

Prevent deflected drill bits (upper left) by nailing pine strip to the plywood's edge (lower left). Tape the hinge in position then bore the pilot holes (right).

CUTTING RINGS

Cutting solid rings using a sabre saw or jigsaw is time-consuming. But with a multiple-blade hole saw and a drill, you can cut perfectly round rings quickly and easily.

Mount two blades in the hole saw's toolhead at the same time. Select two saw blades that will produce a ring of the desired thickness and diameter. This technique works with both a portable electric drill and a drill press.

Cut rings by using two saw blades at once.

Place dowel in drill and contour with file.

TURNING SMALL DIAMETERS

Here's a way to turn small-diameter, decorative finials and spindles on a drill press.

First, select the desired diameter wood dowel and chuck it in the drill press. Then, using a variety of files, rasps and abrasive tapes and cords, contour the dowel to the desired shape. Use very fine-grit abrasive paper for the finishing touches.

For best results, run the drill at its highest speed.

DOUBLE-DUTY DISC

Unless you happen to have two disc sanders in your shop (an expensive luxury), switching from rough to smooth sanding requires changing the discs. But this trick provides you with two different sanding surfaces on one disc sander.

Using a circular template and a razor knife, simultaneously cut out the centers of two sanding discs—one coarse grit, one medium.

Glue the outer ring from one disc and the center portion of the other to the disc sander. Now you can sand both rough and smooth finishes on the same machine. Use the cutoff pieces in reverse order when it's time to replace the sanding surface.

Glue sections from two different abrasive grits for both smooth and rough sanding.

Change splintered dadoes (left) to smooth dadoes (right) by scoring the lines-of-cut.

SPLINTERLESS DADOES

Cutting dadoes will often tear and splinter the crossgrain on a piece of wood. This is especially true of plywood veneer.

To prevent this, score two lines just outside the lines-of-cut with a sharp razor knife. The scored lines will allow the wood's grain to "break off" cleanly as the cutting tool passes. The result is splinterless dadoes and a more professional-looking joint.

This technique is effective with all varieties of dado-cutting tools, including routers, shapers and either radial-arm or table saws with dado heads.

WOODWORKING TIPS

BIG BOARDS FROM SMALL ONES

Not every job requires top-drawer treatment, as in the case of the shop storage shelves shown here. Often, larger stock can be obtained by joining together a number of smaller scrap boards with wood splines to give the overall lengths and widths required.

First, cut the mating board ends straight and square using a planer blade in a table or radial-arm saw. Then, cut matching grooves in the ends to a convenient thickness using a dado head in a table saw. Generally, the spline thickness should equal one-third of the stock thickness. Cut the spline to size, glue and clamp in place.

NEATER JOINTS

When you must make a butt joint between the ends or edges of two boards, the mating surfaces should be in uniform contact. Here's a good way to get a perfect fit.

First, make a crosscut on one board using a table saw. Then butt the edge of the second board against the first so both are in a straight line. In this position, nail one or more scrap lumber strips—depending on length of joint—across the joint using two nails on each side. Elevate the saw blade so it will cut through both boards and slightly into the scrap. Make the cut, remove the strips and the joint should fit perfectly.

MITER-GAUGE CHECK

Don't trust the miter gauge on your table saw to make a true 90° cut. Test it by selecting a piece of scrap wood with two straight, parallel edges. Make a crosscut through the center of the piece and then flip one section over. Press both cut edges together and rest both pieces on the flat surface of the saw table. If the cut is true, both edges will butt perfectly. An angled space between them shows that you need to readjust the miter gauge. A wider space at the top indicates the gauge favors the left. A gap at the bottom shows it is off to the right. Readjust the miter gauge or remark it so you don't have to make trial cuts every time.

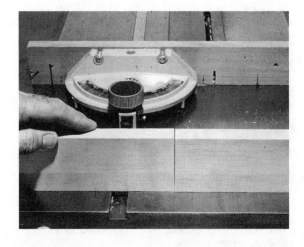

BAND-SAW DUSTER

Mount a stiff-bristled toothbrush so it bears against the lower wheel of your band saw to keep resinous sawdust from building up and affecting the way the blade tracks. To align the brush, bend the plastic handle by softening it with boiling water. Twist the handle so the bristles bear on the driver wheel. You may have to make a wooden mounting block to align the brush. Screws fasten the brush and its mounting block in place.

CUSTOM DRILL SIZE

Need to bore an odd size hole? You can easily grind an equal amount off each side of a spade bit that's the next size too large.

Adjust the tool rest to maintain the same angle on the bit's edge. Carefully align tape markers to guide the grinding. Grind slowly and dip the bit in water frequently to avoid drawing temper from the steel. Bore trial holes in scrap to check progress.

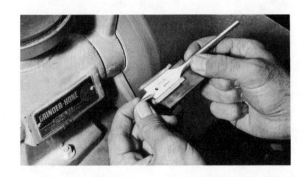

MARKING GAUGE

A tiny nick filed in the blade end of your combination square makes it much easier to draw a straight line along a board.

File the V-notch in the center of the blade edge just deep enough to keep the pencil point from slipping as you move the square along the work. When marking, slant the pencil toward the square. Changing the angle will cause the line to waver.

SANDING DUST

It takes sharp tools to make precise cuts. Whether you are working with finely honed hand chisels or a high-speed router on just-sanded stock, do a thorough job of removing sanding dust. The dust contains dislodged and fractured abrasive grits that will dull cutting edges. Vacuum carefully, then wipe with a tack cloth.

GLUE BRUSHES

One of the best glue applicators is the small metal-handled bristle brush. Sold in hardware and plumbing supply stores for applying soldering flux when sweating copper tubing, these brushes cost about 15 cents and can be reused many times. For best results, cut the 1-in.-long bristles down to ½ in. long.

RECYCLE BLADES

Don't discard broken band-saw blades just because rewelding is expensive or not readily available. Cut them up to make scroll-saw blades. In very short lengths, you might even be able to make usable sabre-saw blades.

Cut the broken band-saw blade into sections the same length as the blades for your scroll saw. Using a scroll-saw blade as a pattern, grind or file the ends of the sections to fit the chucks. To cut the blade, hold it firmly with diagonal cutters or clamp it tightly in a vise while making a sharp bend to break it off. Wear gloves and eye protection.

SQUARE EDGES WITH A JOINTER PLANE

If you have trouble planing narrow edges square with a large jointer plane, then make the simple planing fence shown here.

Bore two holes in the plane bottom, then screw a straight, square-edged board in place. Cut a notch in the area that falls over the blade to allow for blade projection below the surface of the bottom. Adjust the blade to the proper depth and begin planing the board edges. Use full, smooth strokes and apply slight side pressure to the tool so the fence board always remains in contact with the face of the work.

CHECKING WARP

If you are flattening a wood slab using a hand plane, you'll have to start by planing diagonally across the high corners until the top is nearly flat. Check your progress by placing two straight boards of the same width across the end corners. Then sight over the tops of these boards. If the slab is straight, the top edges will line up.

MARKING SOFTWOODS

When working with very soft woods like clear pine, cedar and redwood, you can crush surface fibers with nothing more than a pencil point. The resulting depression will have to be sanded out before the project is finished. Instead, use white chalk for marking wherever possible. It can be removed with a damp rag.

SHOP IDEAS

LOW-COST SHELVES

Here's a simple way to add shelving to your workshop, garage, office or pantry. The shelves are designed for low cost and ease of fit. But they also have some real advantages over conventional support systems.

The suspending flange strengthens the entire length of the shelf, in the same way an angle section is stronger than a flat. The suspending flange also protects the wall from damage when awkward loads are shelved. And heavy loading actually increases the shelf contact with the wall, instead of causing the shelf to sag away from the wall, as with most other supporting methods.

It's important to use only plywood for the wall flange. Inexpensive off-cut strips can be bought at a lumberyard. The shelf must be both glued and nailed (or screwed) to the wall flange. Use wood glue and generous-size common nails, after boring pilot holes.

The table gives suggested widths and thicknesses for the shelves and wall flanges. You can vary dimensions to suit the scrap material you have.

As with all shelving, be sure the wall fastener is secure. For larger shelves fixed to wall studs, use two screws per stud, one above the other. For brick or concrete block walls, space the screws along the top edge of the wall flange at about 12-in. intervals. Finally, be careful not to overload the shelves.

SHELF		WALL FLANGE	
"W"	"T"	"H"	"T"
4"	3/4"	2-1/2"	3/8"
6"	7/8"	3-1/2"	1/2"
8"	1"	5"	5/8"
10"	1-1/4"	6"	3/4"

THICKNESS "T"
HEIGHT "H"
WALL FLANGE
SHELF
WIDTH "W"
ADJUSTABLE SHELF
THICKNESS "T"

MITERBOX GUIDES

Two sections of angle iron fastened to the top of a miterbox can keep the saw at the appropriate angle to the workpiece. Fasten angle iron sections at the 45° slot spaced apart slightly more than the width of the saw band. You can also use a pair of guides at the 90° slot.

MITERBOX HOLDER

A section of heavy angle iron fastened to the bottom of a miterbox can make the box much easier to use. The angle iron, cut to the length of the miterbox, should be clamped in a shop vise. The box will remain stationary, leaving both hands free to manipulate the work and to make the cut.

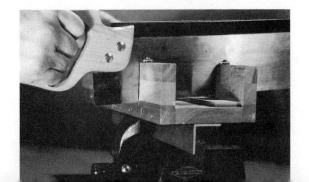

RESAW JIG

This jig was developed to resaw the stock in order to double the covering capacity of a ¾ x 3 in.-wide cedar paneling. The jig was designed for a radial-arm saw but works equally well on table and band saws.

The throat pieces are of 1½-in.-thick material. There is no depth limit within reason for band saws, but for radial-arm and table saws, limit depth to the blade capacity minus ¼ in. Cut the back throat pieces from a 2 x 4. The front throat is a 2 x 4 ripped to 2¾ in. wide. It has two slots bored and chiseled to receive eyebolts.

Make the jig as long as your saw table can accommodate. Size the plywood piece so its's flush with the table edge. The plywood serves as a way to fasten the jig securely to the saw table with C-clamps.

Cut two adjustment blocks. Use a drill and sabre saw to make slots for the threaded ends of the eyebolts. Position the eyebolts in their slots and assemble the front throat pieces to the plywood base with glue and four 1½-in., No. 10 flathead wood screws. Attach the back throat to one end of the adjustment blocks with glue and screws. Run the threaded end of the eyebolts through the slots in the adjustment blocks, then add washers and wingnuts.

To use the jig, first adjust the throat so the stock slides through snugly but freely. Center the space between the throat pieces on the saw blade and secure the jig with C-clamps. Test the cut for accuracy and readjust if needed. Feed stock at a uniformly slow rate so you achieve an attractive resaw pattern and avoid jamming the saw.

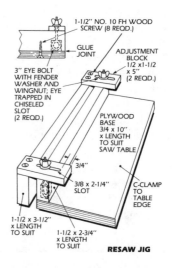

1-1/2" NO. 10 FH WOOD SCREW (8 REQD.)

GLUE JOINT

ADJUSTMENT BLOCK 1/2 x1-1/2 x 5" (2 REQD.)

3" EYE BOLT WITH FENDER WASHER AND WINGNUT; EYE TRAPPED IN CHISELED SLOT (2 REQD.)

PLYWOOD BASE 3/4 x 10" x LENGTH TO SUIT SAW TABLE

3/4"

3/8 x 2-1/4" SLOT

C-CLAMP TO TABLE EDGE

1-1/2 x 3-1/2" x LENGTH TO SUIT

1-1/2 x 2-3/4" x LENGTH TO SUIT

RESAW JIG

SAW PLATFORM

Use your miterbox as a platform to support small pieces of wood while you're cutting them with a sabre saw. The sabre saw blade won't strike the bottom of the miterbox, and the sides are close enough to support even very thin wood pieces while you're cutting them.

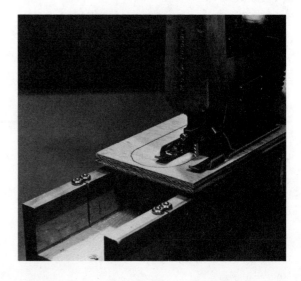

PERFECT JOINTS FROM YOUR ROUTER

Here is a way to cut box joints easily on a table saw or with a router.

Finger or box joints look like dovetails, but without the flair. While box joints are not as strong as dovetails, you can cut them easily on a table saw or with a router using this simple jig.

If your router table does not have a built-in miter gauge, build a miter tabletop from ¾-in. A-C plywood. Dimensions can vary to suit your materials and space, but be sure all four sides are square. Cut a dado about 3 in. from the front edge. If you have a miter gauge from a table or band saw, cut the dado to fit it. If not, make the cut ⅜ in. deep by ¾ in. wide.

Glue the hardwood strip along the front bot-

tom edge of the top to help align it with the router table. Flip over the top to mark and bore countersunk mounting holes. Align these with holes for the router table fence that will not be used. Also bore the holes for the router bit. The jig table mounts with bolts and wingnuts.

The slide fits the dado in the top without slop, but loose enough to slide easily. Notch the backstop for each size finger joint you want to make. A 3-in. strip of ¾-in. plywood a little wider than the table works well. Cut a hardwood finger stop lock to joint-finger width and height by 3 in. long. Notch the backstop for a working cut and again for the finger. Glue the finger in the end cut, making sure it is square.

Make box joints by raising the router bit so its cut equals the thickness of the stock. Clamp two sides of the box together offset by finger width after figuring it so you don't end up with half a finger or less at the end. Match finger width to joint width to avoid 1-in. fingers in a joint only 2 in. long.

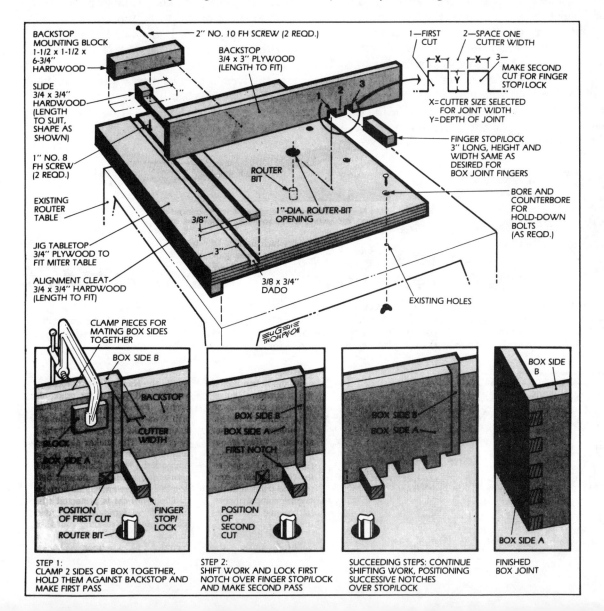

USING HANDSAWS

Each of the common handsaws is designed for specific and specialized uses.

The most useful handsaws for work around the home and shop are the crosscut, rip, compass and coping saws. Two others that are somewhat specialized but still very useful are the dovetail saw and backsaw. And, for cutting metal and other tough materials, a hacksaw is indispensable.

Ripsaws and crosscut saws are similar in appearance, but a close look at their teeth reveals quite a difference. The ripsaw, used to cut wood lengthwise in the direction of the grain, has teeth that are filed straight across to form chisel-like points. These teeth cut by chipping away the wood. The crosscut saw is used for cutting across the grain. Its teeth are beveled on both sides, like knife edges, and the blade cuts by slicing through the wood fibers.

These saws, and the others shown, are classified by the number of saw teeth points per inch (ppi). This factor determines whether the saw will cut fast but rough (fewer teeth per inch) or slow and smooth (more teeth per inch). Ripsaws, for example, are commonly 5½ or 6 points, while crosscut saws are usually 7 or 8

Use thumb knuckle as a guide to start crosscut saw precisely on waste side of cut line. Draw blade back a few times to gain entry, then push blade forward at 45° angle.

points. Saw teeth are also set—that is, alternately bent outward—to create a kerf cut slightly wider than the blade body. This allows the body to move freely through the cut without binding.

The compass saw is used for making cuts where the ripsaw or crosscut saw won't fit and for cutting curves and internal cutouts. But for intricate curves and scroll work, the coping saw is the better choice. It makes a finer cut and its removable blade permits shallow internal cutouts up to the depth of the tool throat. To do this, just bore a blade entry hole into the waste area, thread the blade through the hole, reattach it and make the cut.

The dovetail and backsaws also resemble each other. Both have thin blades with fine teeth and the stiff spline across the blade top to keep it rigid. And both excel at making precise, clean cuts, like the examples shown in the photos.

Start ripsaw like crosscut saw, but use a 60° cutting angle. On long cuts, kerf may close and bind blade. To prevent this, insert nail or wedge to spread kerf open.

Use a compass saw for making internal cuts. Bore a blade entry hole at each corner, then cut out waste between. Draw cut lines on masking tape for greater visibility.

Use a coping saw for curved cuts. For best results, blade teeth should point down so saw works on pulled downstroke. Clamp a V-notched board underneath for support.

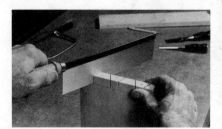

Dovetail saw has thin blade with short, fine teeth for greater cutting accuracy. It's ideal for dovetail depth cuts and for cutting off installed dowel plugs flush to surface.

Use a backsaw in a miterbox for making accurate angle cuts. The saw also works well for cutting tenons and dovetail joints that are too deep for the dovetail saw.

Use a hacksaw for cutting metal. Hold it firmly with both hands and apply cutting pressure only on the push stroke. Lift blade off stock slightly on each return stroke.

USING A COMBINATION SQUARE

The versatile combination square should be a part of any basic tool collection.

The try square and its companion, the miter square, were for many years the basic tools used for marking and checking 90° and 45° angles. Although they served these purposes effectively, both squares have lost their prominence in favor of the more versatile combination square, which functions in both capacities and more.

If you've been working with the limited-duty older squares, perhaps it's time to update your toolbox with a combination square. And if you're in the process of acquiring a beginning basic tool collection, you definitely should include it. It can save you the expense of buying several other tools.

The head or handle of the tool slides along a blade to permit the head's 90° right angle face or the opposite 45° miter face to bear against the work for precise marking. The blade is loos-

ened and tightened with a finger-turned nut.

By adjusting the projection of the blade and locking it into position, the square can be used as a large-capacity (10-in.) marking gauge. Used in a similar way, it can work as a depth gauge. And, the blade can be removed completely for use as a straightedge.

The bubble level vial in the head permits setting and checking components in both vertical and horizontal planes. Some models include a short steel scribing point, shaped like a small marking awl, which stores in the base of the head.

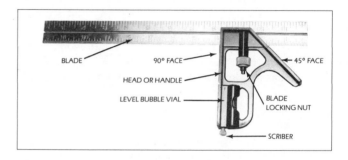

BLADE — 90° FACE — 45° FACE

HEAD OR HANDLE

LEVEL BUBBLE VIAL — BLADE LOCKING NUT

SCRIBER

Typical combination square has a steel head that slides along a slotted blade. It can be locked in place at any point for marking precise 90° and 45° angles.

To check inside corners for squareness, adjust head flush with blade end and lock in place. Then slide head along one board until blade makes contact with other board.

Hold mitered face of head against work edge to mark a 45° angle. Little finger rests on work surface, not blade, to act as brake to prevent slipping.

To use tool as a marking gauge, adjust blade to depth and press head against edge. Hold slightly angled pencil against blade end and pull square backward with pencil following.

To make depth measurements, place head and blade end against pieces as shown and lock blade. Remove and read blade rule.

Check plumb with square by holding blade—with miter face up—against vertical surface. Read bubble position in level vial.

Remove blade from head to use as bench rule. It's 12 in. long and has 1/8-, 1/16-, and 1/32-in. graduations on four scales.

WORKING WITH LEVELS

Levels have many uses in the workshop and in the home as well.

Even the most basic toolkit should contain a level. This simple, easy-to-use tool is a necessity for accurately setting or checking work in a true horizontal plane (called level) and a true vertical plane (called plumb). It is also indispensable for adjusting things such as record players, pendulum clocks and washing machines that must be level or plumb to operate properly.

Levels come in a variety of types, as shown in the photos here. The most widely used are the carpenter's, torpedo and line levels.

Carpenter's levels range in length from 18 to 48 in. and are even longer for specialized mason's levels. The 24-in. size is probably best for overall work. Most come with three bubble vials: a lengthwise center vial for horizontal surfaces, one end vial aligned at right angles to the edges for checking plumb, and a 45° vial at the other end for checking that angle accurately.

The torpedo level is much shorter, usually 9 in. long, and is handy for working in tight spots where a long carpenter's level won't fit. Newer models have three vials like the carpenter's levels, and some have a magnetic edge that will hold the tool on steel or iron workpieces. This

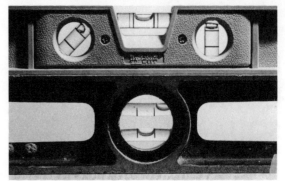

Older-type level (below) with bent-glass vials must be placed on top or bottom edge to read level properly. Newer design (top) has a single straight vial with barrel-shaped inside so that level can be used on edges and sides. Newer vials are also 20 percent larger in volume to provide better visibility.

feature frees your hands to hold the project and mark its proper position.

The line level is shorter still, about 3 in. long, and has two hooks on top so the instrument can hang on a string stretched tightly across a wide span. It's a good reference tool when doing grading or foundation layout and for checking long-span masonry and carpentry work.

Using a level requires no special skill. Just hold it firmly on the surface and be sure both the base of the level and the work surface are absolutely free of debris. You should also get in the habit of periodically checking a level for accuracy. One way to do this is to place the level on a surface and observe the position of the bubble. Then flip the level end over end and see if the bubble is in the same place. If it's not, adjust the vial—if it's possible with your model—or get a new level.

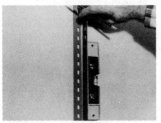

Torpedo level with magnetic edge frees hands when you're working.

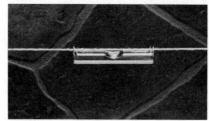

Aluminum line level hooks onto taut line for leveling over long spans. It weighs under 1 oz. so it will not sag the line. Flat bottom allows for its use as a surface level.

Short level can substitute for a longer level by taping it securely to longer board. Board must be straight and have uniform width.

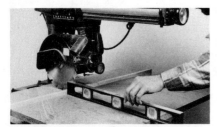

Use level to true up all tables and beds on stationary shop equipment. Level across table (as shown) and along table's length.

Bull's-eye level, on a post, shows plumb in both directions at once, as long as post top is perfectly square to post sides.

Inclinometer (level and angle finder) gives needle readings from 0 to 90° in any quadrant. Tool back has angle and grade chart.

USING CHISELS

Using chisels requires not only following the correct procedures but a tool that is razor-sharp.

The chisel is a freehand tool—which means the results you get with it depend entirely on your manual skill. You can easily master its use with a bit of practice, provided you follow correct procedures and work only with a tool that is razor-sharp.

The chisel is essentially a long knife. It is shaped so the pressure applied to the handle is concentrated on a comparatively small cutting edge that easily enters the wood and severs the fibers.

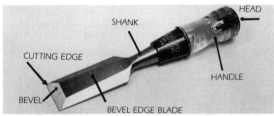

Parts of a chisel are shown above. Pressure is applied to the handle, either by hand or with a mallet. This drives the cutting edge into the wood fibers.

Good work with a chisel requires it to have a sharp edge. Honing on an oilstone maintains the edge. This Stanley honing guide ensures the correct bevel angle.

Outline hinge with knife; chisel vertical cuts on line with mallet, bevel toward waste. Make slant cuts on lines, bevel down. With mallet make score cuts; cut waste, bevel up.

Unless you are applying the driving force with a mallet, both hands are always in contact with the chisel. One hand grips the blade and controls the movement of the cutting edge, while the other hand applies pressure on the handle. The grip may be varied depending on the nature of the cut and personal preference. A comfortable grip aids good blade control.

The blade is flat on one side and beveled on the other. In general, use the chisel with the bevel up for finish (paring) cuts and down for roughing cuts.

In some situations, however, you must make the finish cut with the bevel down. For example, when cleaning out a long groove, the bevel must be down so the handle will be elevated and will clear the workpiece. This also applies when working in confined areas, such as when cutting a mortise. Concave cuts are also easily made with the bevel down; these would be quite difficult with the bevel up.

Whenever possible, hold the chisel at a slight side angle in relation to the direction of travel rather than following a straight path. This presents a smaller leading edge to the wood, resulting in smoother shavings.

Unless you have no choice, always cut *with* the grain. Otherwise, the chisel edge will act much like a wedge and split the wood ahead of it.

Although the chisel can do aggressive cutting when necessary, there's no need to overwork it. Use other tools, such as saws and drills, when feasible, to remove the bulk of the waste before working with a chisel.

To cut a mortise, bore overlapping holes to depth and trim off webs between holes with a chisel. Bore tiny holes in the four corners to simplify squaring corners.

Hold the bevel side of the chisel against the work to cut a concave curve. Push the handle down while pressing blade forward. Work from the edge toward the end grain.

Direct the bevel down when working in confined areas. Here, the left hand is positioned far from blade for photo clarity; it actually should be closer to the cutting edge.

USING POWER PLANES

Power planes do everything hand planes do—and more—with effortless ease.

If you're thinking about buying a power plane, rent one for a weekend the next time you plan to do a lot of planing. Heft the tool about and use it on practice cuts. Once you've mastered the art of getting the spinning cutter on and off the edge to be cut without making a dip—thus a gouge—you'll want your own.

Basically, a power plane does everything a hand plane does. The difference is that the planing job becomes effortless because the tool does all the work. You simply guide it.

The power plane, depending upon its maker, will have a spinning blade with one or more cutting edges, located not quite halfway back from the leading edge of the tool. To obtain depth-of-cut, the front shoe adjusts up or down (in the same fashion that a stationary shop jointer does).

Because the entire cutter on the bottom is exposed when the tool is in use, it should be used with extreme caution. Virtually every manufacturer includes a thorough manual with its tool. Read it through—especially the section dealing with safety. No matter which brand you buy, you'll find that handles and gripping portions of the tool are well away from the blade while the tool is in use. *Make certain you grip the tool as the manufacturer specifies.*

While it's no secret that power planes can make short work out of many planing tasks, they can also cause a great deal of trouble if they are not used properly. The two most common mistakes are improper tool alignment when starting and when finishing cuts. The best way to avoid these mistakes is to spend time practicing on a variety of scrap wood before you put the tool to any finish work.

Tool alignment is particularly crucial when planing the end grain of stock because the edge is normally quite short. To do this properly, hold the tool as shown in the photos and make a short pass in one direction—about 1 in. into the stock—then finish the cut from the other direction. The two cuts should meet flush, keeping you from splitting off any stock when you come to the long edge of the board.

Don't assume power planes are designed only for edge planing. These tools can be used for surface planing as well. Just keep in mind that scant stock removal is the best policy. If you have the cutter set too deep, these powerful tools can make severe gouges in a surface, almost before you know it's happening. It's a better idea to make several shallow cuts until the surface is flat.

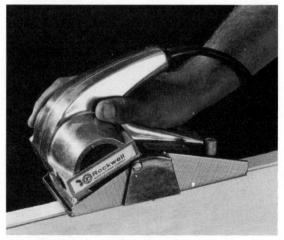

A well-maintained power plane with its supersharp cutter allows for fast removal of large amounts of edge stock. The tool can also be used to remove surface stock.

Here are left and right side views of a power planer. This rugged model is particularly outstanding when you have extensive planing sessions.

Another great use for the power plane is to cut rabbets along a board edge. To do this, you must have a planer equipped with a fence that functions in much the same way that a rip guide operates on a circular saw. By adjusting this fence in and out, you can regulate how far across the board the cutter will extend and, therefore, the width of the rabbet. The depth adjustment on the tool itself regulates the depth of the rabbet.

The depth-of-cut knob is rotated in order to achieve the particular cut you want.

The arrow on the knob serves as the pointer for aligning with index.

Before starting a cut, the shoe should be checked with a straightedge. When both plates are in the same plane, the depth-of-cut knob should be aligned at 0 mark.

It's crucial that the plane be positioned properly before starting. It should rest flat on the board edge, as shown here, with the cutter not yet touching the wood.

This exaggerated pose shows the wrong way to start a planing pass. But even if the back of the tool is just slightly lower than the leading edge, you will get a pronounced dip at the beginning of the cut.

Top board shows scoop that results from dropping rear of plane at beginning of cut. Bottom piece shows edge planed properly.

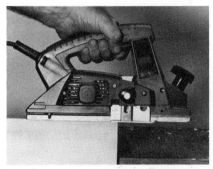

Maintaining the same flat tool alignment is equally important at the other end of a planing pass. Be sure the tool remains level until the cutter has moved completely clear of the board's edge.

This photo shows an exaggerated dip at the end of a cut. Be sure to watch for this tendency until you master the tool.

If you do let the front of the blade dip as it leaves the edge of the stock, you will get a gouge like the one above.

LIGHT CONTROL FOR CLOSE JOBS

Control an incandescent lamp to give you more light for close jobs.

At times when you're doing close work in the shop, a brighter-than-normal worklight would contribute to greater accuracy. This light-control unit regulates a high-wattage incandescent lamp. Most of the time the control holds the illumination at a comfortable working level. When you need more light, twist the control knob to bring the lamp up to its maximum brightness.

The light control shown is intended for mounting on a wall, ceiling or elsewhere within convenient reach from the workspot. The main components of the control are a push on-off dimmer switch of 600-w rating and a grounded duplex outlet that accepts two- or three-prong plugs.

House these two parts in a pair of surface-mounted steel outlet boxes fastened to a plywood base. You can simplify the arrangement by using one double duplex box and a combination outlet-switch plate. The two boxes shown here are linked by a piece of No. 10 copper wire so they both will be grounded. If made with two

The light control shown is tested for use with a No. 1 photoflood lamp on a workbench.

boxes, remove adjacent knockouts where the wires will pass through, and smooth the edges of the holes with a rattail file. Fasten the boxes firmly to the mounting base.

A length of No. 16, three-wire flexible cord brings power to the unit from a conventional outlet. If the power supply outlet isn't grounded, provide the unit with a wire connected to one of the screws holding the box-connecting link, and to a water pipe or other suitable ground.

Attach the wall plug so the dimmer switch is in the power side of the circuit (black wire in the diagram). The black wire should be attached to the brass-colored plug tine, which goes into the small slot in the wall outlet.

Be sure the dimmer you use is rated to handle the wattage of your worklight. This control is *not* suitable for fluorescent lights.

Completed light box is ready for mounting on a wall or other surface. Note box-connecting link near power cord clamp.

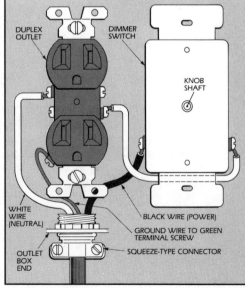

DUPLEX OUTLET

DIMMER SWITCH

KNOB SHAFT

WHITE WIRE (NEUTRAL)

OUTLET BOX END

BLACK WIRE (POWER)

GROUND WIRE TO GREEN TERMINAL SCREW

SQUEEZE-TYPE CONNECTOR

MATERIALS LIST
DIMMER CONTROL

No. Description

1 Dimmer-switch, 600-w rating at 120 v.a.c., push-on action
1 Duplex outlet, grounded, 15-amp., preferably heavy-duty
2 Outlet boxes, surface-mounted, steel (or use one double-duplex, steel, surface-mounted box)*
1 Toggle-switch plate for dimmer-switch box*

1 Duplex outlet plate for outlet box*
1 Squeeze-type cable connector
1 No. 16, three-wire flexible cord, length as needed
1 Grounded three-prong plug
1 No. 10 copper wire (bare), cut to length required by screw spacing, to link boxes
1 ½ x 4½ x 5½" wood base or similar
Misc.: Screws as required, No. 12 insulated wire
* If you use a double-duplex, surface-mounted outlet box, you can use a combination toggle-duplex outlet cover.

GUIDE TO NEW TOOLS AND EQUIPMENT

WOODWORKING TOOLS YOU SHOULD KNOW ABOUT

New tools in the marketplace to make your woodworking easier, safer and more professional-looking.

WOOD-CARVING KNIVES

Whether it's simple whittling or intricate carving, this set of 10 high-quality wood-carving knives does it all. There's a knife for every purpose, including inlaying, shaving, paring, inletting, notching, splicing, incising, and pattern- and model-making. The complete set is available from Fine Tool Shops.

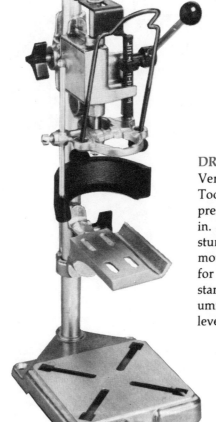

DRILL PRESS STAND

Vermont American, Hardware Tool Division, offers a deluxe drill press stand that converts a ¼- or ⅜-in. portable electric drill into a sturdy drill press. The drill can be mounted vertically or horizontally for use as a bench grinder. The stand has a rigid tubular steel column, die-cast aluminum base and a lever-action feed mechanism.

CORNER CHISELS

These Japanese corner chisels are super for squaring mortises and rounded corners. They have 3-in.-long blades and offset handles to provide clearance. They are available in three sizes from Garrett Wade: ⅜ in., ⅝ in. and 1 in.

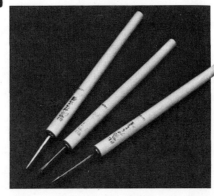

WOODWORKING GIMLETS

These unique Japanese woodworking tools, called gimlets, are used to make a quick hole by either rolling the long handle between your palms or by using it in a screwdriver-like motion. The set of three Japanese gimlets is available from Fine Tool Shops.

RABBET PLANES

These Stanley rabbet planes are available from Fine Tool Shops. The bull-nose rabbet plane, top, has a 1⅛-in.-wide blade. Model 93 has a blade adjustment screw and a removable top to use as a chisel plane. Model 92 is a smaller version of Model 93. The adjustable bull-nose, bottom, has its blade near the toe for working in corners.

INSHAVE SCORP

This is a specially designed inshave called a scorp. It's essentially a draw-knife that can be used with one hand. The scorp is used mainly for roughing out bowls, spoons, chair seats and other woodworking projects that must be hollowed out. It features a 1¼-in.-wide razor-sharp curved blade and a length of about 7 in. The Swiss-made scorp is available from Garrett Wade.

TRY AND MITER SQUARE

The Model TS-2 try square (left) and Model MS-2 miter square are both precision-built tools. Each square has a solid rosewood handle faced on both edges with solid brass wear plates and inlaid with brass rivet seats. The blades are precision-ground ⅛-in.-thick brass. Both are accurate within .002 in. The 8-in. try square and 11-in. miter square are available from Bridge City Tool Works.

WALKING-BEAM SCROLL SAW

The Craftsman 18-in. walking-beam scroll saw makes it easy to produce intricate, highly detailed scrollwork. For bevel-cutting, the blade-drive mechanism tilts 45° right or left while the worktable remains horizontal. Other features include a sawdust blower, miter gauge and clear plastic cutting shield. It's available from Sears.

REDESIGNED DRILL
Black & Decker has redesigned the drill. Model 7144 is a full-feature, ⅜-in. variable-speed reversing drill that is compact and energy-efficient. Its unique square shape allows drilling down along a framing square to ensure perpendicular holes.

MORTISE AND TENON JIG
Morten the Jig is for cutting precise mortise-and-tenon joints using a router with a ⁷⁄₁₆-in. guide bushing and ¼-in. straight bit. It's from Peterson Specialty Products.

RADIAL-ARM ROUTER KIT
A Convert-A-Tool radial-arm router kit attaches a router to a radial-arm saw for pin router operations. The kit fits most 10-in. saws with a double-arm saw carriage. All routers with housing diameters from 3 in. to 4½ in. will fit the U-bolt clamp. It can also plow dadoes and cut grooves and rabbets.

RADIAL-ARM SAW LENGTH GAUGE
The LG500 length gauge is designed to make cutting on a radial-arm saw more accurate, faster and safer. The tool consists of a length rod with a recessed steel measuring tape, a locking cam lever, a U-channel fence and the workpiece stop and carrier. In operation, the gauge is set to the desired measurement and locked in place with the cam lever. The stock is then held against the stop and the fence, and the cut is made. It's available in left- and right-handed mounts from Mertes Manufacturing.

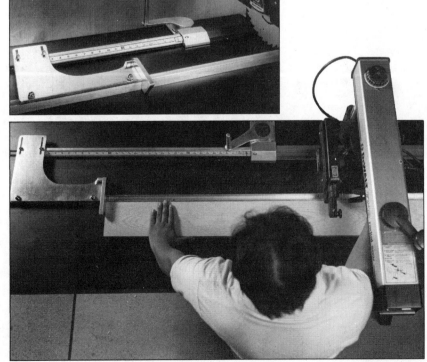

WORK CENTER

Turn your portable power tools into stationary tools with the Sears Work Center. The 25½ x 34 x 35-in.-high table can hold a circular saw and router attached to the tabletop underside while the surface accepts a drill press stand for use with the portable electric drill. The drill stand is optional. The Work Center also features an 18⅞-in.-wide vise with a 5-in. clamping capacity. Pieces up to 12 in. long can be clamped using the bench dogs. Available through Sears.

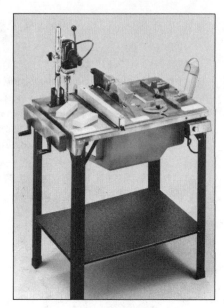

VERSATILE VISE

The quick vise from Black & Decker is a versatile tool for both woodworking and metalworking shops. The 5-in.-wide vise opens to 12 in. and comes with four swivel pegs for clamping irregularly shaped workpieces. The vise jaws can be used in a horizontal or vertical clamping position. The vise swivels 360° and disconnects easily from the base when it's not needed. The 10½-lb. vise is constructed of heavy-gauge steel and can be used as an anvil. The Quick Vise is available at hardware stores and home centers.

FRAME AND TRIM SAW

The Sawbuck frame and trim saw combines the accuracy and portability of a power miter box with the crosscutting capability of a radial-arm saw. When set at 45°, the saw can miter, bevel and cut compound angles in stock up to a 2 x 12. At 90°, the crosscut capacity is 16 in. The unit has a hefty 15-amp, 8-in. circular saw mounted on twin tubular steel guide arms. Die-cast aluminum and tubular steel construction gives the table superior rigidity without excess weight. It folds into a compact 22 x 32 x 50-in. unit and is equipped with two wheels for easy transport. It's made by Delta International Machinery Corp. (formerly Rockwell).

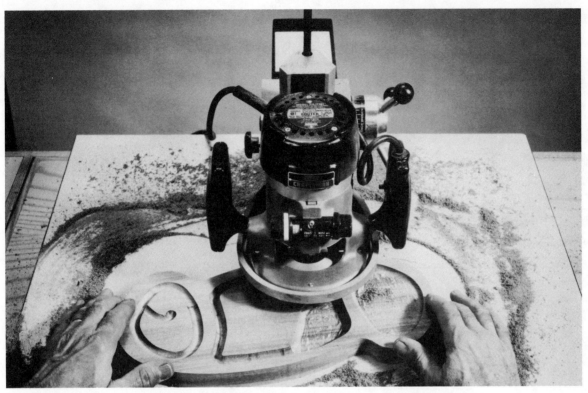

To carve wells in this candy tray, the workpiece is held in a jig and the well outlines are routed. Then, the field in each is routed by moving the workpiece back and forth.

DISCOVER THE PIN ROUTER

Let this revolutionary tool turn your portable router into a precision shaping system.

The router is considered by many craftsmen to be the most versatile and necessary power tool in their shop. In conventional handheld use, the router can perform a wide variety of operations. Here, we'll show you how to increase your router's usefulness and your woodworking skills by mounting the tool to a pin router assembly.

THE PIN ROUTER ASSEMBLY

The assembly looks and operates somewhat like a drill press. The router is mounted in a carriage positioned over the worktable. The depth-adjusting handle raises and lowers the carriage to obtain the desired depth of cut.

The most essential part of the pin router is the ¼-in.-dia. steel guide pin that projects from the worktable's surface. The guide pin is held in the pin block, which is adjusted to center the guide pin directly under the router bit. When the workpiece edge is moved against the guide

pin, the cutter shapes the edge accordingly. One advantage of pin-guided routing is that controlled, uniform shaping is possible using pilotless router bits.

Also, when using cutters with ³⁄₁₆-in.-dia. solid pilots, the problem of edge burning is eliminated. The larger ¼-in.-dia. guide pin creates a gap between the unprotected workpiece edge and the spinning pilot.

TEMPLATE PIN ROUTING

Template-guided routing is the most popular pin router function. Templates of ¼-in. hardboard serve as patterns, allowing you to make exact repetitive cuts with ease, speed and accuracy.

Cut the template to the desired shape and nail it to the workpiece's underside. As the guide pin follows the template, the desired shape is cut into the top surface of the workpiece.

Templates can be used for partial and full-edge trimming of workpieces. When full-edge trimming, cut the workpiece slightly larger than the template. Then, steer the template along the guide pin (which, remember, is aligned with the cutter) to trim the overhanging workpiece edge flush with the template.

Other template cuts include surface carving and surface grooving. Surface carving requires

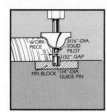

Pin router assembly parts are identified here without router.

BASIC ROUTING TECHNIQUES

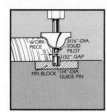

The guide pin creates a gap between the workpiece and the bit's pilot to prevent edge-burning.

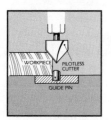

With the guide pin controlling the workpiece, uniform shaping is possible with pilotless cutters.

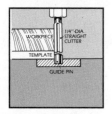

Attach a template to workpiece's underside for full-edge trimming. Depth-of-cut equals edge thickness.

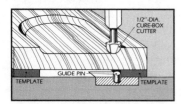
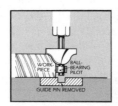

For surface carving, place guide pin against the template's inside edge. Enclose the guide pin completely for carving the workpiece's center section only.

Remove the guide pin from pin block when using ball-bearing piloted cutters.

templates with interior cutouts.

First, place the template over the guide pin, corralling the pin within the cutout. Then, lower the cutter into the workpiece and use freehand movement to carve out the workpiece's surface. The trapped guide pin prevents cutting beyond the template's borders.

Surface-grooving templates are used to cut curved grooves across a workpiece's surface. This method uses two templates spaced ¼ in. apart, forming a channel.

Pass the workpiece over the guide pin, steering the pin into the template's channel. The confined guide pin will keep the workpiece on track, preventing any off-course drift.

BALL-BEARING PILOTED ROUTING

When using router bits fitted with ball-bearing pilots, no template is needed, so remove the guide pin from the worktable. After setting the router's depth of cut, steer the workpiece's edge along the ball-bearing pilot. The bearing will serve to guide the workpiece, establishing a uniform cutting edge.

FENCE-GUIDED ROUTING

With the pin guide removed and a fence clamped to the worktable, the pin router performs much like a stationary shaper. The fence guides the workpiece to produce a variety of straight cuts and mortises.

Full-edge jointing is possible, using an offset fence. Cut the fence's receiving end wider than its feed end. The offset compensates for the amount of stock being removed by the cutter, and work is fully supported for its length. Use a ¼-in.-dia. double-flute straight cutter, and don't offset the fence more than ⅛ in. Avoid trying to remove too much stock at once or you will dull the cutter and overload the router, with possible damage to the motor.

SETTING UP THE ROUTER

The first step in setting up a pin router is mounting the router to the carriage support plate. First, remove the plastic soleplate from the router's base. Routers without soleplates are always mounted as is. *Caution:* Always unplug the router before mounting, making adjustments and changing the cutter bit.

The next step is adjusting the guide pin to align with the cutter bit. The Sears pin router shown comes with a steel alignment pin that's used for this purpose.

First, chuck the alignment pin into the router. Then, lower the carriage, using the depth-adjusting handle until the alignment pin is ⅛ in.

above the guide pin. Tighten the carriage lock knob to hold the carriage in position. Adjust the pin block so the guide pin is directly under the alignment pin. To check for precise final alignment, remove the guide pin and lower the carriage until the alignment pin enters the guide pin hole. If necessary, readjust the pin block to achieve perfect alignment.

PIN ROUTING PROJECTS

Here are techniques and procedures for making three projects—a pediment (ornamental crown detail) using dual templates, a candy tray using a surface carving template and a picture frame shaped with ball-bearing piloted cutters.

Whenever routing, regardless of the technique or type of cutter used, always feed the workpiece against the rotation of the cutter bit. For photo clarity the pin router's plastic safety guard has been removed. During actual routing operations, you should always set the guard ¼ in. above the workpiece.

Pediment. A pair of hardboard templates are used to make the pediment. Cut one template to match the outline of the pediment's back panel. Shape the second template to conform to the built-up molded crown's inside curve. Transfer the shapes of the templates onto two boards. Then rough-cut the boards ¹⁄₁₆ in. larger than the template's outline. Tack-nail the templates to the underside of their respective boards. Use a ¼-in.-dia. straight bit to trim the rough-cut boards flush with the templates.

Two cutters are needed to shape the molded crown's profile. First, rout the crown's lower portion, using a ⅜-in. beading cutter. Then, install a ⅜-in. cove cutter to form the profile's concave upper portion. Cut the crown from the board to match the top outline of the pediment's back panel. Cut the molded crown in half to form the left and right side crown molding. Glue and nail the crown pieces onto the pediment's back panel, allowing the top edges to overhang ¹⁄₁₆ in. Trim the pediment's top edge flush, using a ¼-in.-dia. straight bit. Top off the pediment with a finial turned on a lathe.

Candy tray. Start by nailing a piece of ¼-in. hardboard to a ¾-in.-thick mahogany hardwood board. Then, cut out and edge-sand the candy tray's shape to both pieces simultaneously. Remove the hardboard and cut out the three tray sections. Sand the cutout's interior edges smooth. Then, reattach the hardboard to the workpiece for use as a template.

Next, install a ¾-in.-dia. core box cutter in the router for carving the three tray compartments. Set the depth-stop gauge for an ⅛-in.-deep cut.

Position one of the template's cutouts over the guide pin, start the router and make a plunge cut. Lock the carriage in this position, using the carriage lock knob. With the guide pin against the cutout's inside edge, slowly move the workpiece against the rotation of the cutter to groove the tray compartment's perimeter. Lower the carriage ⅛ in. on each pass until you reach ⅝ in. deep. Repeat this procedure for the two remaining tray compartments.

Once you've grooved all three compartments to ⅝ in. deep, reset the depth-of-cut to ⅛ in. Place one of the template's cutouts over the guide pin, make a plunge cut and lock the carriage.

Using freehand movement, shift the workpiece back and forth to clear out the waste area. Continue, taking deeper cuts in ⅛-in. increments until reaching ⅝ in. deep. Repeat this procedure for two remaining compartments.

Ease the candy tray's sharp outside corners with a ¼-in. rounding-over bit.

Picture frame. The oval picture frame's decorative edge and rabbeted glass recess are both routed with ball-bearing piloted cutters. As is the case with all ball-bearing piloted routing, a template isn't required, so the guide pin is removed.

After sawing the frame's oval shape, finish-sand the inside and the outside edges. Next, rout the decorative outside edge with a ½-in. beading cutter. Then, place the frame face down on the worktable and use a ⅜-in. rabbet cutter to rout a ¼-in.-deep rabbet in the frame's back inside edge.

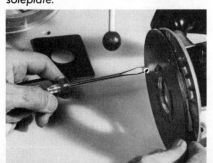

Before you mount the router to the carriage, be sure to remove plastic soleplate.

Use the alignment pin for locating the router bit's exact center. Loosen the pin block's screws. Then shift the guide pin directly under the alignment pin.

Use the knurled depth-stop gauge to control the plunge-cut depths accurately.

PIN ROUTING PROJECTS

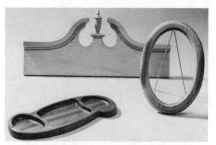

The depth-indicator scale is ruled in 1/32-in. increments to give fine adjustments.

Projects shown prior to shaping: pediment with dual templates, picture frame (which needs no template) and candy tray with surface carving template.

Completed projects: carved candy tray, pediment with built-up molded crown and oval picture frame that was shaped with ball-bearing piloted cutters.

SURFACE-CARVING A CANDY TRAY

Use a straight cutter to trim the crown's top edge flush with the back panel.

Nail the candy tray's surface carving template to the workpiece's underside.

Keep the guide pin against the template cutout's inside edge to groove the perimeters of each candy tray compartment.

Make final leveling passes with the router set for extremely shallow cuts.

ROUTING A DECORATIVE FRAME

Remove the guide pin from the pin block when using ball-bearing piloted cutters.

To shape the frame's outside edge, simply steer it against the ball-bearing pilot.

Rout the glass recess into the frame's back inside edge with a rabbeting bit.

TOOLS THAT WILL SURPRISE YOU

What tools would you buy if you were turned loose in a well-stocked hardware store?

What tools would an active homeowner or woodworking enthusiast select if turned loose in a well-stocked hardware store? *PM's* home and shop editors came up with the tools shown. Their favorites either performed a specialized task, like cutting glass discs or trimming miters perfectly, or performed an ordinary task particularly well, such as smoothing wood or boring tapered screw holes. These are tools you may well want to add to your collection.

PICTURE-FRAMING TOOLS

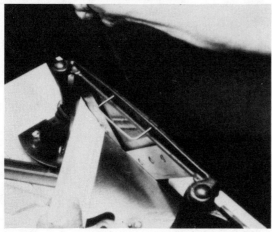

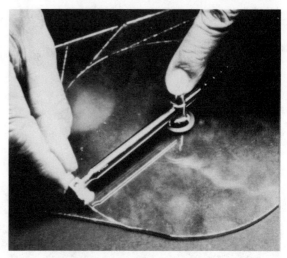

Miter trimmer. After you make a cut with a saw and miterbox, the massive hollow ground blades of this miter trimmer cut like a razor to produce an accurate finish cut that is glass smooth and requires no sanding. A left and a right gauge lock into any angle you desire from 45° to 90° to guide an angled cut. You can use the trimmer on stock up to 4 in. wide when mitering. You can also use it to square ends on stock up to 6 in. wide. The miter trimmer is available from Woodcraft.

Circle glass cutter. The circle glass cutter cuts up to 10½-in.-dia. disks for picture frames, mirrors, clocks and flashlights. Hold the rubber pivot firmly in the center of the glass and rotate the cutter head in a circle. Next, adjust the cutter head for straight cuts and make tangential cuts from the circle to the edge of the glass. Break off the pieces formed and you have a perfect glass disk. The cutter, from Brookstone, comes with three spare cutting wheels and a screwdriver.

WOODWORKING TOOLS

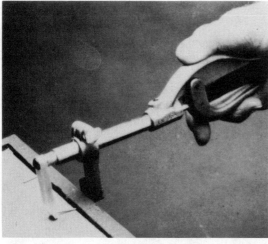

Brad pusher. This lever-assisted brad pusher makes setting the smallest brads a fast, simple and accurate task. You can drive brads without bending them, damaging your fingers or marring the workpiece. It's especially handy for setting the small brads that hold the backing in a picture frame. One jaw padded with rubber protects the frame while the other jaw presses in the brad. The pusher works on molding up to 1¾ in. deep x 3½ in. wide. It's from Constantine.

Block plane. This superb small plane by E. C. Emmerich, West Germany, is available now in the United States. For the same price you'd expect to pay for a first-rate steel plane, you can now enjoy the feel of working with an all-wood one. Its 2⅟₁₆ x 5⅞-in. body is crafted of varnished-steamed beech and the bottom plate is of hornbeam. Surprisingly, the block plane features a depth adjustment knob—no more tapping the blade to depth with a hammer. It's available here from Hammermark Associates.

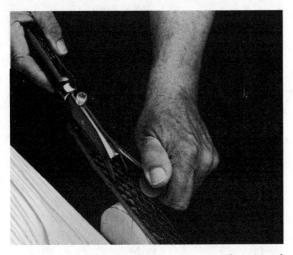

Saw rasp. This Japanese saw rasp planes and shapes wood smoothly and quickly without clogging. It's made of 10 two-sided hacksaw blades assembled so the fine teeth are on one side of the rasp and the coarse teeth are on the other. The overall cutting surface is 1¼ x 10¼ in. To change sides for use, loosen the knurled nut on top and reposition the handle. The round knob gives you an extra hold for two-handed leverage. The saw rasp is available from The Woodworkers' Store.

Spokeshave. This round-face spokeshave works like a plane to smooth concave surfaces. Adjusting screws allow setting for thickness of shaving and provide lateral positioning. Normally, you would set the blade almost flush with the sole. Work with the grain to prevent tearing the wood on curves. The round-face spokeshave is available from Garrett Wade Co. A flat-face spokeshave that helps to chamfer or bevel edges and smoothes flat surfaces is also available from the company.

Cabinet scrapers. With this set of cabinet scrapers, you'll be able to smooth hollows and convex shapes as well as flat surfaces—nearly every shape you'll encounter in the workshop. The set includes a gooseneck 2¾ x 4¾ in., a round-end 2 x 5¾ in. and a straight scraper 2⅜ x 5⅞ in. Besides scraping paper-thin shavings to smooth wood, you can remove paint and fillers in hard-to-reach parts of moldings and in other irregular surfaces. The set comes from The Woodworker's Store.

Hold-down clamp. You can install this handy hold-down clamp anywhere on your bench by simply boring and counterboring a hole and installing a hold-down bolt. The clamp slides onto the bolt head ready to secure work that's up to 3 in. thick. The clamp rotates 360° around the holding bolt to secure work at the right spot or easiest angle for the hobbyist. When it's no longer needed, remove the clamp and let the hold-down bolt drop down out of the way. The hold-down clamp is from Leichtung.

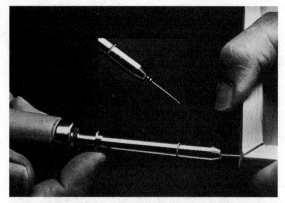

Brad driver. The wood-handled brad driver has a magnetic barrel that picks up a brad (inset photo), drives and sets it. The tool drives up to 1-in., 16- to 19-ga. brads. It is invaluable for paneling jobs, where one hand holds the panel while the other picks up and secures the brad. It's also handy when constructing picture frames, fastening window screens, applying decorative molding and working on miniatures and models. You can find many other uses. The brad driver is from Hyde Tools.

Countersink/counterbore bits. There's a tapered bit for boring holes that conform to the shape of a screw. Each bit comes with a matched fitted stop collar and countersink/counterbore. In one operation you can prepare the wood for the threads, the screwhead and a wood plug. A setscrew, adjusted with the included Allen wrench, secures the stop collar in position to counterbore for a plug or countersink for a screwhead. A set of seven bits for screw sizes Nos. 5 through 12 is from Garrett Wade Co.

HOME IMPROVEMENT AND MAINTENANCE TOOLS

Hole cutter. Finally, there's a hole cutter claimed by its maker to work in a portable electric drill—and it does. The cutter removes disks from 1½ to 18 in. in diameter in wood, plastic and soft metals. You can make portholes and speaker or basin cutouts in wood or plastic laminate, to name a few uses. Push the free end clockwise to get a clean hole (cutout); push it counterclockwise to cut a clean disk. Cutter from Constantine includes a steel case, a bit and an Allen wrench.

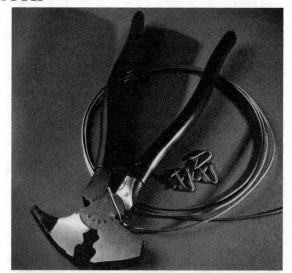

Fenceman's tool. You'll find countless uses for this multipurpose fenceman's tool. For starters, it stretches and twists wire, pulls and drives staples and cuts heavy-gauge wire. In other words, you can use it as a plier, a wrench and a hammer. The handles of the 10½-in.-long tool are clad in soft vinyl to give you a comfortable grip. The driver weighs a hefty 21 oz. and is made of high-tensile-strength alloy steel hot dropforged. Get it from Brookstone.

SUPPLIERS

Brookstone Co., Dept. PM, 695 Vose Farm Rd., Peterborough, N.H. 03458.
Constantine and Son Inc., 2050 Eastchester Rd., Bronx, N.Y. 10461.

Garrett Wade Co., 161 Avenue of the Americas, New York, N.Y. 10013.
Hammermark Associates, Box 201, Floral Park, N.Y. 11002.
Hyde Tools, (Attn: Marketing Dept.), Southbridge, Mass. 01550.

Leichtung Inc., 4944 Commerce Parkway, Cleveland, Ohio 44128.
Woodcraft Supply Corp., Box 4000, Woburn, Mass. 01888.
The Woodcrafters' Store, 2180 Industrial Blvd., Rogers, Minn. 55374.

OTHER NEW TOOLS

Here's a list of some of the new tools introduced recently to help you improve your work.

PROGRAMMABLE SAW

An electronic, 10-in. radial-arm saw is now offered by Sears, Roebuck and Co. The 1½-hp saw has a microprocessor and features a digital display and touch control panel for automatic blade height elevation. This eliminates the need for crank handles. Simply program in the desired blade height on the pushbutton control panel. Then, as the digital display reads out the blade height to .005 of an inch, the saw automatically raises or lowers the blade to the programmed height. An elevation jog button allows you to raise or lower the blade in .005-in. increments with each touch of the button. The digital display also reads bevel and miter angles to a degree.

ELECTRONIC MEASURING TAPE

Calcutape instantly converts English measurements to metric and vice versa. It converts length, volume, temperature and weight. Also instantly computes circumference to a circle from its diameter. Calcutape is a calculator featuring constant, square and power, reciprocal and memory functions. It is also programmed to give you Pythagorean calculations. So at the touch of a button, you get the hypotenuse of a right triangle. This can be very useful in determining the pitch of a roof line or the cross-squaring method to get a true 90° angle. Calcutape can be mail-ordered from Innovations in Owings Mills, Maryland.

ELECTRONIC STUD FINDER

Magnetic stud sensors can't really locate studs—they find only the nails. This stud sensor locates actual studs. Using a technology called "diaelectric constant," the Stud Sensor measures change in density and is capable of locating not just the general areas of studs but their exact dimensions and center. Now you can install shelves, hang pictures, put up heavy mirrors, suspend hanging plants, install new wiring—all without drilling exploratory holes or ruining your wall surface. Works on sheetrock, plaster, wood or acoustic ceilings. It's available from Innovations in Owings Mills, Maryland.

OLD LADDER LEARNS NEW TRICKS

No other ladder can do the things new Flexladder can, claims distributor Innovations in Owings Mills, Md. Use Flexladder as a 12-ft. straight ladder, a double-sided 6-ft. stepladder, a scaffold or one of dozens more unusual shapes to help with any job. The key to Flexladder's versatility is its ingenious hinges. They rotate and flex to any of three positions, then lock tight. Has anti-slip rungs and stay-put rubber feet for safety.

THREE-TOOL CUTTING GUIDE

For the do-it-yourselfer who wants to add accuracy and safety to paneling and remodeling jobs, the Panel Crafter portable guide will come in handy. You can use it with a circular saw, sabre saw or router to cut sheet material such as plywood, paneling, particleboard and hardboard. The guide permits cuts from ½ to 24 in. wide and bevel cuts of up to 45°. Normal depth-of-cut capacity is reduced by about ¹¹⁄₁₆ in. when using the guide. The Panel Crafter is available at hardware stores. For details, contact Vermont American, Hardware Tool Divison.

ADJUSTABLE DRILL GUIDE

Get drill press accuracy with your portable drill by using the Precision Drill Guide (No. 36). It allows accurate boring of right-angle holes or adjusts for angled boring up to 45°. Anchor pin centers guide for boring the workpiece edge. Contact General Hardware Co. for the hardware store nearest you carrying the product.

RADIAL-ARM MITER GAUGE

The Radial-Miter attachment lets you cut precise 45° left and right miters on a radial-arm saw without moving the saw's arm. It's made of sturdy aluminum with the guide edges machined to a true 90° for producing square joints. The Radial-Miter has a built-in C-clamp for mounting to the front edge of the saw table. A wood cam is supplied for securing the workpiece against the guide edge to prevent creeping and kickback. It's available from Topper Manufacturing Co.

AFFORDABLE POWER PLANE

Skil now offers an affordable power plane with features usually found on professional planes. The Model 94, 3¼-in,. 4/10-hp plane features an adjustable depth-of-cut knob, rabbet-cutting capabilities, a double V-groove footplate for chamfering and two reversible high-speed steel cutters.

QUICK-LOCK C-CLAMP

The Peterson Manufacturing Co., makers of Vise-Grip hand tools, has introduced a new line of quick-locking C-clamps that feature self-leveling swivel pads. The swivel pads let you clamp together tapered or uneven surfaces. The clamps are available at hardware stores and home centers in three sizes: 6 in., 11 in. and 18 in.

ABRASIVE ERASERS

Sanding Insurance is the name of giant erasers made by Granlund Engineering Co. The company claims the erasers are effective in removing all kinds of embedded material from sanding belts, disks, drums and sheets, thereby increasing the life of all abrasives.

SUPER ROUTER

If you do a lot of routing in hard materials, consider this brute from Black & Decker. With 3½ hp, it offers a 20,000-rpm operating speed for wood and other soft materials and a 16,000-rpm speed for harder workpieces, such as aluminum. Even with that much power, the tool still has an electronic speed control and overload protection system. The 15-lb. tool's other features include a topside on/off thumbswitch for operator safety and control and a shutoff probe device.

DOVETAIL JIG

Here's good news for both the amateur and professional woodworker. It's now possible to make through dovetail joints using a router, thanks to the Leigh dovetail jig. Ordinarily, dovetail jigs cut only half-blind joints with pins and tails of one size and spacing. But the Leigh jig helps cut true *through* dovetails just as you would by hand, only with greater speed and precision.

To use the jig, first position the mating workpieces flush under the adjustable guide fingers. Then secure them by tightening the clamp bars. Space the fingers as desired and lock them in place. The fingers guide the router, which is fitted with a guide bushing, to cut the joint. The pins and half-pins are formed with a straight cutter while following the angled guide fingers. Make the tails by following the square-end fingers using a dovetail cutter.

SAFER CHAIN SAWING

The Lift'N Guard chain saw attachment allows you to cut wood right where it lies—no more lifting heavy logs onto a sawbuck or similar log-holding device. This unique attachment eliminates chain pinching while protecting the bar and chain from hitting the ground. When cutting larger logs or when felling trees, the Lift'N Guard pivots upward, allowing the saw to be used normally. The product comes from Energy Equipment complete with a new bar and chain in 14-in., 16-in. and 20-in. lengths.

SANDING SAW BLADE

Smoother, faster and more accurate cuts with no splintered edges—even in plywood or particleboard—are possible with Sanblade's 7¼-in. or 10-in. saw blade. Sanblade combines a two-faced sanding disk with a circular saw blade. High rpm enables the 40-grit aluminum oxide abrasive bonded to both sides of the blade to sand-cut edges as smooth as 120-grid used normally. Diamond-honed carbide teeth cut up to 50,000 board-feet before dulling, according to the manufacturer. Kerosene and an old toothbrush remove gum from the abrasive on the blade. It's supposed to last almost indefinitely, but can be recoated and the teeth resharpened by a dealer. Clemson Group offers both sizes.

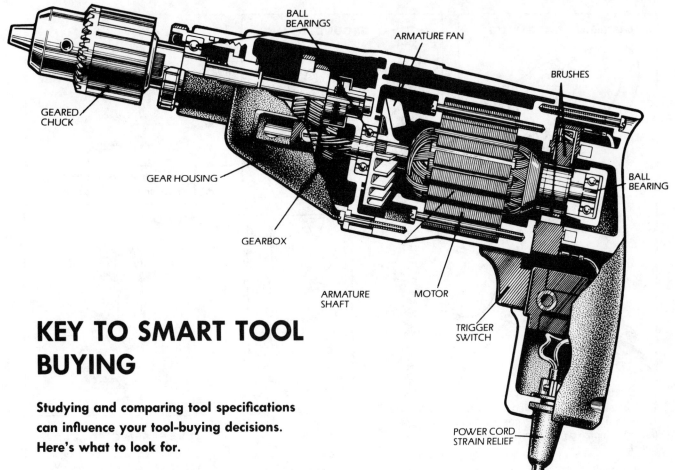

BALL BEARINGS

ARMATURE FAN

BRUSHES

GEARED CHUCK

BALL BEARING

GEAR HOUSING

GEARBOX

ARMATURE SHAFT

MOTOR

TRIGGER SWITCH

POWER CORD STRAIN RELIEF

KEY TO SMART TOOL BUYING

Studying and comparing tool specifications can influence your tool-buying decisions. Here's what to look for.

At one time, buying a portable power tool was fairly simple. You'd go to the local lumberyard or hardware store and buy a tool with a brand name you trusted. It was often the same tool your father used. Purchases were based mostly on personal preference and past experiences. Although these are still two valid reasons for purchasing a tool, they alone are not enough.

THE TOOL MARKET

Today, manufacturers are offering more tools than ever before, and it's important to study the details, the specifications, before buying. The introduction of foreign tools has created a competitive market similar to the situation found in the automobile industry—quality products available in a wide range of prices.

Today's toolmakers recognize the need for a wide range of products to satisfy all skill levels. It wasn't long ago that the homeowner had only two choices: Pay top dollar for a high-quality, professional-grade tool or buy a light-duty, low-quality tool. There were no middle-range tools for the average do-it-yourselfer. Now, manufacturers commonly produce a consumer, tradesman and professional line of tools.

Tools are also available at more places than

ever before. Besides the lumberyard and hardware store, power tools are sold at home centers, discount department stores, mass merchandisers, manufacturer's service centers and through mail-order tool companies. So it's easier to buy the tool that is just right for your budget and skill level. But deciding on a specific model is more difficult because of the many choices available. For example, Skil makes 14 different circular saws and Black & Decker offers more than 50 drill models. The first step in making an intelligent buying decision is to research the tool market so you can compare and evaluate the tool specifications of different brand tools. By doing this, you'll learn which ones are best suited to your purposes.

DO YOUR HOMEWORK

All major toolmakers offer a catalog that describes each tool in detail (see source list). Studying the catalogs is a great way to compare the specifications—amps, horsepower, weight, capacities, bearings, rpm—of one tool to another. Tool specifications can be clues to the expected performance of a hand tool and can

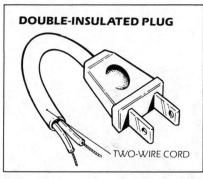

DOUBLE-INSULATED PLUG

TWO-WIRE CORD

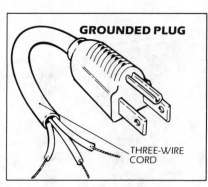

GROUNDED PLUG

THREE-WIRE CORD

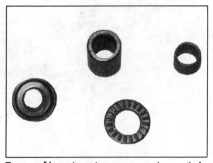

Types of bearings in power tools are (left to right); ball, roller, needle and sleeve.

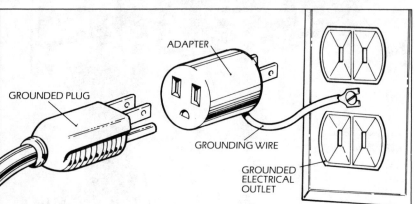

ADAPTER

GROUNDED PLUG

GROUNDING WIRE

GROUNDED ELECTRICAL OUTLET

Tools have a double-insulated, two-wire (top, left) or a three-prong grounded plug (top, right). Use an adapter (lower) to match a grounded plug with a two-wire outlet.

BALL BEARING

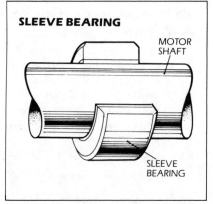

SLEEVE BEARING

MOTOR SHAFT

SLEEVE BEARING

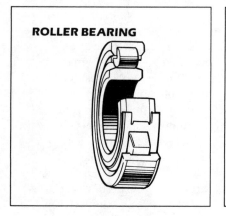

ROLLER BEARING

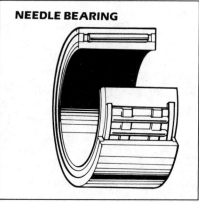

NEEDLE BEARING

Drawings show cutaway views of four bearings. The rolling elements, balls, rollers and needles, are held in position by the cage. Sleeve bearings have no rolling elements.

justify the price difference between two seemingly identical tools. Tool catalogs also provide valuable information about warranties, accessories, service center locations and tool operator safety. When ordering a catalog, be sure you ask for a current retail price schedule, too.

After studying the catalogs, bring them to the stores for use as reference guides. You'll find that most stores carry only a few models of each tool from two or three manufacturers. Contact the manufacturer if you're having trouble locating a specific tool and ask for a list of tool

dealers in your area.

Another important factor to consider before purchasing a power tool is the location of the nearest authorized service center. If the tool breaks down, you shouldn't have to send it back to the manufacturer for repairs. Check the tool catalog for the nearest service center. Call them and ask a technician about the speed of repairs and the availability of replacement parts. Porter-Cable, for example, pledges to have a disabled tool operating within 72 hours or they'll provide a loaner tool.

LOCATING TOOL SPECIFICATIONS

There are four places to find tool specifications: in the tool catalogs, on the tool's packaging, in the owner's manual and on the nameplate affixed to the tool. The catalogs contain the most helpful information regarding tool specifications.

The specifications that will influence your buying decisions the most include the ampere rating (amps), horsepower, what type of bearings are used and if the tool carries an Underwriters' Laboratories (UL) label.

Amp rating. Amps are the standard unit for measuring the strength of an electric current. The amp rating of a tool is usually found on its nameplate.

It's commonly thought that higher amp ratings mean more power, and in most cases this is true. But don't use amp rating as the single deciding factor when comparing tools. A low-grade tool often requires more current to perform the same job as a high-quality, highly efficient tool. The lower-grade tool, therefore, may have a higher amp rating.

Horsepower. The horsepower rating of a tool motor represents the maximum horsepower the tool can develop, rather than the actual horsepower output when operating at the specified amp rating. In actuality, motors can run for only a very short time at maximum horsepower without burning out. But the horsepower rating does give you an idea of the motor output when comparing tools.

Horsepower ratings are most important when buying a router or circular saw. Choose the horsepower rating depending on the job you're doing. Don't expect a ⅝-hp router to perform the heavy-duty operations of a 2- or 3-hp router. When you're looking for power, look for more horsepower.

Bearings. Discovering what kinds of bearings are used in a tool is probably your most important quality consideration. It's a simple fact that high-quality bearings improve performance and the life of the tool. The types of bearings used are usually listed in the manufacturer's catalog or in the owner's manual.

There are basically four types of bearings used in tool construction (see drawing): ball, roller, needle and sleeve. Occasionally, you'll see ball-thrust bearings, a special type of ball bearing that is designed to resist loads acting in an axial direction to the armature shaft. They're commonly used in hammer drills. Sometimes, a combination of bearings is used, such as ball and roller or ball and sleeve. All ball-bearing construction is considered the most desirable, with ball and roller construction a close second.

Ball bearings consist of steel balls that move within an enclosed circular channel called a cage. Roller bearings, on the other hand, are made of cylindrical rolling elements. Needle bearings are similar to roller bearings except that the rolling elements are longer and generally have smaller diameters. Their one advantage over roller bearings is that they require less space. In every other respect, though, needle bearings perform with far less efficiency than either ball or roller bearings.

A sleeve bearing has no true rolling element and is the least efficient bearing. Sleeve bearings are commonly used, though, in combination with ball and/or roller bearings in quality tools. They're used in areas where the least amount of load will be exerted on the bearing.

Single-sleeeve bearings (see photo) are made from powdered bronze or iron impregnated with lubricant at extremely high temperatures. As the sleeve heats up during tool use, the lubricant is released from the metal. Single-sleeve bearings are commonly used in drills.

As you compare tool specifications, you'll find the bearings are often the difference between the regular-duty tool and a heavy-duty model.

Underwriters' Laboratories. While most tool specifications affect a tool's performance and durability, the most important specification, the UL label, assures tool operator safety. The UL label means the tool has been tested and met stringent electrical and mechanical safety standards. Look for the UL label on the tool nameplate, packaging and owner's manual. All major toolmakers carry the UL listing, and we strongly recommend buying only UL-listed tools.

Also, make certain the tool is either double-insulated or has a three-prong grounded plug (see drawing). Both provide protection from the danger of electrical shock.

All power tools have a basic or functional insulation system to separate the current-carrying parts from each other and from the metallic motor components. Without this functional insulation, the tool would not operate. In double-insulated tools, an extra insulating system is provided for additional protection against electrical shock in case the functional insulation fails. Double-insulated tools have a two-wire cord with a two-prong plug.

Grounded tools have three-wire cords and a plug with three prongs, one of which is the ground. A wire connects the ground prong to the tool's metal housing.

Caution: Use a grounded plug only in a matching outlet. Never break off the grounding prong for use in a two-wire outlet. An adapter, as shown, can be used with a two-wire outlet, but *only* if the outlet itself is grounded and the adapter pigtail is attached to the facing plate mounting screw as shown in the drawing. If necessary, you should have an electrician check the electrical outlet for ground.

Double-insulated and grounded tools are equally safe when they are used properly. The average homeowner will find double-insulated tools are more versatile since many homes have two-wire outlets.

DRILLS

The portable electric drill is by far the most popular consumer power tool. It's available in a variety of styles, capacities, power ratings and prices.

Drills are sized according to the maximum diameter bit accepted by the chuck. The most common sizes are ¼, ⅜ and ½ in. Active homeowners will find a ⅜-in. drill provides a nice combination of power and versatility in a medium price range. Drills are rated by amps and by the no-load speed (rpm). Amps generally range from 2 to 6. The higher the amp rating, the more powerful the drill. The rpm, on the other hand, drop as the power increases. So, if you're looking for power in a drill, buy lower rpm and higher amps.

Two popular drill features are variable-speed trigger control and a reversible motor. Variable-speed allows you to control the bit speed with finger pressure, and the reversing mode is necessary for removing screws and jammed drill bits.

Next, handle the drill. It should feel balanced and comfortable in your hand. Some models have center-mounted handles to distribute the weight evenly, making the tool less nose-heavy. Also, check to be sure the drill manufacturer offers a full line of accessories.

CIRCULAR SAWS

When fitted with the appropriate blade, the portable, powerful circular saw will cut wood, metal, plastics and masonry materials. Circular saws are classified by the diameter saw blade they use. Common sizes range from 4½ to 10¼

in. The 4½-in. saw is a specialty tool used for cutting plywoods, paneling and trim stock. The 10¼-in. saw is an industrial heavyweight that has no practical use for the homeowner. The middle-range models, 7¼- and 8¼-in., better suit the consumer. The principal difference between these two is that the larger saw has a greater depth-of-cut.

When comparing saws, the tool specifications that influence your buying decision the most include horsepower, amp rating, bearings and maximum depth-of-cut at 90° and 45°.

The safety features to look for when buying a circular saw are an electric brake that stops the blade within seconds of releasing the trigger, and a slip-clutch that prevents dangerous kickback and motor burnout. Should the blade bind in a cut, the clutch will override the connection between the blade and the motor. This allows the motor armature to rotate even though the blade is stopped.

Also, check the saw's retractable blade guard. See that it slides up smoothly, closes quickly when released and operates without excessive play that could cause the guard to hang up. Choose a saw that has a front handle or knob for additional control and a heavy-gauge, sturdy wraparound shoe.

Most circular saws are rated standard-, heavy- or super-duty based on the amps, horsepower and bearings. The best buy would be a standard-duty, 7¼-in., 1½- to 2-hp. 10-amp ball-bearing circular saw.

SABRE SAWS

The lightweight, portable sabre saw, or jigsaw, is unsurpassed for cutting curves in a variety of materials including softwood and hardwood, plywood, metal, plastic, leather and rubber.

Sabre saws are rated according to horsepower, blade speed and blade stroke length. Consumer saws range from ⅙ to ⅝ hp. As with other tools, more horsepower means greater cutting power. A ⅓-hp sabre saw is adequate for the average do-it-yourselfer.

Saw blade speed is measured in strokes per minute (spm). Saws are available in single-speed, two-speed and variable-speed models. The variable-speed model offers greater versatility and control.

The blade stroke length is the distance that the blade travels in one stroke. A 1-in. stroke length is the most common. Some sabre saws have a scrolling mechanism that allows the blade to pivot 360°. Scrolling sabre saws are worth the additional cost if you need to do intricate, highly detailed scrollwork.

Other points to look for when comparing sabre saws include the cutting capacities in wood and metal and if the shoe is adjustable for cutting angles. Also, examine the saw blade clamp, the fixture that holds the blade in the saw. This is a common weak link in sabre saws. Be sure the blade clamp fits on the saw shaft without excessive play. Any wobbling in this clamp will be transferred to the blade. Be certain the clamp accepts universal, straight shank saw blades. Avoid a saw that uses only specially shaped blades. And finally, choose a saw in which adjustments and blade changes are made with a screwdriver, not a hex-key wrench. It seems you can always find a screwdriver.

BELT SANDERS

A portable belt sander is a quick, easy way to smooth rough boards and remove old finishes. Sanders are identified according to their belt size and belt speed.

The most popular size sanders are 3 x 21 in., 3 x 14 in. and 4 x 24 in. The 3 x 21-in. sander is a good, all-purpose tool for the home workshop. For light-duty sanding, Skil and Black & Decker each makes a small, easy-to-handle 2½ x 16-in. sander. The power of a belt sander is determined by the amp rating and horsepower. But generally, the larger the belt size, the more powerful the sander.

The belt speed is rated as surface feet per minute (sfpm). Look for this information in the tool catalogs. The best-performing 3 x 21-in. belt sanders operate with a belt speed between 1,000 and 1,300 sfpm. Be sure the sander has an adjustment knob for keeping the belt on track. Some Skil sanders have an automatic tracking system that eliminates the adjustment knob.

Next, check the belt-changing procedure. The simple practice of changing sanding belts shouldn't be a troublesome task. Choose a sander with a belt release lever for quick, easy belt changes. Other desirable features in belt sanders include a dust-collection system and a flat-top design that allows you to secure the sander upside-down for use as a stationary sander.

ROUTERS

Routers are rated by rpm, horsepower and amps. They're sized according to the maximum diameter bit accepted by the collet (chuck). A ¼-in.-capacity collet is the best choice for do-it-yourselfers. Rpm range from about 15,000 to 30,000. As with a drill, the lower the rpm, the more powerful the tool. Horsepower ranges from a ⅝-hp light-duty laminate trimmer up to a 3½-hp professional router. The mid-range 1- and 1½-hp routers will provide enough power to handle most woodworking operations.

Next, check the router handles for comfort and the on-off switch for convenient location. The trigger switch is the safest because you can squeeze it while keeping both hands on the tool. Toggle and slide switches can seldom be reached from the handles.

CATALOG SOURCE LIST

The following major toolmakers and suppliers offer catalogs free of charge, unless otherwise noted.

Black & Decker, 701 East Joppa Rd., Towson, Md. 21204. (Request literature on specific tools.)

Bosch Tool Corp., MAS Dept., 3701 Neuse Blvd., New Bern, N.C. 28560.

Hitachi U.S.A., 4487-F Park Dr., Norcross, Ga. 30093.

J.C. Penney Co., Box 2028, Milwaukee, Wisc. 53201. (General catalog, $3.)

Jepson Inc., 23140 Kashiwa Court, Torrance, Calif. 90505.

Makita, 12950 East Alondra Blvd., Cerritos, Calif. 90701. (Attention: Catalog request.)

Milwaukee Electric Tool Corp., Advertising Dept., 13135 West Libson Rd., Brookfield, Wisc. 53005.

Montgomery Ward, Box 4695, Dept. PM, Chicago, Ill. 60680. (General catalog, $4.)

Porter-Cable, Advertising Dept., Youngs Crossing at Highway 45, Box 2468, Jackson, Tenn. 38302.

Ryobi America, Power Tools Div., 1158 Tower Lane, Bensenville, Ill. 60106.

Sears, Roebuck and Co., Dept. 139H-PM, 925 So. Homan Ave., Chicago, Ill. 60607. (Send $1.)

Skil Corp., Advertising Dept., 4801 West Peterson Ave., Chicago, Ill. 60646.

Wen Products, Literature Dept., 5810 Northwest Highway, Chicago, Ill. 60631.

HOME ENERGY GUIDE

SOLAR SYSTEM-HEAT PUMP WATER HEATER

An investigation of alternative methods of heating water.

Approximately 15 percent of a home electric bill can go to heat water. Yours could be higher. While this cost may not break the bank, it is a continuing year-round expense. Many people looking to save on energy costs find themselves in a morass of new and innovative water-heating products. Some of these work, some don't; others have such a long payback period that it hardly matters whether they work or not.

A solar-assisted, heat-pump water-heating system was tested. Savings added up to about 300 to 400 kilowatt hours per month.

The first component installed was one of the new hot-water heat pumps. These air-to-water devices are touted to cut the cost of heating water dramatically, whether you live in Alaska or Alabama. They operate by removing some of the heat from the surrounding air and using it to heat water.

Next, two separate systems were added that heat water with solar energy. The first consists of three collector panels mounted on the roof. The second makes use of two porcelain-lined tempering tanks suspended from the trusses in an attic. Potable water circulates through both systems, and each operates independently of the other. Because of the experimental nature of this project, both were installed; most people would use one or the other.

Keep in mind that going solar in the northern latitudes is not always economically beneficial. Since the house used in the test is in northern Illinois, the plan was to use the solar parts of the system primarily during the summer months. You'll save more with a year-round system, but there are several benefits to a warm-weather-only system: To begin with, summer is the time of year when many utilities raise their rates because of the huge increases in demand. In northern Illinois, this rate increase is about 19 percent. Second, summer is also the time when most families use more hot water: They shower and launder more frequently during hot, sticky weather.

The last advantage is strictly an investment consideration. A summer-only system eliminates the need for a closed-loop arrangement, which requires antifreeze to keep the circulating fluid from freezing, and a heat exchanger, to remove heat from the toxic antifreeze line and apply it to a second line containing potable water. The antifreeze, additional plumbing and heat exchanger add substantially to the startup costs and simultaneously reduce the overall efficiency of the system by some 15 to 20 percent.

HOW THE SYSTEM WORKS

The drawing gives the best layout for the entire system. The best way to understand it is to follow the water, step by step, as it moves through the various components.

To begin with, there is a 267-ft.-deep well to supply water with very high mineral content to a pressure tank (L).

This hardness is not only a problem for everyday home use, but also presents a distinct liability for the new installation. The minute iron and other mineral particles suspended in the water could raise havoc with the small, narrow tubes in the collector panels, the heat pump, circulating pump and the many valves in the system. To prevent this, the minerals are removed by a water softener [E]. This device exchanges salt for the minerals in the water, protecting the components farther down the line.

But there are a couple of drawbacks to using the softening system. First, many physicians today discourage the use of excess salt because it is believed to contribute to high blood pressure, and second, salt treatment of the water is an added expense.

To offset both of these concerns, hot water was diverted to two places before it went to the softener. The first was the outside spigots that provide water for gardening and lawn care. The second diverted water to a separate faucet at the kitchen sink. Water passes through a charcoal filter [C] that removes particles as small as one micron (1/25,000th of an inch). This improves the taste of the water used for drinking and preparing food, without adding salt.

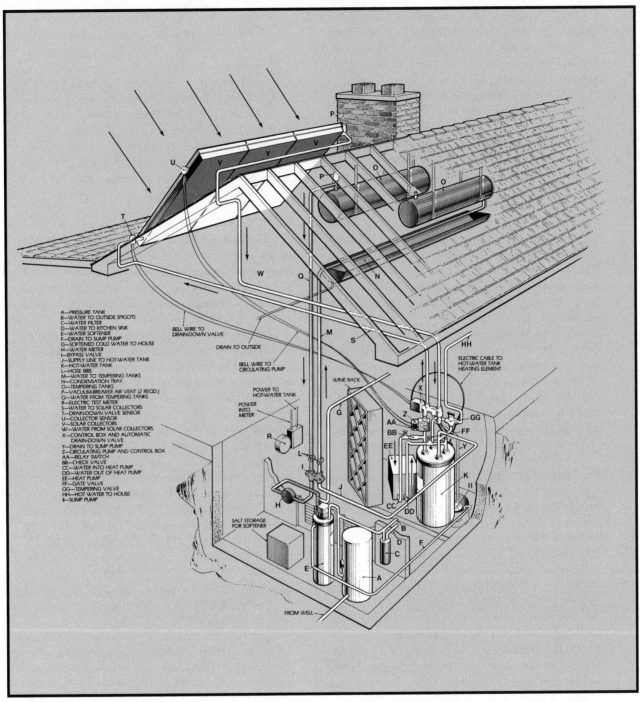

A—PRESSURE TANK
B—WATER TO OUTSIDE SPIGOTS
C—WATER FILTER
D—WATER TO KITCHEN SINK
E—WATER SOFTENER
F—DRAIN TO SUMP PUMP
G—SOFTENED COLD WATER TO HOUSE
H—WATER METER
I—BYPASS VALVE
J—SUPPLY LINE TO HOT-WATER TANK
K—HOT-WATER TANK
L—HOSE BIBS
M—WATER TO TEMPERING TANKS
N—CONDENSATION TRAY
O—TEMPERING TANKS
P—VACUUM-BREAKER AIR VENT (2 REQD.)
Q—WATER FROM TEMPERING TANKS
R—ELECTRIC TEST METER
S—WATER TO SOLAR COLLECTORS
T—DRAIN-DOWN VALVE SENSOR
U—COLLECTOR SENSOR
V—SOLAR COLLECTORS
W—WATER FROM SOLAR COLLECTORS
X—CONTROL BOX AND AUTOMATIC
        DRAIN-DOWN VALVE
Y—DRAIN TO SUMP PUMP
Z—CIRCULATING PUMP AND CONTROL BOX
AA—RELAY SWITCH
BB—CHECK VALVE
CC—WATER INTO HEAT PUMP
DD—WATER OUT OF HEAT PUMP
EE—HEAT PUMP
FF—GATE VALVE
GG—TEMPERING VALVE
HH—HOT WATER TO HOUSE
II—SUMP PUMP

BELL WIRE TO
DRAIN-DOWN VALVE

DRAIN TO OUTSIDE

BELL WIRE TO
CIRCULATING PUMP

POWER TO
HOT-WATER TANK

POWER
INTO
METER

WINE RACK

SALT STORAGE
FOR SOFTENER

FROM WELL

ELECTRIC CABLE TO
HOT-WATER TANK
HEATING ELEMENT

Water out of the softener goes to the cold supply line [G] for the rest of the house, including the baths, laundry, dishwasher and so forth. The other side of this tee is the beginning of the water supply to the hot water tank. At this point, a water meter [H] was installed so the water being used during the test period could be measured.

From the meter, the water travels to a specialized bypass valve [I] that diverts it to the tempering tank system. This manual valve is opened or closed, depending on the time of year. During the summer the attic gets extremely hot, often reaching 120°F and higher. Water circulating through the tanks is preheated before it goes to the hot water storage tank. Because the temperature of the well water is a consistent 55°F, using the tempering system makes sense only when the temperature in the attic is consistently (and considerably) higher than 55°F. In locations farther south, its benefits would be greatly increased.

When the temperature falls below the useful point, the valve is moved and the tempering system is bypassed. The tempering system is drained for the year by attaching a garden hose to each hose bib **[L]**—situated just above the bypass valve—running the hose to the sump pump and opening the valve.

With the tempering tanks out of service, the water goes directly to the storage tank **[K]**, where it enters the top and goes through an internal tube to the bottom of the tank. Near the bottom of this special solar hot water tank is a sensor that monitors the temperature of the entering water. It is connected to another sensor **[U]**—through the circulating control pump control box **[Z]**—mounted on the solar collectors on the roof. Together they regulate the circulating pump that supplies the collectors with water. If the temperature of the water inside the tank falls below that of the water inside the collectors, the pump will force the collector water down into the tank.

While two solar collectors will often suffice in other parts of the country, in the northern Illinois test home, three 3 x 8 units were installed. They are angled at 42°, corresponding to the latitude. This angle is a good average for summer solar efficiency. If you are going to use your system all year round, add 5° to the collector angle to compensate for shifts in the sun.

If, at some point, the collectors cannot meet the demand for hot water, then a relay **[AA]**, on the pump control box, will immediately switch power to the heat pump, which will heat the water until the demand subsides. Then the heat pump will kick off and the water will go back to being preheated by the solar collectors.

Keep in mind that when the heat pump is operating, it is drawing heat from the surrounding air. As such, it acts like an air conditioner. For this reason, the device must be installed in a well-ventilated area. If it is placed in a confined room, the surrounding air will quickly become cooled to the point where the heat pump no longer operates efficiently.

If, at any point, the surrounding air temperature drops below 49°F, the heat pump will shut off and the electric resistance heating element in the water tank will take over. This element functions only as a last resort.

Unlike the tempering tanks, the solar collectors do not have to be manually drained when the cold weather arrives. This is handled automatically by means of a drain-down valve **[X]** that spans both the inflow and outflow lines **[S and W]** to the collector. The drain-down valve is regulated by another sensor **[T]** located at the bottom on the bottom side of the roof collec-

tors. When the water temperature inside the panel drops to 45°F, the drain-down valve immediately blocks water from going up to the collectors and drains what is up there down into the sump pump through plastic tubing **[Y]**.

The final component of the system is a tempering valve **[GG]**, installed for safety. This device automatically mixes colder water with the hot water before it goes out of the system for home use. The valve operates only when the water heated by the solar collectors, on the hottest days, is too hot to use.

SYSTEM COSTS

A solar-assisted heat-pump system like this one is an expensive installation. The combination solar water tank and three collectors cost about $3,100. The heat pump adds another $1,000 and the pipes, fittings, valves and pipe insulation another $700.

The tempering tanks, while certainly not as efficient as the collectors, go for about $350—including the $100 condensation tray made at a local sheet-metal shop. These can be installed with any hot water tank system. Because the system is manually operated, it also eliminates the need for costly sensors and complex valves.

Both the solar-collector system and the tempering system will save money when it comes to heating water, but don't expect a quick return on your investment, especially with the collector panels and solar tank. When this system was installed in 1982, the Federal Renewable Energy Source tax credit did change the investment picture substantially. It allowed a tax credit of 40 percent of the first $10,000 spent on materials and labor for a solar energy installation. Instead of costing $3,100, the solar collectors and water tank effectively cost $1,860.

Unfortunately, the heat pump did not qualify for the tax credit and neither did the tempering tanks because they are not mounted in the direct path of the sun's rays. One way to ease the financial burden is to stretch out your solar investment by installing the system in stages: first the heat pump, then the tempering tanks or solar collectors and solar tank, and ultimately the pipe insulation on the hot water lines.

Finally, no matter what you plan to do, remember there is no guarantee that these federal tax credits will be renewed by Congress. By far, your best money-saving technique is to do the whole installation yourself. By following the installation instructions for the products you buy and the basics of good plumbing, you can cut costs drastically.

ENERGY-SAVING TIPS

Helpful tips and products to save both energy and money in the winter months.

REDIRECTING AIR

Many times the furnace room, or one near it, is the hottest room in the house. Many times it is the workshop room. One way of recovering this heat would be to put an intake vent in the cold air return plenum near the ceiling of the basement room. This, however, would cause workshop dust to circulate all over the house.

A compromise is to remove the cover panel across the fan and filter compartment so the warmed air could pass upward. To combat dust circulation, close off the space below the in-furnace filter with a 16 x 20-in. washable filter. It is held in place by 22-ga. copper wire secured to one of the existing filters, to form a tight seal inside the door frame. Washable filters are stiff enough to stand when supported this way, but flexible enough to be worked behind the door frame.

Then, tape two disposable fiberglass filters over the entire cover opening with masking tape. Air coming from the upstairs cold air return ducts still passes through the original set of filters, but air from the workshop room in the basement must pass through two sets of filters to recirculate through the house.

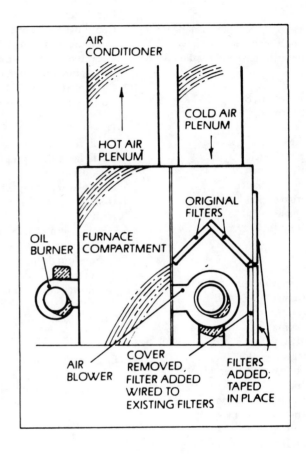

SHARING WARMTH

Circulating air warmed by a wood stove into adjoining rooms can be a problem. Warm air rises easily, but won't move laterally unless pushed or pulled mechanically. Solve the problem using ductwork and a fan installed at ceiling level.

Above the doorway in the warm room, insert a 3¼ x 1¼-in. grille, 1½ in. below the ceiling. On the cold side, use a transitional duct (3¼ x 10¼ in. expanding to 9 in. round) to connect the grille with a 9-in. circular fan drawing 75 cfm. Beyond the fan, use another transitional duct to connect the fan with rectangular ductwork. (Materials are available at heating equipment suppliers.) Wire the motor with metal-sheathed cable to a nearby light switch. Suspend the ductwork from right-angle strips of metal screwed into the ceiling joists and ductwork. Finish by painting it the same color as the ceiling.

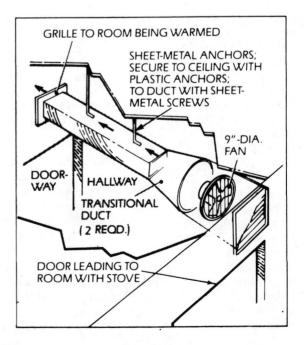

Index

The page number refers to the first page on which specific information can be found.

METRIC CONVERSION

Conversion factors can be carried so far they become impractical. In cases below where an entry is exact it is followed by an asterisk (*). Where considerable rounding off has taken place, the entry is followed by a + or a – sign.

CUSTOMARY TO METRIC

Linear Measure

inches	millimeters
1/16	1.5875*
1/8	3.2
3/16	4.8
1/4	6.35*
5/16	7.9
3/8	9.5
7/16	11.1
1/2	12.7*
9/16	14.3
5/8	15.9
11/16	17.5
3/4	19.05*
13/16	20.6
7/8	22.2
15/16	23.8
1	25.4*

inches	centimeters
1	2.54*
2	5.1
3	7.6
4	10.2
5	12.7*
6	15.2
7	17.8
8	20.3
9	22.9
10	25.4*
11	27.9
12	30.5

feet	centimeters	meters
1	30.48*	.3048*
2	61	.61
3	91	.91
4	122	1.22
5	152	1.52
6	183	1.83
7	213	2.13
8	244	2.44
9	274	2.74
10	305	3.05
50	1524*	15.24*
100	3048*	30.48*

1 yard =
.9144* meters

1 rod =
5.0292* meters

1 mile =
1.6 kilometers

1 nautical mile =
1.852* kilometers

Fluid Measure

(Milliliters [ml] and cubic centimeters [cc or cu cm] are equivalent, but it is customary to use milliliters for liquids.)

1 cu in = 16.39 ml
1 fl oz = 29.6 ml
1 cup = 237 ml
1 pint = 473 ml
1 quart = 946 ml
    = .946 liters
1 gallon = 3785 ml
    = 3.785 liters
Formula (exact):
fluid ounces × 29.573 529 562 5*
  = milliliters

Weights

ounces	grams
1	28.3
2	56.7
3	85
4	113
5	142
6	170
7	198
8	227
9	255
10	283
11	312
12	340
13	369
14	397
15	425
16	454

Formula (exact):
  ounces × 28.349 523 125* = grams

pounds	kilograms
1	.45
2	.9
3	1.4
4	1.8
5	2.3
6	2.7
7	3.2
8	3.6
9	4.1
10	4.5

1 short ton (2000 lbs) =
907 kilograms (kg)
Formula (exact):
pounds × .453 592 37* = kilograms

Volume

1 cu in = 16.39 cubic centimeters (cc)
1 cu ft = 28 316.7 cc
1 bushel = 35 239.1 cc
1 peck = 8 809.8 cc

Area

1 sq in = 6.45 sq cm
1 sq ft = 929 sq cm
    = .093 sq meters
1 sq yd = .84 sq meters
1 acre = 4 046.9 sq meters
    = .404 7 hectares
1 sq mile = 2 589 988 sq meters
    = 259 hectares
    = 2.589 9 sq kilometers

Kitchen Measure

1 teaspoon = 4.93 milliliters (ml)
1 Tablespoon = 14.79 milliliters (ml)

Miscellaneous

1 British thermal unit (Btu) (mean)
    = 1 055.9 joules
1 calorie (mean) = 4.19 joules
1 horsepower = 745.7 watts
    = .75 kilowatts
caliber (diameter of a firearm's bore in hundredths of an inch)
    = .254 millimeters (mm)
1 atmosphere pressure = 101 325* pascals (newtons per sq meter)
1 pound per square inch (psi) = 6 895 pascals
1 pound per square foot = 47.9 pascals
1 knot = 1.85 kilometers per hour
25 miles per hour = 40.2 kilometers per hour
50 miles per hour = 80.5 kilometers per hour
75 miles per hour = 120.7 kilometers per hour